LIBERALISM DISAVOWED

LIBERALISM DISAVOWED
Communitarianism and State Capitalism in Singapore

Beng Huat Chua

CORNELL UNIVERSITY PRESS
Ithaca and London

First published 2017 by NUS Press, National University of Singapore
First published in the United States of America in 2017 by Cornell University Press
First printing, Cornell Paperbacks, 2017

Library of Congress Cataloging-in-Publication Data

Names: Chua, Beng Huat, author.
Title: Liberalism disavowed: communitarianism and state capitalism in
    Singapore/Beng Huat Chua.
Description: Ithaca: Cornell University Press, 2017.|Includes bibliographical
    references and index.
Identifiers: LCCN 2016050361|ISBN 9781501713439 (cloth: alk. paper)|
    ISBN 9781501713446 (pbk.: alk. paper)
Subjects: LCSH: Singapore—Politics and government.|Communitarianism—
    Singapore.|Liberalism—Singapore.|People's Action Party (Singapore)
Classification: LCC JQ1063.A58 C48 2017|DDC 320.95957—dc23 LC record
    available at https://lccn.loc.gov/2016050361

Cornell University Press strives to use environmentally responsible suppliers and materials to the fullest extent possible in the publishing of its books. Such materials include vegetable-based, low-VOC inks and acid-free papers that are recycled, totally chlorine-free, or partly composed of nonwood fibers. For further information, visit our website at www.cornellpress.cornell.edu.

Cover image courtesy of Timothy Chua Yi-neng.

Printed in the United States of America.

CONTENTS

PREFACE

EDUCATED SINGAPOREANS ARE VERY KNOWLEDGEABLE about national affairs. They cannot help it because the People's Action Party (PAP) government carefully orchestrates its messages to the public. These messages, in turn, are frequently repeated by all the cabinet ministers during their appearances at big and small social events and everyday by the local media, which are obliged to report/broadcast speeches of political office holders. The government is everywhere, inescapable, as long as you are on the island.

Everyone acknowledges the undeniable fact that the material life of the entire nation has improved massively under more than half a century of PAP rule as a single-party dominant government. Everyone is also acutely aware of the equally undeniable fact that this improvement has been paid for with a significant quantum of social, cultural and political repression, strewn across the political history of the island nation, particularly in the first 30 years under Prime Minister Lee Kuan Yew. The PAP, in its own defense, would insist that repression was necessary to produce an improved material life for all.

Singaporeans are aware of being caught between these two undeniable facts of their everyday life and navigate consciously between them. It would be fair to say that the overwhelming majority accepts, broadly, political repression in return for an improved material life, especially since repression is only visited on selected individuals. The willing acquiescence of the majority is often misread as "apathy" and/or "fear" of repressive punishment by the PAP government. That fear has little to do with it becomes obvious when a particular repressive policy that is excessive and morally unacceptable has generalized effects. Rebel they did against the morally unacceptable "Graduate Mother" policy and against poorly thought-out and equally poorly executed public policies in the 1984 and 2011 general elections. During those elections, in which the PAP suffered symbolically significant drops in popular electoral support, Singaporeans demonstrated a rather sophisticated understanding of the rational basis for electoral democracy.

The first-generation leadership that was primarily responsible for the heavy repression has passed. The second generation that lived under the tutelage of the first has also come and gone, replaced by a third generation, currently incumbent parliamentarians who are already preparing the ground for succession. During the rule of the second and current generations, many aspects of social, cultural and, indeed, political life have been progressively liberalized, sometimes voluntarily undertaken by the government, at other times undertaken reluctantly under pressure from Singaporeans and/or the outside world. In spite of the palpable liberalization, past repression casts a long, if fading, shadow on many Singaporeans. For example, the undergraduates that I have taught, who have no serious criticisms of the government beyond the normal complaints about the inconveniences of life, think that they cannot speak "freely," as if their complaints amount to rousing fellow citizens to revolt. Social memory of repression continues to generate, among many Singaporeans, cynicism and distrust towards the long-ruling government. These memories, stoked every so often by aggressive lawsuits that are financially ruinous to non-PAP politicians and other political critics, continue to induce psychic stresses caused by self-censorship, self-abnegation, a sense of powerlessness, defeat and even cowardice. How can such damage not fail to result in people who are resentful of repression, past and present?

Under such conditions, it is understandable why political liberalism is immediately attractive to most Singaporeans, given that it espouses the primacy of constitutionally guaranteed individual rights and freedoms by a popularly elected government that is constitutionally bound to uphold these rights and freedoms. Reinforced by a world history of more than 200 years of intellectual debates, elaborations and refinements—speaking against feudalism in the French Revolution, against colonialism in the American Revolution, against patriarchy in the suffragette movement, against Fascism and Communism and Western colonialism in Asia and Africa during and after the Second World War, against racism in the 1960s to the present—political liberalism is skeptical, if not suspicious, of any and all talk of the "social," "collective" and "community," because these terms are often invoked as thin veils covering intentions to suppress the individual. Although political liberalism is intuitively appealing, the reality of the "social" holds that appeal in check. One's freedom is existentially and unavoidably constrained by the network of social obligations and responsibilities that one has to a whole range of intimate and distant others, from family to nation.

Perhaps it is the "Asian" cultural heritage of Singapore's citizens, but the smallness of the island that is also the "nation" most certainly imposes upon all but the most committed "liberal" Singaporeans a certain realism of the importance of the "social," the "collective." This sense of social realism is a very significant part of what is often alluded to, by PAP politicians and Singaporeans alike, as the "conservative" Singapore society. It is this conservatism that the PAP government regularly invokes to justify the necessity of facilitating incremental rather than speedy or radical social change. While the depth of Singapore society's conservatism will likely remain a matter of social attitudinal surveys and public debate, the overall "collectivist" orientation of the state has been embedded in some of the most important public institutions since the early days of nation building, largely as a consequence of the social democratic origin of the PAP. The institutionalization of the "social" in these key institutions constitutes the basis of the PAP's claim to embrace communitarianism as its ideology, which has displaced the PAP's pragmatism of its earlier years.

This book examines the relative coherence of the key institutions as a "system" of governance—the Singapore system as such—which is likely to endure not only beyond the incumbent generation of PAP leaders but beyond the PAP government should it be displaced from power in the future.

The book has taken a long time in its writing. Parts of it have appeared in different publications over the years; the most recent journals include *Housing Studies*, *International Journal of Housing Policy*, *The Pacific Review*, *boundary 2* and *positions*. In the process, much intellectual goodwill and debt have been accumulated. I would like to thank Garry Rodan, Kwok Kian Woon, Wee Wan Ling, Ho Kong Chong, Tay Kheng Soon, Lily Kong, Arun Mahizhnan, Nirmala Purushotam and William and Lena Lim, all with abiding interests in Singaporean matters, for years of ongoing conversations; Kanishka Jayasuriya, Daniel Goh, Teo You Yenn and Kurtulus Gemici for reading and commenting on different chapters of the book; Wong Meisen, Ng Hui Hsien, Caryn Tan and Quek Ri An for research assistance; and Peter Schoppert for his confidence in this book when it was only an idea. Funding for the project was largely provided by the Provost Professorship Research Fund and Heads and Deanery Research Support Scheme, Faculty of Arts and Social Science, National University of Singapore, for which I am grateful. This book is a small tribute to fellow Singaporeans on the fiftieth anniversary of our independence.

INTRODUCTION

SINGAPORE IS EASY TO DENIGRATE FROM a distance—the arrogant authoritarianism of the first and long serving, Prime Minister, the late Lee Kuan Yew; the long-term detention without trial of political opponents, an estimated 800 individuals detained from 1963–87; the financially ruinous libel suits against opposition party members through the 1980s and 1990s; the bank of repressive legislation on labor relations, race relations, media and civil society organizations, which are all constantly under threat of proscription and deregistration; and, finally, the aggressive gerrymandering of electoral boundaries and changes in electoral rules that have ensured the People's Action Party's (PAP) uninterrupted one-party domination of parliament since 1959. The aggregated effects of these measures have been seen through the lens of liberal ideology as a "suffocating atmosphere" of political and cultural repression. Liberal critiques assert that under such conditions, the continuous support of Singaporeans in every general election of such an authoritarian government must be motivated by factors other than good reason, such as fear of punishment by the government, political powerlessness, political apathy or striking a Faustian bargain in return for improved material life. The PAP has indeed transformed Singapore from a regional trading economy in the twilight of the British Empire to a first-world economy in one single generation, since independence in 1965. An authoritarian state with popular support that works is a distressing idea in a world defined by liberal democracy!

Up close, ironically, it is easy to be seduced, as Singaporeans themselves have been, by the city-state's obvious success as a nation—the gleaming downtown banking district that signifies a global financial center; the smoothly integrated transportation network of roads, highways and mass rapid transit trains; the endless expanse of high-rise public housing estates that house the entire nation; the strong sense of orderliness and public security without the ubiquitous police or armed soldiers that one has come to expect of an authoritarian state; and, finally, the high standard of material life of the citizens, all under an efficient, efficacious and uncorrupt government that makes and carries out long-term, future-oriented plans. Economic success has elevated the small island-nation in the esteem of the world and given Singapore a voice in the global economy and political arena that belies its small size. It is now frequently regarded by many developing nations as a "model" for development. Obviously, even its harshest critic will not be comfortable reducing the political economy of Singapore's success to simply authoritarianism at work, or its staunchest supporter seeing this success as simply the triumph of free-market capitalism.

It would be easy to attribute Singapore's economic success to its small and readily manageable size, with all the advantages of an urban economy without the drag of a rural hinterland except, as the PAP government habitually warns Singaporeans, smallness has its disadvantages. The island is devoid of natural resources, including land and population. Even Singapore's supposedly advantageous geographical location is dubious; until the opening of the Changi International Airport, Bangkok was the international transit point for air travel from the West to northeast Asia. It is dependent on the regional and global markets for all its imports, which makes it a very open economy that is extremely vulnerable to the fluctuations of external conditions. This "vulnerability" has been ideologically harnessed to generate a string of political consequences: fear of becoming irrelevant to the global market, thus constantly in search of niches of opportunities for economic growth; fear of fragmentation, thus an insistence on tight social control to ensure social cohesion; fear of political polarization by different political parties with different ideologies that might jeopardize national development, thus an emphasis on the administrative advantages of a one-party dominant government. In sum, a generalized anxiety about the long-term viability of the social, economic and political foundation of the island-nation has been transformed into a set of ideological justifications for and instrumental practices of tight social and political control, which taken together constitutes the authoritarianism of the regime. The much-criticized politics of the single-party dominant parliamentary system is for the PAP the critical element of Singapore's economic success.

Single-party dominant parliamentary states are not uncommon in Asia. The Liberal Democratic Party (LDP) in Japan and the India Congress Party are two political parties that have dominated their respective governments since the end of the Second World War. However, in neither India nor Japan has there been absolute and undisrupted rule; both parties have been occasionally voted out of power. Indeed, the dominance of the Indian Congress Party has been severely eroded by the rise of regional parties in a federal system. Although the LDP's and PAP's situations seem similar, there are differences. The LDP's dominance appears unassailable, because the other Japanese political parties have withered into political insignificance. However, the LDP is a deeply fractional political party while the PAP leadership is tightly united. The specific criticism of the PAP is thus less about one-party dominance than its history of authoritarianism.

Against the critique of authoritarianism, one should note that during the early 1960s till the end of the 1970s, when political repression was most intense in Singapore, authoritarian regimes were practically the norm in decolonized nations and economic failure was the rule in these regimes. These failed states were characterized by the propensity of the authoritarian postcolonial elite to plunder the national wealth; endemic corruption at every level in both the public and private sectors of their economies; tribal or ethnic antagonism, often encouraged by the self-interested elite; unscrupulous tampering of ballot boxes accompanied by violence during elections; and, finally, the increasingly alienated and restive population that could only be controlled by state violence involving the police and military. From the struggle to political ascendancy, the first-generation PAP leaders learned that if they were to defeat their once erstwhile radical left-wing comrades and win the hearts and minds of the newly enfranchised citizens, they would have to equal if not better the asceticism and self-sacrificing attitude of the radical left. Thus, from the outset anti-corruption was the moral basis of its rule. To this day, this spirit to serve and anti-corruption remain core values of the PAP. In addition, the holding of general elections every five years has been retained although the playing field has never been entirely equal or fair. The PAP is not beyond using its incumbent governmental prerogative to modify the rules of electoral contest to its advantage. In the early years, this prerogative included the jailing of opposition leaders before elections and heavy-handed gerrymandering. Beyond these tactics, elections have always been conducted without violence and without the tampering of ballot boxes, as the PAP realizes that "clean" elections are critical to its justification and legitimacy to rule in the eyes of the citizens and international observers.

After 50 years of sustained economic growth, Singapore is now an overwhelming middle-class society of public-housing homeowners with an increasingly better educated, culturally diverse and informed citizenry that is globally connected and globally mobile, as students, tourists or managers in homegrown or foreign multinational corporations. Given these changes, the continuing simplistic and reductionist characterization of the Singaporean as "docile," culturally race-bound and living in fear of political authoritarianism is descriptively inadequate. It is a view that reflects an increasingly misinformed understanding of contemporary Singapore society. With the cultural diversity engendered by education and financial affluence, liberalization in the cultural sphere is inevitable. Under the watch of Prime Minister Goh Chok Tong and his successor, the current Prime Minister Lee Hsien Loong, the boundaries of public behavior, films, art and theater have all been pushed back by artists and cultural activists, with the government accepting the changes, often reluctantly. Whereas the Cold War was a convenient excuse for the first-generation PAP leaders to exercise a heavy-handed repression of their opponents, the same instruments of repression are no longer readily at hand for the present or future generations. The potential loss of its esteem in the global political and economic arenas, including the risk of economic and political sanctions that unnecessary and/or excessive political repression could bring, is a price too high for the current and future PAP leaders to contemplate. In this sense, the liberalization of culture and politics is inevitable; however, this is not the same as embodying liberalism in the polity.

Political liberals, at home and abroad, are keen to see Singapore develop politically towards a multi-party liberal democracy. They pin their desire and hope upon the general understanding that the rise of the middle class, which is abundantly evident in Singapore, would lead to a demand for political liberalism and ultimately liberal democracy, as it has in Taiwan and South Korea. Sadly, they have been consistently frustrated in the case of Singapore, most recently in the 2015 general election. Buoyed by the worst result suffered by the PAP in the 2011 general election, in which it lost six parliamentary seats and received only 60 percent of the popular vote, there was a widespread expectation that opposition parties would gain further parliamentary seats in the 2015 general election. Instead, the PAP romped home with close to a 10 percent increase in the national popular vote, winning nearly all the contested electoral constituencies; the top leaders of the Workers' Party, the main opposition party, barely retained the six seats they had won by a comfortable margin in the 2011 general election. In this latest general election, gerrymandering was kept to a minimum, and there is no gain saying that the election was without credible opposition candidates and alternative policy proposals to those of the PAP regime. The final result can only be interpreted as a ringing endorsement of the PAP government by an overwhelming majority of Singaporeans.

The 2015 general election result showed that the PAP is likely to continue to stay in power well into the third decade of the twenty-first century. The general narrative of the PAP government and the economic development of Singapore are by now legendary. However, details of its ideological commitments and the concomitant economic and social political practices remain mired in simplistic explanations of authoritarianism in politics and apparently unstinting support for free market capitalism in Singapore's economic policy. Indeed, the PAP government itself might be said to have encouraged the simplistic view of its governance and economic policies. What this "encouraged" understanding veils, intentionally or otherwise, is the social democratic origin of the PAP, which explains some of the fundamental social and economic programs which are critical to the economic and political success of the PAP government, and from which it has not wavered in more than its 50 years in power. The PAP's social democratic origin, not authoritarianism, explains the Party's vociferous disavowal of liberalism as the basis of politics and government. This book locates the social democratic traces that are embedded in, and continue to determine, the political economy of contemporary Singapore under the PAP government.

Embedding Social Democracy

The PAP was founded in 1954, in a world when decolonization was the preoccupation of every politically minded colonized subject and the prevailing political sentiment was invariably anti-colonial and left-wing. Communism, socialism and social democracy, ideologies of progressive movements in post-World War II Europe, were also the prevailing ideologies of the decolonization movements in Asia and Africa. The PAP, a political party of its time, was constituted by a coalition of two factions: a group of radical left-wing unionists, many with no more than secondary school education in local Chinese-language schools, with an ability to mobilize the masses against the colonial government; and a group of privileged British-university-educated professionals whose interest in politics was ignited during their student days in immediate post-World War II Britain and who were influenced by British social democratic ideology. The coalition was one of political expediency: the British-educated "social democrats" needed the ability of the radical left to mobilize the masses, while the latter needed the protective legitimacy of the English-speaking, British-educated professionals. In the first general election for a fully locally-elected parliament in 1959, the PAP won an overwhelming majority to constitute the first elected parliament. All the right-wing political parties were decimated; from then on, politics in Singapore was dominated by the left (Devan 2009: 29). Soon after, the inevitable split between the two factions in the PAP followed. In 1961, politically outmaneuvered, the radical left faction split off to form the Barisan Sosialis, while the British-educated faction retained the PAP name and parliamentary power. From then on, with the convenience of the emerging Cold War between Communism and the so-called "Free World," the latter "anointed" themselves as the "moderates" and persistently labeled their former comrades as "communists" or "pro-communists." On 2 February 1963, more than 100 individuals, among them Barisan Sosialis central executive committee members, were arrested in Operation Cold Store and detained without trial under the Internal Security Act. The subsequent boycott of the 1968 general election by the Barisan left the PAP in absolute control of parliament and free to define and craft the future of Singapore. As shall be argued here, this future has been marked by the legacy of the coalition and social democratic beginning of the PAP.

At the abstract ideological level, arguably the PAP government's continuing emphasis of placing the "collective" or "societal" interests above those of individuals has had its roots in its formative history as a social democratic party. This was reinforced by the perceived need for tight social cohesion because of the vulnerabilities of a small nation. This emphasis on "collective" ideologically translated into its vehement ideological anti-liberalism. In the early years, this anti-liberalism was often conflated with the personal authoritarianism of Lee Kuan Yew. This conflation began to be untangled in the early 1990s, when a second generation of PAP ministers, under Prime Minister Goh Chok Tong, assumed office. At that time, the "Confucian-communitarian" explanation for the "East Asian model" of capitalism development was in vogue. Under Goh's administration, the social democratic emphasis on the "collective" was ideologically reconfigured as an Asian culture, specifically Confucianism, communitarianism. This ideological communitarianism facilitated the reinterpretation of the vocabulary of democracy: election to office was interpreted as being entrusted by the electorate to govern in the latter's best interest rather than being elected to represent the narrow interests of different electoral constituencies.

Concretely, several areas of public policies continue to reflect social democratic ideas in the present. The most obvious is the national public housing program. This was initiated a year after the PAP was elected as the first parliament, when its left-oriented politics were still fully intact. Nearly universal state-subsidized housing was only possible partly because the government radically nationalized land through a draconian compulsory acquisition of private landholdings, in complete disregard of the sacred liberal right of private property. With the acquisition and extensive reclamation, the government ultimately owned about 90 percent of the total land in the nation, a portion of which has been used for public housing. The promise of affordable homeownership for up to 90 percent of the population remains the most concrete social democratic "welfare" program of the PAP government. It is fundamental to the PAP's political legitimacy to govern.

Economically, given that an "open market" is the lifeline of the Singapore economy, it is understandable that the PAP government would espouse support for "free trade" in global forums. However, it is concurrently unapologetically and actively engaged in building and expanding its state-capitalist sector at home and abroad. Against the prevailing neoliberal mythology that only a free market constituted by private enterprises can be competitive and efficient, the PAP government has built a network of state-owned enterprises that started out to service domestic needs but which have grown to become very successful global enterprises, which are bundled together under a state-owned holding company. The profits of the holding company are in turn reorganized into a separate sovereign wealth fund, which invests in established global corporations and in domestic private enterprises that have the potential to regionalize or globalize their businesses. The Singapore state is a significant entrepreneur in global capitalism. A substantial portion of the annual profit derived from the state capitalist sector goes to underwrite part of the cost of governance, effectively creating a mode of social redistribution without specific target recipients.

The ideological emphasis on the "collective" is most apparent in the official policy of multiracialism. Devoid of the conventional conditions of an ethnically homogenous population who share the same history, language and mythological "blood," Singapore declared itself a constitutional "multiracial" nation, in spite of an overwhelming majority of Chinese in the population. The decision to be multiracial was largely determined by regional geopolitics. With communist China within striking distance, to declare Singapore as a "Chinese" nation would not be accepted with equanimity in a region where Malays are indigenous. Official multiracialism emphasizes the "equality" of race-groups under a generalized ideology of racial harmony as a public good. Ironically, the maintenance of "racial harmony" often requires discriminatory social policies targeting particular race-groups for different reasons. Official multiracialism thus serves as the framework for rationalizing and justifying discriminatory social control strategies to maintain "racial harmony" as essential for Singapore's social stability and national security.

Four institutionalized political and economic practices grounded in social democracy can be identified: ideological anti-liberalism, the national public housing program, state capitalism and multiracialism. Their primacy is reflected in the fact that other significant social policies and administrative practices, which are politically important in their own right, can be enfolded within the operating logic of one or more of these four institutions. The most obvious example is the use of public housing allocation to carry out other significant social policies, such as pro-family policies and the enforced spatial distribution of the three major races, in indirect support of multiracialism and "racial harmony." At a more abstract level is meritocracy, which the PAP government insists is the Achilles-heel in the equitable distribution of economic opportunities and rewards. Meritocracy has been an explicit ideology/policy not only because of the multiracial composition of the population but more importantly, it is necessitated by the geopolitical conditions. Singapore needs to demonstrate the absence of racial discrimination in the Malay-dominant region, in contrast to Malaysia's insistence on political supremacy and privileging of Malays as its indigenous people.

It is critical to note that the policies and practices in the four areas identified have been contingent developments or, in the government's term, "pragmatic" solutions to changing circumstances. Put in place at the very outset of the PAP government, the substance and trajectory of these policies and practices have unfolded and been modified in conjunction with the ongoing changes wrought by the policies themselves, such as the inflationary costs of public housing, or changes in global conditions, such as the end of the Cold War. Over time, each area has also generated internal systemic contradictions and problems that require constant vigilance and solutions, which are more often temporary rather than permanent. However, to the extent that other significant practices of governance can be enfolded into one of the four identified political and economic practices, they may be conceptually considered as the "defining" features and central operating "principles" of the Singapore system under the PAP. Arguably the four areas of policies and practices may be said to constitute the foundational and defining features of the Singapore state. They are likely to endure not only while the PAP controls parliament but even in the event of the PAP losing parliament. Their obvious importance to the economic, social and political stability of Singapore would make it difficult, if not foolish, for any incumbent government to remove them without undermining its own legitimacy to rule. Conceptually, the four areas of practices provide relative coherence to Singapore as a social, political and economic unit, demonstrating the possibility of a non-liberal electoral polity with a successful capitalist economy in the contemporary world. It is the intention of this book to make this case.

Chapter 1

CONTEXTUALIZING SINGAPORE
Antipathy to Liberalism

> Singapore did not believe in the Western liberal democratic model which developed in the last half-century as the pinnacle of human achievement and the solution for the whole of the world (Prime Minister Lee Hsien Loong, *Straits Times* 23 July 2009).

IN THE QUOTE ABOVE, THE THIRD Prime Minister of Singapore, Lee Hsien Loong, states categorically that the People's Action Party (PAP), which has governed continuously since 1959, or close to 60 years, is not interested in transforming the Singapore polity into a Western liberal democracy. This very explicit declaration is indicative of how the PAP government in Singapore sees itself as operating within and against the global ideological environment of liberal democracy. In the present post-socialist world where liberalism enjoys "a position of dominance not only within the academy but in general public discourse in all contemporary democracies around the world" (Chatterjee 2011: 2–3), the constellation of the three terms in the phrase, "liberal-capitalist-democracy," has become conventionally understood as the desired common system (Fukuyama 1992). All other modes of governance are decried as deviations from this righteous path, including the single-party dominant PAP government. While its anti-liberalism stance is likely to be read by critics as a mere ideological rationalization of its uninterrupted rule as a single-party dominant parliament, the PAP's disavowal of liberalism in fact has deeper roots in the social democratic orientation of the people who founded the party in 1954. Through a series of political twists and turns—the first fully elected self-government in 1959, the purge of its radical faction in the early 1960s, the brief membership in Malaysia starting in 1963 and Singapore's subsequent independence in 1965—the PAP has been able to monopolize parliamentary power since 1968. Since then, the single-party dominant parliament has proved so expedient in enabling the government to efficaciously execute long-term political, social and economic planning that the PAP has been motivated to entrench its political system and practice, in defiance of domestic and international pressures to embrace liberal democracy. Against liberalism, it has proposed communitarianism as the preferred national ideology. However, because communitarianism has also been heralded as part of the national ideology by authoritarian political leaders in other East Asian nations with endemic corruption at all levels of government, the PAP's ideological claim has been inevitably entangled in the skepticism and criticism of generalized "communitarianism in Asia." To understand the current PAP government's disavowal of liberalism, it is therefore necessary to know, first, how it conceptualizes liberalism as the ideology against which it defines itself and, second, how it distinguishes itself from the other governments that claim to be communitarian.

Trajectory of Liberal Individualism

Given the status of the US as a global power, the contemporary concept of liberal democracy arguably embraces a largely American version of liberalism. It should therefore not be surprising that it is this version which looms large in the PAP government's antipathy to liberalism, especially its emphasis on individualism. Rooted in its unique history of being never burdened by a feudal aristocracy nor oppressed by colonization, the liberal ethos was inscribed into the US constitution in the 1776 American Declaration of Independence: "We hold these truths to be self-evident, that all men are created equal, that they are endowed by their Creator with certain unalienable Rights, that among these are Life, Liberty and the pursuit of Happiness" (Hartz 1955). Over the years of repetition, reiteration and reformulation, the phrase, "self-evident truths," has crystallized into a set of vernacular values and beliefs of the American people. As summarized by the first black US President, Barack Obama, this liberty includes

> …the right to speak our minds; the right to worship how and if we wish; the right to peaceably assemble to petition our government; the right to own, buy and sell property and not have it taken without fair compensation; the right to be free from unreasonable searches and

seizures; the right not to be detained by the state without due process; the right to a fair and speedy trial; and the right to make our own determinations, with minimal restrictions, regarding family life and the way we raised our children. (2006: 86)

As "self-evident" truths, these freedoms of individuals extend by definition to all people at all times, that is, they are universal. As Lukes points out, American individualism refers "to the actual or imminent realization of the final stage of human progress in a spontaneously cohesive society of equal individual rights, limited government, *laissez-faire*, natural justice and equal opportunity, and individual freedom, moral development and dignity" (1973: 26). Achieving these individual freedoms thus constitutes the teleological end point of social political development of all societies.

Liberalism and Democracy

For the post-socialist world, the conjoining of liberalism and democracy may be a matter of course. In fact this coupling is historically a relatively recent phenomenon. As political theorist, Alan Wolfe, notes, "Any important political theorist of the nineteenth century would have been puzzled by the expression 'liberal democracy'" (1977: 3). First, formally, in democratic systems "the political authority of citizens takes precedence over citizens' personal freedoms" (Rodan and Hughes 2014: 8). Second, liberalism and democracy take diametrically opposite stances towards capitalism (Wolfe 1977: 4). The difference turns on their respective understandings of the concept of "equality." Both capitalism and liberalism promote "equality in the abstract" to ideologically enable individuals to engage in economic exchange as "equals," including the free exchange of labor power for wages between workers and employers. However, capitalists will fight equality "bitterly in the real world" of capitalism (Wolfe 1977: 5), as capitalism necessarily produces inequality, privilege and hierarchy as the unavoidable outcomes of competition. Liberalism serves to gloss over this inequality.[1] In contrast, for democrats, equality implies social justice and civil rights, which must be

---

[1] "[N]atural rights were transformed into property rights, individualism became the rationale for the buying and selling of labour power, community became the exercise of authority necessary to ensure the stability of civil society, individual differences became class distinctions, and the social contract became the primary justification for a market economy" (Wolfe, 1977: 4).

protected "against the excesses of an unfettered, market-driven ethos" (Ong 2006: 2). Social justice "presupposes social solidarities and a willingness to submerge individual wants, needs, and desires in the cause of some more general struggle" (Harvey 2005: 41); demands of social justice and individual freedom are thus potentially incompatible. Therefore, to formally conjoin liberalism and democracy as conceptually seamless basically involves the displacement of the demand for social solidarity by privileging individual freedoms and desires. However, displacement is not erasure; conflicting ideological/political positions derived from democratic demands for social solidarity and social justice remain political possibilities.

Political Liberalism and the Welfare State

After the Second World War, the demand for social justice manifested itself in the development of the "welfare state," as a compromise between capitalists and the working classes in democratic nations (Esping-Andersen 1990). David Harvey (2005) and, before him, Daniel Bell (1960) suggest that after the Second World War, the US polity had the following features: a "focus on full employment, economic growth, and the welfare of its citizens, and that state power should be freely deployed, alongside of or, if necessary, intervening in or even substituting for market processes to achieve these ends;" the state also "actively intervened in industrial policy and moved to set standards for the social wage by constructing a variety of welfare systems (health care, education, and the like);" finally, in societal management, the interventionist state fostered a "social and moral economy," in which class compromise between capital and labor was seen as "the key guarantor of domestic peace and tranquillity" (Harvey 2005: 10). The broadly similar social welfare provisions had different political labels across the Atlantic. In Europe, it was called social democracy; in the US, political liberalism. This was because in post-war Europe, socialism and communism remained salient anti-capitalist ideologies, and socialist and communist political parties remained serious contenders for state power, until at least the late 1970s. Consequently, European democrats, including liberals, generally place emphasis on the social/collective responsibility; hence their label, "social" democracy. In contrast, communism and socialism in the US were thoroughly routed by McCarthyism in the 1950s. As a result, all left-of-liberal political language has since been suppressed in the public sphere. Social welfare advocates were thus called, by default, "liberal democrats" or "political liberals" to distinguish them from anti-welfare "conservatives" and "classic liberals" committed to individualism, private property and free market.

By the 1970s, the economic and political contradictions inherent in managing the tensions between the need to simultaneously maintain the conditions for capital accumulation and the mass loyalty of the citizens in the welfare state had become apparent. First, to maintain its source of revenues, taxation, tariffs and even borrowings for its fiscal needs, the state is compelled to ensure continual capital accumulation, that is, the profitability of private investments. To secure the conditions of capital accumulation, the state must provide and improve physical infrastructure, services and the quality and productivity of the workforce by investments in public education, health and housing, that is, increase "social capital" investments (O'Connor 2002: xix). The state cannot neglect its "accumulation function" without risking a capitalist revolt of withholding investments, without which all state revenues through taxation and tariffs would cease.

Second, capitalist production incurs externalized undesirable costs, including environmental degradation, urban transportation gridlock, unemployment, poverty, and "various groups whose life chances had been damaged systematically by market exchange processes" (Keane 1984: 13). To maintain the mass loyalty of citizens from whom it derives its mandate to govern, that is, to achieve its "legitimacy function," the state needs to recognize the demands for compensation from organized civil society groups who have been affected by these negative externalities of capitalism. Consequently, beneficiaries of social expenditure in education, health care, housing, unemployment insurance and other financial assistance have been able to ideologically and substantively transform these provisions into an extensive set of "entitlements" and "rights" of citizenship (Keane 1984: 17) and state bureaucracy has to expand to cope with the workload. In the 1970s, capitalist resistance to increased taxation caused by welfare expansion resulted in a persistent fiscal deficit which affected the implementation of public policies, causing mass disaffection with the state. In short, the welfare state has been in a permanent state of fiscal crisis (O'Connor 2002) and has suffered an on-going deficit of legitimacy since the 1970s (Offe 1984; Habermas 1973). Meanwhile, the 1970s also saw the political right raise objections to social welfare entitlements as the weakening of work ethics and the ever-expanding state bureaucracy as "big" government. This led political conservatives to call for the return of classical liberal values.

Neoliberalism Interlude

By the early 1980s, US President Ronald Reagan (1981–89) reactivated a classic principle of Jeffersonian liberalism: "That government is best which governs least" (Lukes 1973: 82). To downsize the government, market regulations were reduced, state enterprises and state-owned assets were sold off, some state social responsibilities were outsourced (Niskanen 1988: 5), and social welfare provisions were cut back to "wean" citizens off state dependency. Meanwhile, the notions of free market, self-reliance, self-management and individual enterprise were ideologically emphasized. American political philosopher Irving Kristol saw this as America redirecting itself back to the original "liberal vision and liberal energy" (quoted in Williams 1997: 82), however, under a new name for a new time—neoliberalism.

The same strictures were undertaken in Britain by Prime Minister Margaret Thatcher, an ideological sibling and ally of President Reagan. Emphasizing individual self-reliance, she famously declared, "There is no such thing as society: there are only men and women, and there are families."[2] The family was added as an afterthought. For example, to reduce state responsibility in housing provision, she sold off state-subsidized council housing with a very significant one-off subsidy to sitting tenants, transforming many households into home owners but simultaneously driving those who were unable to purchase houses to residual units of the worst quality housing (Saunders 1990). Throughout the 1980s and 1990s, neoliberalism was embraced by the multilateral financial institutions under the control of the US, namely the International Monetary Fund (IMF) and the World Bank, and imposed on nations in need of their loans.

Two decades of continuous market deregulation resulted in a corporate world that focused almost exclusively on short-term profit for shareholders. Complicated financial "products" and transaction schemes —derivatives, hedge funds, securitizations, structured investments and collateralized debt obligations—which defy the understanding of most lay investors were invented to churn money and profit, which in turn justified hugely exaggerated salaries and bonuses for executives in financial industries. By 2008, the deregulated financial industries finally blew up. The undoing came with the unravelling of the US sub-prime

---

[2] https://www.google.com.sg/?gfe_rd=cr&ei=tjyDV4DfCOuL8Qe8wLaQDg&gws_rd=ssl#q=margaret+thatcher+quotes [accessed 25 Apr. 2016].

mortgage system. Residential properties were sold, with minimum or no down payments or monthly mortgage payments for a sustained period, to households who had no means of meeting the regular financial obligations of their purchases. Such gain-without-pain schemes encouraged property speculation. These high-risk mortgages were in turn repackaged as "securitized" assets and sold to the next financial institutions in the global financial market. The sub-prime bubble finally burst in late 2007. Many financial institutions in the US and elsewhere globally that were exposed to the sub-prime mortgage industry either went bust or tottered on the brink of insolvency. The total global loss from the crisis was estimated by the IMF to be in excess of USD 4 trillion, with the US accounting for USD 2.7 trillion (*Straits Times* 22 Apr. 2009). The US sub-prime crisis turned into a global depression. Governments in the US and Europe had to bail out some of the biggest banks, insurance companies and industrial manufacturers. The state as the default rescuer of the last resort for private capital has always been just beneath the surface of the neoliberal rhetoric. With the government bailouts, de-regulation and privatization were turned on their heads! Close to a decade later, the central banks of the world are still at a loss as how to "revitalize" the global capitalist economy. Significantly, Asian economies were largely spared from the crisis but not from the global recession.

Critiques of Liberal Individualism

Every ideology engenders its own critics and opposition, and liberalism is no exception. Criticism is frequently focused on its individualism. British conservative philosopher, John Gray, argues that the asocial individual of liberalism is a conceptual fiction, as such a person would be one "without history or ethnicity, denuded of the special attachments that in the real human world give us the particular identities we have" (1995: 5). The critique of asocial individualism is often accompanied by a counter-conceptualization of a socially embedded individual who realizes and reproduces his/her everyday life in and as a community. This is true also in America (Mudhall and Swift 1992). As recently as the early 1990s, a group of American intellectuals and public figures noted with concern a rise in the excesses of individualism—private desires re-scripted as individual rights and freedoms—and a corresponding decline of "public spiritedness" (Etzioni 1998). This group issued a communitarian manifesto, "The Responsive Community Platform: Rights and Responsibilities" (Etzioni 1998: xxv–xxxix), advocating

a political and ideological re-balancing of self-interest and social responsibility in public life. However, characterizing themselves as "liberal
communitarians" they were not interested in displacing and replacing
individualism with communitarian values. Indeed, in America the debate between communitarians and liberals is always "carried out on the
terrain and under the auspices of liberal universalism, with communitarianism playing at best a subsidiary or remedial role" (Dallmayr 1996:
281) and, in the end "preserves the liberal order" (Williams 1997: 78).
Unsurprisingly, Daniel A. Bell concluded that "it must be conceded that
1980s communitarian theorists [among whom he was affiliated] were
less-than-successful at putting forward attractive visions of non-liberal
societies" (2004).[3]

The same debate between liberal individualism and communitarianism was to be played out in East Asia in the early 1990s. Ironically,
just as the teleological narrative of liberal democratic capitalism appeared
to have triumphed over other political and economic narratives, it was
disrupted by the rise of non-liberal capitalism in East Asia (Fukuyama
1992: 238). Seeing the expansion of liberal individualism as a source
of social dissolution and a destructive force of community, many East
Asian political and thought leaders regularly espoused anti-liberal social
values, including communitarianism. At the front of the East Asian
resistance to liberal individualism was the PAP government. It hit a
wall of skepticism about the general idea that East Asian societies are
essentially communitarian, and a barrage of criticism that so-called
communitarianism was no more than a thin veil for authoritarianism
and corruption among political leaders in Asian nations where corruption is endemic at every level of government but worse at the top.
Given its history of political repression and the authoritarianism of
Prime Minister Lee Kuan Yew, the inclusion of the PAP government
in such critique was not groundless. Nevertheless, it has distinguished
itself in very significant ways from the guilty-as-charged political leaders
in East Asia.

Democratic Deficit in East Asia

The rejection of liberalism in East Asian nations has much to do with
their respective histories of state formation. All the East Asian nations
are post-World War II nations; additionally, all Southeast Asian nations,

---

[3] Bell has since then embraced a more collective definition of communitarianism
based on his reading of Confucian philosophy (see Bell and Hahm 2003).

except for Thailand, are post-colonial nations. All experimented with electoral democracy in the early phase of state formation; the experiments mostly failed. The contemporary non-communist nations have all conceded to some form of electoral politics as the means of selecting political office holders but they are far from being liberal democracies. Accordingly, they have been labelled as "hybrid" regimes under different names, such as "illiberal democracies" (Bell, et al. 1995; Zakaria 2003), "semi-democracies" (Case 2002) and "competitive authoritarianism" (Levitsky and Way 2010). Most political analyses of these hybrid regimes are framed within the expectation of their "transition" to liberal democracy, "rather than seeking to understand or explain these so-called hybrid regimes in their own terms" (Jayasuriya and Rodan 2007: 768). To date, only Taiwan (Alagappa 2001), South Korea and perhaps, Indonesia, may be said to have transited from military-supported authoritarian regimes into relatively liberal democracies. In the other states, an uneven playing field, restricted franchise, corruption, violence and tampering with ballots and other violations of the electoral process persist, which is painfully illustrated by the contemporary Philippines (Hutchcroft and Rocamora 2003). Furthermore, these violations or "democratic deficits" have become embedded in the existing stable states, making it difficult to honor their claims to being democratic, let alone liberal.

Several historical reasons stand in the way of democracy, particularly in post-colonial Southeast Asian nations. First, where there was a protracted violent anti-colonial struggle, military and political leaders who led the armed revolution often assumed that they, having shed blood for the birth of the new nation, were entitled to lead the new nation, as in the case of Aung San in Burma. Or, when a fledgling elected government ran into the normal prolonged negotiations among competing interests, causing delays in policy decisions that intensify economics and social issues, the supposed "instability" would serve as an excuse/opportunity for military leaders to intervene directly or stand ready to be "invited" by civilian political leaders to impose emergency rule, such as the regular coups in Thailand. Second, with or without an armed struggle for decolonization, indigenous political leaders could legitimately "reclaim" their homeland and re-impose, in whole or in part, the resurrected pre-colonial governing structure as the structure of government in the new nation. For example, the Sultans of the West Malaysia provinces are reconstituted as the Council of Rulers—an upper level of government with significant symbolic if not direct governing power. Furthermore, as postcolonial states tend to be multi-ethnic in composition due to immigration and the arbitrary boundaries of the new states, the primacy of indigenous people in the political, cultural and economic life of these new nations have been imposed, thus relegating non-indigenous groups to some form of "second class" citizenship or denying them citizenship. In such instances, ethnic inequalities and potential ethnic conflicts are built into the governance structure and, in the name of pre-empting possible ethnic conflict, highly undemocratic laws that restrict the freedoms of individuals or groups have been enacted, as in Malaysia (Liow 2015). Third, newly minted East Asian nations are still very much insecure objects in-the-making. They continue to tightly embrace their citizens, incorporating them within a bounded "national" space, inscribing upon them a "national" identity and incorporating them into the ongoing nation-building project. Nationalism remains an important and vital social and political force that exercises a strong affective hold on their respective peoples. With the multiple anxieties of nation building, the individualizing tendency and the demands of liberalism for a minimalist state constitute threats to the "unity" of the emergent nation, as in the case of Singapore. For all these reasons, the political leaders and citizens of post-colonial Southeast Asian nations are inclined to rebuff political criticisms from the West as hypocrisy against the latter's disinterest in democracy as colonizers in the past. They have often insisted that local history and cultural traditions should be given serious consideration in the shaping of the particular local political system, just as liberal democracy is a unique historical contingent development of the West.

Communitarianism, Authoritarianism and Corruption

Capitalist industrialization and urbanization in contemporary East Asia have lifted millions out of poverty. At the same time, it has also fragmented the extended household and generally loosened social constraints on individuals. The individualizing effect is celebrated as liberating new freedoms in money-making opportunities, expanding consumerism and, perhaps, an even greater demand for more freedoms (Chua 2000a; Zhao 1997; Davis 2005). However, it would be grossly simplistic to equate this as evidence of an emergent totalizing liberalism in these societies. At the ideological level, Aihwa Ong (2006: 12) observes: "Many ordinary people remain ambivalent and sceptical about market criteria and its assault on collective values and community interest." Indeed, the ambivalence and skepticism of ordinary citizens are often shared by their political and thought leaders. Supposedly drawing from their own historical and cultural resources, politicians have resurrected, reinvented and rendered local/traditional ideas and values as "indigenous values" to be re-inscribed on the nation. Predictably, these local values valorize the idea of "community," the "collective," and the "social": *gotong royong* for Indonesia (Bowen 1986), "Asian Values" for Singapore and Malaysia (Chua 1999), Confucianism for Korea (Lew, Choi and Wang 2011), and in China (Bell 2008) the addition of "socialism with Chinese character." If there has been one common element, it is the family as the foundational, quintessential social institution.

In and outside of Asia, the claim that East Asian societies are essentially communitarian has been met with skepticism by various liberal and left-of-liberal commentators. One would be hard to empirically prove the above claim (Kim 1994). For example, while the family may remain a relatively stable institution in most East Asian societies, a strong sense of social responsibility and obligation to the family often justifies nepotism and corruption that militates against the welfare of the larger community (Chang 2009). The essentialist communitarian culture claim is best viewed as a "clumsy" attempt to develop an ideological concept in resistance and opposition to liberal individualism (Rodan 1996: 337).

As mentioned above, the communitarian claim has been also subjected to the criticism that it is no more than a thin veil to hide the authoritarianism and financial corruption of the political leaders who espouse supposedly local communitarian traditions. However, the tendency for authoritarianism, corruption and the communitarian claim to be co-present is neither causally nor logically inevitable. One of the responsibilities of an elected government is to define the interests of the nation as a community. The temptation of elected individuals to turn this responsibility into their exclusive right to define, impose and demand adherence of the governed to a set of "national" interests is always present.

When the so-defined national interests are self-serving, corruption ensues. A prime example was the late President Suharto of Indonesia. Suharto joined the Indonesian army during the armed decolonization struggle and rose to the rank of major-general after independence. The alleged communist coup in 1965 turned him into the "savior" of the nation from communism. Installing himself as President and "father" of economic development, he ruled for 31 years. Ideologically, he had "vigorously propagated a set of 'communitarian' morals and ideological values under the rubric of *kekluargaan* (literally 'family-ness' from *keluarga*, family)" (Heryanto 2008: 20) and insisted on the principle of consensus through deliberations among elected representatives in government (Ramage 1995). Meanwhile, his family members and crony business partners were using the president's authoritarian power to usurp monopolistic business licenses for massive financial gains (Chua 1993). His New Order regime became emblematic of *Korupsi, Kolusi dan Nepotisme* (*KKN*—corruption, collusion and nepotism) in government (Robison 1996), which was exposed by the 1997 Asian regional financial crisis that led to the fall of Suharto.

In this sense, leadership risks authoritarianism and corruption but this is not inevitable. In a democratic society, this risk is contained partially by periodic elections that can remove and replace the corrupt authoritarian in power. In postcolonial Asian nations where electoral democracy is unstable, the tendency towards authoritarianism and corruption often comes from individuals who, for the reasons discussed above, presume their "right" and "entitlement" to govern the new nation.

Singaporean Antipathy to Liberalism

As mentioned, the PAP government faced the same skepticism and criticism suffered by the likes of Suharto but it has distinguished itself in significant ways. First, let us dispense with charges of corruption. In defense of the much caricatured "Asian Values," Lee Kuan Yew argued that within the Confucian (read: communitarian) idea of duty:

> You're supposed to look after your family and your extended family, and to be loyal and supportive of your friends. And you should do it from your private purse and not from the public treasury. Now, when you have weak governments and corruption seeps in, then this private obligation is often fulfilled at the public expense, and that's wrong. (*Straits Times* 23 May 1998)

The PAP government's signal pride is that it is scrupulously financially incorruptible. The PAP government, therefore, compels us to conceptually and empirically disaggregate communitarianism, authoritarianism and corruption as discrete ideas and practices that can be assembled in different ways by different individuals or groups, under different historical circumstances and to explain each instance only in its historical specificity.

At the ideological level, unlike other governments the PAP's rejection of liberalism is not ideologically opportunistic. The party was founded as a social democratic party in the generally left-infused atmosphere of post-World War II anti-colonialism. The first generation PAP political leaders had their ideological misgivings about liberalism in general and excessive individualism in particular, from the very beginning. It rejected the idea of "minimal" government, thus it ignored all neoliberal calls for deregulation and privatization of state enterprises. Instead, it continues to consolidate and extend state capitalism at home and globally. Ideologically, since the early 1990s, it has been experimenting with a different ideological framing for a more robust communitarianism. Given its expressed abhorrence for "ideology," its communitarianism may be said to be a beguiling simple formula—"society above individual"—in the governing of the economy, polity and social life. "Society" and "individual" take on different relative scales in different contexts. In the communitarian context, the nation is made up of different ethnic and/or religious communities; ethnic communities are made up of families which are constituted of individual members. Above all is national social and political stability, without which economic development and, in turn, the well-being of all individuals would be jeopardized (Chua 1995).

However, as an integral part of global capitalism, Singapore must out of necessity adopt certain capitalist values and accept their social consequences. For example, it actively promotes individualistic self-reliance and competition in education and employment, through the ideology of "meritocracy." The policy is "to reward work and work for reward" (PM Lee Hsien Loong, quoted in Rodan and Hughes 2014: 76) and Singaporeans just have to accept the social and economic inequalities and class divisions that the policy produces. It is this emphasis on self-reliance and meritocracy that has led critics to suggest that the PAP government is neoliberal (Tan 2013), in spite of the Singapore state's presence in the domestic and global economy through its state-owned enterprises and sovereign wealth funds. As a social mechanism for rewarding work, meritocracy was partly a response to the anti-welfare ideology that social welfare creates a mentality of entitlement and saps work ethics. According to Lee Kuan Yew, in the early 1960s,

> Through Hong Kong watching, I concluded that state welfare and subsidies blunted the individual's drive to succeed. I resolved to reverse course on the welfare policies which my Party had inherited or copied

from British Labour Party policies. I scaled back on subsidies except where they made the person more productive through better education, better health and better housing. (1997: 6–7)

Social expenditure is to be rendered as "human capital" development: education enhances the employability of workers and improves their productivity which, in turn, enhances capital accumulation; better employment rates, housing and public health improve the material condition of life for Singaporeans; finally, the ways through which human capital investments are funded underwrite the PAP government's legitimacy to rule and recuperate the PAP's claim to be a "social democratic" party.

Chapter 2

SINGAPORE STATE FORMATION IN THE COLD WAR ERA

IN ITS EFFORTS TO REMOVE THE last vestiges of colonialism from an independent Singapore, the PAP government made a conscious ideological decision that the official history of independent Singapore would consign the island's past glory as a notable trading post in archipelagic Southeast Asia (Kwa, Heng and Tan 2009) and its place as an island in the Malay world (Imran 2016) to prehistory. The official history would begin with the arrival of Stamford Raffles in 1819 and its founding as a free port of the East India Company (Hong and Huang 2008: 15–8) to avoid foregrounding the long, politically complex histories of contemporary Singapore's Chinese, Indian and Islamic peoples which would complicate the anticipated nation-building process.

Knowledgeable in the history of the Malay world, Raffles knew of the political rivalry between the Bugis and Malay factions within the Johor-Riau Sultanate to which the island belonged. The death of the Sultan of Johor in 1812 left the sultanate without a clear heir apparent, and with two surviving sons vying for their father's position, each supported by their respective factions. In 1819, Raffles opportunistically "proclaimed" the elder son, Hussein, to be the Sultan of Johor and signed an agreement with him, which granted the East India Company control over the port of Singapore. To compete with more developed ports in the region, such as Riau and Batavia, Raffles made Singapore a free port. Traders paid no import or export duties, no port fees, and no corporate or personal income taxes. Revenue was derived from license fees for businesses, property taxes, excise taxes and especially "vice taxes" on gambling, cock fighting, opium and local alcohol.

Although running a loss for many decades, Singapore became a vibrant port. It drew migrants from across Asia in search of employment and trade opportunities (E. Lee 2008: 4–6). Malays came from the archipelago, particularly the Bugis who had deep historical regional trade connections. Others came from the Malayan peninsula because of social disorder in the Malay states, such as succession disputes within chiefdoms, general lawlessness caused by Chinese coolies' secret societies (Baker 1999) and the threat of Siamese aggression in the northern states (Kennedy 1970). The Malay language, the regional lingua franca of the Southeast Asian archipelago, and Islam forged the Malay immigrants into a single community early on, largely replacing their family and community ties to their places of origin (Baker 1999: 111).

The closing of the British penal colony at Bencoolen, with the signing of the Anglo-Dutch Treaty in 1824, led to the arrival of Indian convict laborers until 1873, when the Andamans became the main penal colony (Baker 1999: 45). Also, Indian traders, primarily Chettiars or Muslims from Tamil Nadu, who already had extensive regional trade networks, found in Singapore a convenient base for their expeditions. However, large-scale Indian labor migration started only in the late nineteenth century when coolies, particularly low caste Tamils, were enticed to Singapore with three-to-five year contracts. In addition, a small number of *sepoys* (Indian soldiers) were employed and later, in 1879, Sikhs arrived to serve as a local police force (Lal, Reeves and Raj 2006: 32–65, 176–88).

Chinese, overwhelmingly men from the southern coastal provinces of Guangdong and Fujian, began to arrive in large numbers as opportunistic traders/merchants or impoverished laborers (Kwa, Heng and Tan 2009: 112). By the 1860s, the Chinese made up more than 65 percent of the population and they have been the demographic majority ever since. With the opening of the Suez Canal in 1869, Singapore's economic importance rose and Chinese immigration, especially coolies, increased significantly in the 1870s (E. Lee 2008: 28). (Two years earlier, in 1867, Singapore had been transferred from the East India Company to the British Empire, governed by the Colonial Office in India.) In the late nineteenth century, as the Qing dynasty reversed its traditional sanctions against emigration and began to regulate migration (E. Lee 2008: 30–1), new arrivals increased again, especially women who began to migrate to Singapore on a large scale (Wang 1989: 557). By the first decade of the twentieth century, the Chinese constituted about 70 percent of the population, with an increasing number of locally born residents. Immigrants continued to arrive until the eve of the Second World War but their numbers were slowly being overtaken by the locally born Chinese population.

Based on the 1947 Malaya and Singapore census, the total population was 940,824. Of this total population, 60.7 percent (or 571,331) were born in Singapore or Malaya while 39.3 percent (or 369,493) were immigrants.[1] However, for the majority of both locally born and newly immigrated Chinese, their respective homelands continued to be the reference points for emotional investment and life trajectories. Only a small portion of the population had developed local loyalties. After the collapse of the Qing Dynasty and the establishment of the Republic of China in 1911, the Chinese community was divided into three segments: the pro-Kuomintang, pro-Communist and "Malayans." The English-educated Chinese especially identified with the last group (Wang 1989: 561; E. Lee 2008: 53). In the early 1950s, many local-born Chinese-educated youth identified with the "new" China, the communist People's Republic of China, and "returned" to help rebuild their "motherland." By the 1920s, the immigrant Indians in Singapore became concerned with India's struggle for independence. During the Japanese Occupation (1942–45), the Japanese Imperial Army used the Indian nationalist, Chandra Bose, to reorganize the captured Indian soldiers of the British colonial armed forces into an Indian National Army, as a decolonization force. After the Japanese Occupation, the Malays were oriented to decolonization developments in Peninsular Malaya and Indonesia (Rahim 1998: 14). Each racial community was oriented politically toward a homeland outside Singapore.

It was only with independence in 1965 that the population began to be able to invest in a sense of permanence through citizenship in Singapore, the "nation." Singapore's history of migration and its transition from a trading post to a colony to a politically independent nation is unlike the "normal" history of colonization. There was no violent massacre of the indigenous population, no erasure of indigenous culture and no dismantling of local governmental and administrative structures by a conquering race. Furthermore, with its non-white Chinese majority,

---

[1] Washington, D.C. Migration Policy Institute, http://www.migrationinformation.org/charts/singapore-apr12-table1.cfm [accessed 25 Apr. 2016].

Singapore as a "settler" nation is unlike Canada, the US and Australia, where the majority were descendants of the colonizing country. This history obviously had a determining effect in the state formation of an independent Singapore.

The Left Beginning of the PAP

After the Second World War, the British colonial administration returned to find the people of Malaya no longer acquiescent to colonial rule. It found itself immediately engaged in a 10-year insurgency war with the Malayan Communist Party (MCP) (Chin 2003). With the defeat of the MCP, Peninsular Malaya was granted political independence in 1957. Singapore was retained as a colony. In 1955, an advisory legis-lative council with locally elected members, under a British colonial governor, was instituted in Singapore. The PAP was founded in Novem-ber 1954 to contest this election. At its founding, the PAP consisted of a coalition of left-wing unionists and British-educated professionals, who were influenced by the social democracy of post-war Britain. Lee Kuan Yew, a British-trained lawyer, came into contact with the left wingers fortuitously, when he was brought in as an assistant to Queen's Counsel, D.M. Pritt, to defend the office holders of the Socialist Club, a University of Malaya student organization, against sedition charges brought by the colonial government (Liao, et al. 2012). "[I]t was this trial, with its wide publicity and the public sympathy for the students, that launched Lee into left-wing circles in Singapore, and began his reputation as lawyer for the left" (Puthucheary 1998: 14).

An uneasy partnership ensued. The professionals, led by Lee, needed the unionists for the support of the working masses and marginalized Chinese-educated youth, while the unionists led by locally Chinese-educated Lim Chin Siong, faced with persistent threat of suppression by the colonial administration, welcomed the veneer of "legitimacy" pro-vided by the British-educated PAP members. The two factions were very distinct from each other, as events would show, despite their mutual need for each other and their shared anti-colonial and left-leaning poli-tical sentiments.

In the April 1955 legislative council election, the Progressive Party, a conservative bastion of English-educated, Straits-born Chinese, was decimated. The Labour Front, a pro-labor socialist party which had failed to forge a coalition with the PAP (Chan 1984: 75), won the majority of seats under the leadership of David Marshall, a brilliant criminal lawyer. The PAP won three of the four seats it contested, enough "to secure a forum in the Legislative Assembly to propagate the Party's objectives" (Fong 1980: 26). One month after the election, unionized bus drivers at the Hock Lee Bus Company went on strike. They were joined in solidarity by the Chinese middle-school unions. The students had been politically mobilized in the previous year by their resistance to the colonial government's expressed intention to conscript male students into military service.[2] Chief Minister Marshall was disinclined to use force to suppress the strike. Skirmishes between the police, workers and the workers' student sympathizers turned violent on 12 May, leaving three people dead, including a 16-year-old youth whose body was paraded through the streets. Two days later, the strike was settled largely in favor of the strikers (Clutterbuck 1984: 84–6), whose legal counsel was provided by PAP leaders. During the election, Marshall had promised that he would obtain full political independence from Britain. When he failed to do so after an all-party negotiation trip to London, he resigned. His tenure as Chief Minister was a brief 14 months (Chan 1984).

Knowing that crushing popular political unrest was necessary to gain British confidence in granting of independence, Marshall's successor, Lim Yew Hock, deregistered radical student associations and labor unions and imprisoned their leaders. In 1957, the British colonial office agreed to self-government in all domestic affairs but defense and foreign relations; however, real power remained in the hands of *ex-officio* colonial administrators and the governor (Lee B.H. 1989: 91). An election for a self-governing parliament was held in 1959. By then, with its record of violent political repression, the Labour Front had lost its credentials and credibility as an anti-colonial socialist political party. This left the PAP as the sole claimant of the anti-colonial movement. It campaigned vigorously during the election and won 43 of the 51 parliamentary seats, reducing all other political parties into insignificance, if not irrelevance. Lee Kuan Yew, 37 years old, accepted the office of the first Prime Minister of Singapore, after securing the release of left-leaning PAP unionists from political detention.

---

[2] An autobiographical novel, *The Mighty Wave*, by He Jin (2011), provides evidence that Malayan Communist Party members had infiltrated the Chinese Middle School student movement.

Having gained parliamentary power, the fateful reckoning of intra-party differences was inevitable. The untimely death of a PAP Member of Parliament (MP) in 1961 created the need for a by-election. The leftist PAP faction threatened to throw their support to the ex-Chief Minister, David Marshall, if the Lee faction refused to redress the faction's grievances against a whole battery of politically repressive measures. These included the absence of civil liberties, continuing political detention under the Internal Security Act, denial of citizenship to left-wing individuals, attempts to control the radical trade union movement instead of assisting it to consolidate its political base and, finally, the absence of intra-party democracy (Rodan 1989: 67). The issue over intra-party democracy arose because the cadre system of electing PAP party executives, which had been introduced while the left-wing leaders were in detention under the previous government, deprived these imprisoned leaders of access to power in the party (Bloodworth 1986: 185).[3] The Lee faction stood firm. The left delivered its threat. The PAP lost the by-election.

The loss of the by-election gave Lee the opening to force the intra-party division into the open by calling a confidence vote on his own government. In the ensuing vote, eight of the left-leaning faction crossed the floor in support of a no-confidence vote and five abstained; nevertheless, the government survived with a majority of one vote. The 13 defecting members were immediately expelled from the PAP. They, in turn, formed the Barisan Sosialis (Socialist Front; henceforth Barisan). A massive groundswell of defections from the PAP followed, leaving the Lee faction with little organized popular support but with the control of the party, the government and the wherewithal to continue its consolidation of power. Henceforth, Lee's faction would call itself, and what remained of the PAP, "moderates." It would also liberally label the purged left faction as "hidden" communists serving as the "open front" of the criminalized underground communist movement (Poh 2013: 194–7). Lee argued that the "communists" were in fact "pro-colonialist" because they preferred Singapore to remain a colony, so that their political activities could be seen as taking the moral high ground in the "anti-colonial" struggle. However, their struggle against the duly

---

[3] Dennis Bloodworth's history of the PAP may be said to belong to the "official" or "mainstream" history from the side of the victors. For a critique of these histories, see Hong and Huang (2008).

popularly elected government exposed their anti-nationalist sentiments (Lee 1962: 45). By implication, what remained of the PAP government was the "true" anti-colonial nationalist party of the future nation. The division rewrote the party's history: the radical left was expelled, with many subsequently imprisoned, deported or banned from politics after being coerced into confessing that they were "communists," while the social democrats re-labelled themselves as "moderates" and re-oriented themselves towards capitalist nation building.

Exit Malaysia

During the Cold War years, the formation of the Barisan as a viable left-socialist party, with its formidable popular support and alleged affiliation with the underground MCP, could be readily "imagined" as a threat not only to the colonial regime but also to all non-left political parties. It caused then Malayan Prime Minister, Tengku Abdul Rahman, hitherto disinterested in any political merger with Singapore, to propose the formation of the Federation of Malaysia, which would incorporate Peninsular Malaya, Singapore and the two small British colonies, Sarawak and North Borneo (the latter would be later renamed Sabah), on the large island of Borneo. The Malaysian proposal was quickly accepted by the British colonial office. A referendum for Singaporeans on the merger was held on 1 September 1962. Predictably the referendum was controversial.

The Barisan argued that the terms negotiated by the PAP government, where the Singapore retained certain rights in matters of labor and education, made it not a "true" merger. It proposed that Singapore should have the same terms as those for Penang and Malacca, the other two Malayan territories of the colonial Straits Settlements. The government suggested that since none of the political parties were in principle against the merger but differed only on conditions, the electorate's choice would be between the different terms for the merger; a "no" vote to the merger should not be an option. Outmaneuvered, the Barisan encouraged protest through the casting of blank votes. The government countered by adding a provision that all blank votes would be considered votes for the option selected by the majority of the voters. The government's option won an overwhelming majority.

After the referendum, the PAP government mounted Operation Cold Store on 2 February 1963. More than 100 left-wing individuals were detained allegedly for communist or pro-communist activities.

Among them were the Barisan leaders, including Lim Chin Siong. The operation was authorized by the Internal Security Council of seven members—three from the Singapore government, three from British colonial officials and one from Malaya, ostensibly the deciding vote. This composition provided the PAP government with a possible alibi to displace its responsibility for detention onto the Malayan representative. Operation Cold Store was undoubtedly the darkest episode in the history of Singapore's road to independence. Many people were imprisoned without trial in excess of 10 years, with Chai Thai Poh detained the longest for 23 years. Published counter-historical narratives and memories of detainees protesting their innocence from charges of being communists (Poh, Tan and Hong 2013) continue to ruffle the PAP government and official historians (Lau 2014; Ramakrishna 2015), because the supposed "life and death struggle with communism" in the 1950s and 60s has been one of the ideological foundations of the PAP government. However, with the death of Lee Kuan Yew in March 2015, the surviving Cold Store detainees have lost their target for condemnation and denouncement. Consequently, the ideological significance of Operation Cold Store is likely to have diminishing affective impact to successive generations of Singaporeans.

After the detention, Malaysia was formally constituted on 16 September 1963, following which the PAP called for a snap election. Despite having most of its top tier leaders in detention, the Barisan managed to win 33 percent of the popular vote, giving it 13 parliamentary seats, against the PAP's 47 percent, giving it 37 seats. The last seat went to the former first and only elected mayor of Singapore, Ong Eng Guan, who had been expelled earlier from the PAP for challenging Lee Kuan Yew's leadership. The result clearly suggested the possible emergence of a two-party parliamentary system. However, even before the new parliament was sworn in, three of the elected Barisan MPs were arrested and another two went into exile. In protest, its secretary general imposed a boycott of its remaining eight members sitting in parliament. They finally resigned in 1965, giving the PAP the opportunity to pick up all the vacated seats in by-elections. By this time, constant disagreements between the PAP government and the Malaysia federal government led to the separation of Singapore from Malaysia (Tan 2008). Singapore became independent on 9 August 1965.

As Singapore did not attain political independence through a protracted violent armed struggle, there were no authoritarian-revolutionary military generals who could emplace themselves as the "rightful" leaders to govern the new state. Although Malays were constitutionally "recognized" as the indigenous people, this is in reference to the Malay world of the Southeast Asian archipelago, rather than specific to the island of Singapore, where they were demographically a minority.[4] The majority ethnic-Chinese population, neither indigenous nor descendants of the colonizing race, had no proprietary claim to the right to govern. Finally, as a colonial territory Singapore had only known the British system of government and public service (E. Lee 1989: 4–6). Therefore, postcolonial independent Singapore arguably had to be founded on a "modern" footing, namely, as a constitutional democracy with an elected parliament; with the conventional guarantees of liberal individual equality, freedoms and rights; and with a rational civil service bureaucracy and an independent judiciary. The only unique feature is its declaration that Singapore is a constitutional "multiracial" nation, rather than one that is constituted by a singular homogenous indigenous ethnic people with a supposedly shared history, blood and cultural inheritance. The Barisan boycotted the first election after independence which was held in 1968. Because the Barisan was the only other viable political party, this left the PAP to win all the contested parliamentary seats and consolidate its absolute monopoly of political power, which spelled the end of a two-party system in parliament, a situation that still exists today.

National Survival

With absolute parliamentary power, the PAP government was in control of the state machinery to aggregate the common interests of individuals and racial groups and meld them into the "national" interest of an ideologically non-communist Singapore, upon which they could emotionally invest in their new identity as Singaporeans. Of immediate concern after independence was the very viability of the island's "survival" as a nation. Although Singapore was possibly the most prosperous city relative to the other cities in Southeast Asia, it was nevertheless still a non-industrialized economy with a high rate of underemployment and

---

[4] Indeed, Prime Minister Lee Kuan Yew had "challenged the special constitutional position and privileges of Malays in Malaysia by alleging that Malays were no more indigenous than the Chinese, Indians and other immigrant communities" (Rahim 1998: 16), and that they "should be on the same footing as the other immigrant communities" (Rahim 1998: 17).

unemployment plus a high birth rate. The continuing "survival" as a nation became the primary preoccupation, and it has remained central to the logic of the PAP government until today despite being one of the wealthiest countries in the world (Chan 1971). As former Minister for Foreign Affairs, George Yeo, put it,

> There is always certain anxiety in Singapore that our geographic, econo-mic and political positions are vulnerable. The anxiety is a galvanizing force, in some way an obsession. Our success is a result of anxiety, and the anxiety is never fully assuaged by success. Perhaps all city-states feel that way. It keeps people on the ball. (quoted in Kraar 1997)

This collective anxiety drives the underlying determination of the PAP government and Singaporeans to succeed; failure is not an option. Ironically, economic success only aggravates the anxiety as current success is always ephemeral against the permanence of vulnerability-and-survival. Against this logic, the massively improved material life has produced in the majority of Singaporeans a political conservatism that is highly protective of the hard-earned material gains, a conservatism that dovetails with the government's emphasis on the need to maintain social and political stability.

"Survivalism" has become a constitutive element of the PAP's ideology; what was a historically contingent fact has been naturalized as a permanent state of the nation (Chua 1995). Vulnerability-and-survival is an open concept without a fixed substance, which makes it an all encompassing and highly efficacious ideological frame. For example, any social issue can be interpreted as a vulnerability that threatens the nation's survival and used to justify various policies. This open concept thus exercises a disciplining function: to ensure national survival, the population must "be transformed into a tightly organized and highly disciplined citizenry all pulling in the same direction with a sense of public spiritedness and self-sacrifice in the national interest" (Chua 1995: 18). Deviation from the collective effort could potentially be framed as threatening national survival and thus justify calls for state intervention, including political repression.

Concretely, the government sees several persistent or permanent threats and vulnerabilities to national survival within and beyond the nation. Domestic threats include economic stagnation with high rates of unemployment; potential "communalism" or "racial conflict" which always lies just beneath the surface calm of a multiracial society; and until recently, communism. Fear of economic stagnation has resulted in the government's obsession with economic growth at all costs, which has been politically reflected in its taming of labor as an organized force. Fear of "communalism" and racial conflict has led to the government's policy of multiracialism which has preemptively put in place a comprehensive network of commissions, state-sponsored organizations, legislations and administrative practices that act concertedly to prevent imagined racial conflicts from becoming realities. Fear of communism justified the PAP government's constant hunt for communists from the 1950s until as late as 1987, when it discovered and exposed a supposedly "Marxist conspiracy," when communism had been defeated nearly everywhere in the world!

Threats from the outside include worldwide economic competition and military aggression from unnamed nations. Singaporeans are constantly reminded that they cannot rest on past and current achievements and slow down because other "hungrier" countries are ready to displace and replace Singapore from its competitive position. Military threats cannot be spelt out explicitly without causing diplomatic difficulties. They can, nevertheless, be alluded to in the idea of Singapore being an ethnic-Chinese-majority nation in a Malay Sea. Indeed, during the 1997 Asian regional financial crisis, Indonesian President Habibe reminded the visiting Minister for Defense of Singapore, lest he had forgotten, that Singapore is but a "little red dot" in a sea of green, the color of Islam. Since then the "Little Red Dot" has been popularly adopted by Singaporean leaders, citizens and media as a self-referencing metaphor not only of vulnerability but also, perhaps more significantly, pride in the nation's achievements and progress. To fend off military threats, in addition to the conscription of all male citizens into military service, defense constitutes the largest item in the annual national budget; an enormous amount of money is spent on high-tech military hardware, relative to the smallness of the practically indefensible island. As the respected veteran Singapore diplomat Tommy Koh put it, "The world is, however, a dangerous place and small fish will always be vulnerable to big predators of the ocean" (2013). The point is to deter potential predators by making them realize that it would be very costly to try to "swallow" tiny Singapore.

With these and other imaginable domestic and external threats in mind, pre-emptory interventions and controls, whether big or small, or in different modes from film censorship to detention without trial, are constantly being put in place rather than withheld until threats have occurred and wreaked havoc on the nation. Following this logic of pre-emption, laws become tools of "legitimate" repression: laws against vandalism are used to suppress political expressions in graffiti form; laws regulating the media are partially motivated to control the alleged Chinese chauvinism of the Chinese language press; and religious harmony laws are aimed at keeping religion out of public debates which have political implications (Rajah 2012). With an absolute majority in parliament, the PAP government can readily enact, with due parliamentary process, new laws, as well as make amendments to existing ones to suppress activities in social and political life. The use of laws as tools of social control reinterprets and transforms the liberal notion of the "rule of law" to a state of "rule by law" (Jayasuriya 1997; Rajah 2012).

In matters of national interest, the government must distance and place itself structurally above all individuals and groups so that it can, and be seen to, act as a "neutral" umpire in adjudicating without discriminating or privileging any individual or group. For example, the first Foreign Affairs Minister, S. Rajaratnam, pointed out that the PAP "has come to realize that the workers are a class with vested interests, and that as a political party, the PAP must work for the interest of the whole country and not for one class" (quoted in Pang 1971: 21), in spite of the supposedly "symbiotic" relationship between the PAP and the National Trades Union Congress, as shown in the next section. The PAP's ability to insulate itself from socially generated pressures has been greatly facilitated by its very high degree of autonomy vis-à-vis the citizenry afforded by absolute parliamentary power. As will be shown in the chapter on multiracialism, this power has been used to great effect in the management of race.

Taming Labor

Concretely, "national survival" must be disaggregated into specific interests and public policies that contribute to the survival itself. One immediate and obvious survival demand was the creation of employment through economic growth in the 1960s: "Political problems ultimately mean the problem of how we make our living, how we can give everyone a fair and equal chance to study and work and have a full life" (Lee 1962: 83). To create employment, industrialization was essential. Ironically, the loss of the anticipated Malaysia market due to political separation resulted in an expansion of horizon and vision. The Minister for Foreign Affairs, S. Rajaratnam, declared in 1972 that Singapore "is transforming itself into a new kind of city—the Global City," one which embraces the world as its hinterland (Rajaratnam 1972). To access the global market, the PAP government adopted the export-oriented industrial strategy that had propelled Japan from the devastation of war into an advanced industrial nation by the 1960s and that South Korea, Taiwan and Hong Kong successfully adopted later. However, at the time, Singapore was lacking the two key elements for successful industrialization, namely, an industrial labor force and industrial capital.

Regarding labor, according to the first Minister for Finance, Goh Keng Swee, Singapore's unemployed and underemployed population lacked industrial work skills and habits; therefore, the population had to be remoulded into economically productive citizens by inculcating in them an interest in "rising incomes and improved standard of living," which could be achieved through the willingness and ability to work hard (Goh 1976: 81). But, first, the restive left-leaning labor movement under the radical faction of the PAP had to be tamed and workers brought under control. Then-Prime Minister Lee Kuan Yew was very explicit about the need for the government to dominate labor, stating that "[p]olitical leaders must triumph [over unions], if necessary, by changing the ground rules to thwart the challenge [by unions], using legislative and administrative powers, and when necessary backed by the mandate of the electorate" (quoted in Wong 1983: 265). Thus, the Singapore Association of Trade Unions (SATU) and its affiliates of radical trade unions were deregistered. Radical union leaders were detained during and after the 1963 Operation Cold Store and non-citizen leaders deported.

The PAP government in turn established the National Trades Union Congress (NTUC) in 1964, under the leadership of C.V. Devan Nair, a veteran left-wing unionist and ex-political detainee who switched political affiliations to join Lee Kuan Yew's team. The NTUC brought workers under direct PAP control. Its members constituted a new mass support base for the party, replacing the ground it had lost to the Barisan. From then on organized labor was yoked to the PAP, party and government, in a so-called "symbiotic" relationship. This relation has been institutionalized through (1) the concurrent appointment of the Secretary General of NTUC as a cabinet minister in the Prime Minister's Office; (2) the regular employment of PAP-MPs as so-called "labor MPs," ranging from union advisors to managers in the various NTUC cooperative enterprises; and (3) the regular election of labor MPs as members of the NTUC Central Committee.

The PAP did not stop at incorporating organized labor into the party and government. A string of legislation was enacted to progressively constrain the rights of unions from taking conventional industrial actions, such as work-to-rule, walkouts and strikes, which effectively further reduced the political power of the already compliant unions. This string of legislation was aimed at redirecting the unions away from confrontational relations with employers, towards a tripartite relation of "trust and cooperation" among unions, employers and the government, in which obviously the government supersedes capital, which in turn supersedes labor.

In 1968, to stabilize labor costs during the first five years of operation of pioneer industries, the Industrial Relations (Amendments) Act prohibited unions from bargaining beyond the minimum standards set by the Act. Strikes and lock-outs were prohibited and replaced by compulsory conciliation and arbitration. In 1972, the union's role in the collective bargaining of wages was further eroded by the establishment of a "tripartite" National Wage Council. The primary role of the council is to recommend annual wage increase guidelines which are largely followed by employers and unions. In 1982, a Trade Union (Amendments) Bill further emphasized cooperative industrial relations by specifically defining union activities as promoting "good" (read: cooperative) industrial relations, improving work conditions and helping to increase productivity. The NTUC itself also initiated the breaking down of large industrial unions into "house unions" thereby reducing the collective strength of labor as a whole. In 1984, the Employment Act gave the employer greater discretion in the scheduling of work to maximize the productivity of employees.

In 2000 and 2002, the Trade Union Act was further amended. One amendment, which still holds today, empowered the Minister for Manpower to freeze funds to trade unions if there is satisfactory evidence that unions are misusing funds and to make financial institutions, where the funds are deposited, withhold these funds. Finally, strikes which do not follow the legislative guidelines are criminalized and striking workers can be fined or imprisoned.[5] All these "amendments

---

[5] This criminalization was carried out in 2013, when a group of migrant workers from China, who worked as bus drivers, collectively failed to show up for work. Their action was declared an "illegal strike" by the Minister for Manpower and the workers' leaders were tried, jailed and deported.

are a systematic attempt to remove any legal obstacles in the way of the nation's objectives" (*Straits Times* 30 Sept. 1981); namely, industry peace that is essential to keeping workers employed, keeping production going, furthering capital accumulation for employers and generating national economic growth and government revenue. The need for government intervention to keep industry peace is justified in these terms. For example, in 1982 when the government was criticized for eroding workers' rights and benefits through legislation, then NTUC Secretary-General Lim Chee Onn conceded that workers might indeed be working under less than desirable legislation and state-controlled unions but "had they not however benefitted from economic growth?" (Wong 1983: 266).

Concerning the lack of local industrial capital, the government set out to attract foreign investors with attractive tax packages, including a tax-free pioneer industries status. The timing was felicitous. It was just when manufacturing industries in the developed economies of the US, Europe and Japan, facing high domestic labor costs, went in search of offshore locations that had abundant surplus labor for the low-cost production of low-end consumer goods. Fortunately, too, China had yet to open up its massive labor force to global capitalism. Also, neighboring Indonesia had just discovered oil and was not competing for foreign direct investments. The result was investments flowed into Singapore, creating employment for its citizens. Where foreign capital was not available to set up particular industries, the government developed its own state enterprises. Over the years, many of these enterprises have been corporatized and developed into successful multinational corporations, with long-term investments regionally and globally. Their annual profits have become an important revenue source for the Singapore government. (The details of Singapore's industrial development will be analyzed in the chapter on state capitalism.) By the mid-1970s, Singapore was transformed from a country with high unemployment to one with a permanent labor shortage, attracting different types of migrant labor, from top-end managers to low-end unskilled workers from both developed and developing countries around the world.

Reining in the Media

Having decimated its political opposition and brought labor under its direct control, the hegemonic one-party government continued to consolidate its power over society by reining in the media. As radio and television were already state enterprises, control of the media focused on newspapers. The Chinese-language newspapers were the first to be targeted. In May 1971, Lee Mau Seng, a former general manager, Shamsuddin Tung Tao Chang, the Muslim-Chinese editor-in-chief, Ly Singko, senior editorial writer, and Kerk Loong Seng, public relations officer of the established Mandarin newspaper, *Nanyang Siang Pau*, were arrested under the Internal Security Act (E. Lee 2008: 305). They had allegedly criticized the government's pro-English policies and accused the government of being "pseudo-foreigners who forget their ancestors." Such criticism was allegedly a "deliberate campaign by the *Nanyang Siang Pau* to whip up Chinese racial emotions," seeking to "sharpen conflict along race, language and culture lines" (*Straits Times* 3 May 1971). The detained would be released if they agreed to change the newspaper's editorial policy. They refused and were sentenced to two years of detention (Seow 1998: 46), but the newspaper continued publication.

In 1982, the government suggested that given its relatively small domestic readership, *Nanyang Siang Pau* should merge with the other Mandarin newspaper, *Sin Chew Jit Poh*. The backroom intervention of the government led to the two publishers merging to form the Singapore News and Publications Limited (SNPL). The two newspapers were dissolved and replaced by *Lianhe Zaobao* (morning edition) and *Lianhe Wanbao* (evening edition). In 1984, the government further arranged for the merger of the SNPL, Straits Times Press and Times Publishing Board to form the Singapore Press Holdings Ltd (SPH), thus consolidating the English-language, the Malay-language and Chinese-language newspapers, under one news corporation.[6] Eventually, the family-run Tamil-language daily, *Tamil Murasu*, was also absorbed by the SPH. Ostensibly, the business-minded logic for merging all the newspapers under one corporation was to reduce redundancy and pool resources to improve publication quality. The result, however, was to create an easily controllable, single channel and single definition of news in different languages (Tan and Soh 1994), which obviously contradicts the logic of competition as the basis for a healthy media environment essential for a well-informed citizenry.

The second newspaper to draw the wrath of the government was the *Singapore Herald*. Started in 1970, it soon became controversial for three reasons. First, it allowed citizens to complain about the government through its letters to the editor (Baker 1999: 371), and it was critical of the government's arrest of the *Nanyang Siang Pau*'s editors

---

[6] For a detailed account of Lee Kuan Yew's role in the merger see Cheong (2012: 192–4).

(Seow 1998: 58). Second, it supposedly had pro-Western editors. Founder-editor Francis Wong, who resigned only after one year, was allegedly sympathetic to Western "decadent" behavior, such as men having long hair, which threatened the government efforts to develop a disciplined labor force for the economy (E. Lee 2008: 536). Foreign editor Bob Reece, his Malaysian wife Adele Koh, who was features editor, and M.G.G. Pillai, another features editor, were asked to leave Singapore. Third and most importantly, it relied heavily on foreign funds and, according to the government, was possibly involved in "Black Operation," that is, clandestine anti-government activities organized overseas by foreigners with an interest in undermining Singapore's system of state control (Tan and Soh 1994: 5). The newspaper was in debt by SGD 4.5 million to Chase Manhattan Bank. The government "encouraged" the bank to foreclose on the loan (*Straits Times* 20 May 1971). However, an enthusiastic public campaign to "Save the Herald" ensued, raising at least SGD 70,000 (*Straits Times* 29 May 1971). Following this campaign, the government mandated that the financial supporters of the *Herald* must be locals, to avoid foreign interference. On 24 May, the *Herald* announced that it had found a willing Singaporean investor, but he apparently retracted his offer on 27 May (Seow 1998: 81–4). The government revoked the *Herald*'s license on 28 May and the newspaper ceased publication the next day (*Straits Times* 29 May 1971).

The end result of all the government actions was to leave Singapore's print media under a single publisher, the SPH, for ease of media control. Under the 1920 Printing Press Act of the colonial government, if a publication causes "ill-will" towards the authorities, ethnic/communal unrest or promoted political violence, its permit could be revoked. The Act was amended in 1972 to require would-be publishers to agree to these conditions *before* a permit was issued, thus reinforcing the colonial rules (Tan and Soh 1994: 36). In 1974, the entire Act was replaced by the Newspaper and Printing Act with the following conditions:

- publishers must renew their licenses every year;
- publishing houses must be publicly listed companies, with special "management shares" which carry 200 times more voting power than ordinary shareholders and which are issued only to people approved by the government;
- all directors must be Singaporean citizens; and finally,
- sources of foreign funding are subject to government approval (Tan and Soh 1994: 37).

In addition, government nominees are to sit on the board of directors for each newspaper, and the government can appoint or remove any person from any post in a newspaper (Lim 1985: 107 and 113). A separate Undesirable Publication Act (1967) prohibits "objectionable" content relating to sex, violence, drugs and ethnic hostility. Finally, under the Internal Security Act, the government can ban publications and detain any journalist for publishing news which it deems to have incited violence or jeopardized "the national interest" or public security. Cumulatively, these laws have effectively imposed on the media severe self-censorship (George 2012: 44) in order to stay in print.

On Social Groups

Not surprisingly, censorship was extended beyond the media to cultural productions by independent cultural organizations. Surveillance and punishment were also extended to other activist social groups. By the mid-1960s, rebellious Chinese-educated students were effectively suppressed as part of the larger post-war decolonization process (Hong and Huang 2008: 137–62). Student protests shifted to the University of Singapore. In 1968, students protested to no avail against the appointment of former Deputy Prime Minister, Toh Chin Chye as Vice Chancellor, on the grounds that he was concurrently the Minister for Science and Technology, and thus would give the government too much influence over university affairs (E. Lee 2008: 404). In 1974, the University of Singapore Student Union (USSU) led by student, Tan Wah Piow, became particularly active, supporting a range of causes from protests over local bus-fare increases to supporting workers' rights and humanitarian fund-raising for the Bangladesh Flood Relief. Things came to a head when Tan was accused of inciting a riot during a protest against the American Marine Pte Ltd factory which had laid off employees for a few weeks due to a worldwide economic recession (*Straits Times* 23 Feb. 1975). Tan and six USSU executives were arrested. Five of them were Malaysians and one was from Hong Kong. The six foreign students were accused of involving themselves in local political activities and deported (*Straits Times* 12 Dec. 1974).[7]

---

[7] One of them initially managed to escape deportation and hid in Singapore until August 1975, where he clandestinely wrote articles critical of the Singaporean government and posted them on notice boards throughout the university's campus (*Far Eastern Economic Review* 5 Sept. 1975).

Tan was placed on trial on 11 December 1974. Hundreds of students and workers came to the trial to support Tan while other students held a three-hour rally at the campus (*Straits Times* 12 Dec. 1974). Students also held a 48-hour boycott of classes (E. Lee 2008: 407). In addition to causing riot, Tan was also charged for using the USSU as a "political machine" to serve as an advocate for workers' rights, and more generally to be a source of opposition to Parliament (*Straits Times* 22 Feb. 1975). Tan denied both charges and argued that there had been no riot and thus he had been framed.[8] After a trial of nearly two months, Tan was sentenced to one year of prison. He was let out after eight months in order to do military national service. Upon hearing of the planned release of Tan, students planned to gather at the prison's gates to give him a hero's welcome; in response, the authorities released him two hours ahead of schedule (*Far Eastern Economic Review* 14 Nov. 1975). Instead of enlisting, Tan escaped to Britain, where he has remained in exile until today; in the eyes of the Singapore government and the law, he is a fugitive. Following these events, the University of Singapore Amendment Bill was enacted to regulate university political associations. USSU leaders were no longer directly elected by students, foreign students were prohibited from participation in the election and funds were controlled by the university administration (George 2012: 101). The Bill marked "the end of student activism" (Turnbull quoted in Huang 2006: 405).

On Communists

Through the 1970s and 1980s, alleged communists continued to be uncovered. According to the *Straits Times* (28 May 1976), in March 1976, in a room at No. 24 Kay Poh Road authorities found two detonators, a checklist for intelligence information, SGD 1,000 in cash, 23 types of communist pamphlets, photographs from a guerilla training camp on the Thai-Malaysian border and other suspicious documents. The documents uncovered suggested a group had developed the following plans: recruiting new members; engaging in guerilla warfare in Southern Thailand and Western Malaysia; infiltrating the government, schools and

---

[8] Meanwhile, Foreign Minister Rajaratnam claimed that Singapore University student activists were being manipulated by foreign elements, such as Australian leftists, Malaysian Chinese (to promote re-merger with Malaysia) and the CIA (*Far East Economic Review* 1 Mar. 1975).

cultural groups; setting up factories, businesses and shops to manage underground operations; collecting information on the government; working with secret society gangsters; and setting up underground arsenals and manufacturing weapons. Fifty people were subsequently detained for hatching "a communist plot to start a new phase of subversion and terrorism in Singapore" (*Straits Times* 28 May 1976).

Among the detained were Kuo Pao Kun, a playwright and his wife, Goh Lay Kuan, a ballet dancer. Goh, trained in Australia, had allegedly gone to the Malayan Communist Party guerilla training camp on the Thai-Malaysian border, where she was assigned to recruit students, doctors and engineers in Australia, as well as raise funds for the cause. Kuo supposedly converted to communism while receiving theater training in Australia. He returned to Singapore in 1965 and set up a performance arts studio, supposedly "to propagate leftist dance and drama" with working class and peasantry issues (Quah 2012). In early 1974, Kuo was allegedly inducted into the Malayan People's Liberation League. He also allegedly visited the guerilla training camp and was selected to form and cultivate a chapter of the League in Singapore (*Straits Times* 28 May 1976). Goh was released after two and a half months, after making a TV confession, but Kuo remained in prison until 1 October 1980 (*Straits Times* 19 Oct. 1980). After his release, Kuo continued to write and produce allegorical plays on local issues, including multilingual productions. In 1990, he was awarded the national Cultural Medallion for his contribution as a pioneer in Singapore theater and some of his early banned plays have been reprised by his theater company, under his daughter's directorship.

1987 Marxist Conspiracy

Just as communism was in defeat globally, a Marxist Conspiracy aiming to topple the PAP government was uncovered. In March 1987, 22 young Singaporeans were detained as part of the conspiracy, allegedly masterminded by Tan Wah Piow, the self-exiled student activist from the 1970s. Many of the detained were also accused of infiltrating several Catholic student groups and welfare centers (*Straits Times* 27 May 1987). Others had allegedly infiltrated the opposition Workers' Party, "evidenced" by their helping the party's candidate, J.B. Jeyaratnam, during by-elections in 1981 and 1984 (Seow 1994: 79). Vincent Cheng, supposedly the group leader, had been allegedly acquainted with the

Filipino insurgency movement, Christians for National Liberation (CNL), since 1972. Moreover, throughout the early 1980s, Cheng was supposedly in frequent contact with visiting members of the New People's Army, a Filipino communist insurgency group, whose members had come to Singapore to give guidance to the drama group, Third Stage (*Straits Times* 29 May 1987). This drama group, founded in July 1983, was accused of using drama as a means to politicize and radicalize the audience by consistently presenting a negative image of Singaporean politics and society (*Straits Times* 27 May 1987), for example, *Esperanza*, a play about an abused Filipino maid (*Straits Times* 5 May 1986). Several of its members were among the detained. Within four months, most of the 22 detained young Singaporeans were released.

Nine of the released later issued a statement claiming they were framed by the government, physically tortured in detention and forced to issue fake confessions. Eight were re-arrested (the ninth was outside Singapore) along with their lawyer, Patrick Seong (E. Lee 2008: 468). All but the lawyer Teo Soh Lung were subsequently released after they retracted their press release (Teo 2011). (Several of the detainees describe graphically the physical abuse in the documentary film, *Unravelling the Conspiracy*, in 2016.) The idea of the Marxist Conspiracy lacked credibility among Singaporeans. Indeed, the government quickly dropped its claim that Tan Wah Piow was the mastermind of the plot (Singh 1988: 8). The government's story was ultimately discredited when the current Minister for Finance and Second Deputy Prime Minister, Tharman Shanmugaratnam, who was a friend of several of the detainees and who was himself interrogated by the police "day and night for a week but escaped detention," said, "Although I had no access to state intelligence, from what I knew of them, most were social activists but not out to subvert the system" (quoted in Hong and Huang 2008: 145).

The detention of defense lawyer Patrick Seong further complicated the situation. He was detained for keeping US-based human rights groups informed of the legal proceedings against the detainees, especially at a time when Prime Minister Lee Kuan Yew was visiting the US, thereby causing Lee great embarrassment (Seow 1994: 90). During interrogation, Seong made a statement linking his own defense lawyer, Francis Seow, to E.M. Hendrickson, first secretary of the US Embassy in Singapore. Hendrickson was accused of seeking to develop Seong and Seow as viable opposition candidates (E. Lee 2008: 470) for the upcoming 1988 parliamentary election. According to Seow, the statement was extracted under duress from Seong, whose wife had apologized on her husband's behalf and had further warned Seow to leave Singapore as the latter's detention was inevitable. In May 1988, Seow was arrested while visiting Seong in detention, accused of being a proxy for foreign powers (E. Lee 2008: 472). He was released after two months and advised to stay out of politics, after allegedly being subjected to extensive interrogations and torture (Seow 1994: 244).

In defiance, Seow stood in the 1988 election as part of the Workers' Party slate of three candidates in the Eunos Greater Representative Constituency (GRC) along with Lee Siew Choh, former secretary general of the Barisan Sosialis, and Mohamed Khalit bin Baboo, a Malay radio personality. (A GRC is constituted by binding several electoral constituencies into a single electoral unit. Contesting political parties have to field a slate of candidates; the slate that wins the most votes wins all the seats.) Seow's team lost to the PAP slate of candidates by a very slim margin of less than 2 percent of the total votes cast. However, as the team that drew the highest number of votes among those who lost the election, Lee and Seow were in line for the Non-Constituency Member of Parliament seats. Before Seow could take up his seat, he was charged with tax evasion. He chose exile in the US rather than face the charge against him. He was nevertheless tried in absentia, where he was further accused of deceiving the court by claiming to be physically unfit to fly (*Straits Times* 16 Mar. 1989). In 1991 he was again tried in absentia for 60 tax summonses, for all of which he was found guilty and sentenced to pay a fine of SGD 80,000 or 95 months in jail (*Straits Times* 17 Oct. 1991). He died in exile in January 2016.

Ruinous Libel Suits

Another mode of repression takes the form of PAP MPs, especially heavy-weight cabinet ministers, suing opposition politicians (although ordinary citizens are not entirely exempted) for libel, and making large financial claims for supposed damages to the claimant's personal reputation and, by extension, the reputation of the PAP government. "Between 1971 and 1993 'there has been 11 cases of opposition politicians who had been made bankrupt after being sued'" (Thio 2004: 189). The person who bore the heaviest brunt of this mode of "punishment" was the late J.B. Jeyaratnam, whom Lee Kuan Yew promised to "crush" the moment the former stepped into the political arena as the leader of the

Workers' Party. The determination to "destroy" Jeyaratnam intensified when he managed to win the parliamentary seat in the 1981 by-election in the Anson constituency, breaking what had been the all-PAP parliament since 1968. The chronicle of Jeyaratnam's sufferings in his lifelong confrontation with the PAP government is well documented by Lydgate (2003: 312–4). A quick summary of instances in which opposition political leaders were sued include:

> Prime Minister Lee Kuan Yew sued Jeyaratnam for making defamatory innuendoes in his speech about the Tat Lee Bank [license] in 1976. Lee sued him again for asking about the suicide of Teh Cheng Wan [then incumbent Minister of National Development] in 1988. Lee sued United Front [political party] Seow Keng Leng in 1989. Lee sued the *Far Eastern Economic Review* in 1989. Lee and his son, Lee Hsien Loong, sued Workers' Party candidate Wee Han Kim in 1992. Five PAP MPs sued the Workers' Party in 1995. Lee Kuan Yew, his son Lee Hsien Loong, and prime minister Goh Chok Tong sued the *International Herald Tribune* twice in 1995. (Lydgate 2003: 260)

The list continues:

- S. Jayakumar, Minister for Law and four Indian PAP MPs sued the Workers' Party in 1995.
- Lee Kuan Yew and Lee Hsien Loong sued Tang Liang Hong [a Workers' Party candidate in the 1997 parliamentary election] and Hong Kong magazine *Yazhou Zhoukan* in May 1996.
- Prime Minister Goh Chok Tong, Senior Minister Lee Kuan Yew, Deputy Prime Minister Lee Hsien Loong and five PAP MPs sued Tang in December 1996.
- Lee Kuan Yew and Lee Hsien Loong sued Tang in January 1997.
- Goh Chok Tong and Lee Kuan Yew sued Tang in January 1997.
- Goh Chok Tong, Lee Kuan Yew and six other PAP leaders sued Tang in January 1997.
- Goh Chok Tong, Lee Kuan Yew and nine other PAP MPs launched separate suits against Jeyaratnam in January 1997.
- Goh Chok Tong and Lee Kuan Yew sued Chee Soon Juan of the Singapore Democratic Party in 2002.

The outcomes of these suits were quite predictable. Jeyaratnam, Tang Liang Hong and Chee Soon Juan were all made bankrupt and thus disqualified from electoral political contests. Tang left for Australia in self-exile and has never returned to Singapore. Jeyaratnam finally discharged his bankruptcy in 2005. He died in 2008. Chee finally discharged his bankruptcy in 2012 after Lee Kuan Yew and Goh Chok Tong agreed to a very substantially reduced settlement, from SGD 500,000 to SGD 30,000. He was finally able to stand in the 2015 general election, as the leader of the Singapore Democratic Party. Although he did not win, he did emerge as a formidable contestant whose campaign speeches at the political rallies won him much attention and praise from his audiences as the electioneering progressed.

Conclusion

Becoming independent during the Cold War, the PAP government of Singapore, along with other Southeast Asian countries, was willing to be cast as a "frontline" state in resisting the spread of communism. Alliance with the US-led "free world" provided various forms of economic benefits—development aid, investment capital, development of domestic service enterprises, including the morally dubious "rest and recreation" services to the American military fighting in the Vietnam War and generally policing the regional seas. Fighting communism was not only financially lucrative but also a convenient excuse for domestic political repression by any politician with a tenuous hold on power. Instead of condemning excessive and often violent repression, the "free" world shored up the authoritarian regimes, materially and ideologically, to contain if not defeat communism at all costs. In Singapore, where "anti-communist" repression had already been carried out before independence, the PAP government further turned up its anti-communist rhetoric as that of a "life and death" struggle for the survival of the nascent island-nation.

There can thus be no doubt that the road to the PAP's monopolization and longevity in parliamentary power, uninterrupted since 1959 until today, was paved with the ruthless repression of organized groups, social institutions and individuals. It dismantled alternative power bases by detaining dissidents, emasculating existing organizations, such as labor unions, placing the media on a short leash with multiple legal restrictions; and, where possible, bringing dissident individuals and organizations under the wing of the PAP itself or enfolding them into the government's effort in economic development. These repressive measures have effectively discouraged individuals, especially those who are professionally and financially successful, from entering political contests against the PAP.[9] Although the number of individuals and groups subjected to these repressive measures has been small and selective, or as George (2007) put it, "calibrated," the repression has nevertheless cast long and lasting shadows and engendered a fear that penetrates deeply into Singapore society, reaching ordinary citizens who might not even be particularly concerned with politics. For example, young university students often believe that they should not voice their opinions publicly. They exercise self-censorship, lest they incur the wrath of the PAP government and be imprisoned without trial. Such fear may be perversely self-satisfying as it allows individuals to imagine that their opinions might be subjected to state repression. Such fear is ironically self-fulfilling; if one says nothing, one has no problem with the government.

Of greater consequence was the widespread rumor that the compulsory vote during elections was not secret and that the government could ferret out for "punishment" those who voted against the PAP. This was clearly unfounded because in every general election an average of 25 to 30 percent of the electorate consistently voted against the PAP. This number rose to 40 percent in the 2011 general election, in which the PAP lost six parliamentary seats and two years later, another seat as the result of a by-election. It is obviously impossible for the government to go after each and every one of these voters. However, at the constituency level, the PAP government is not beyond punishing any constituency that elects a non-PAP MP. Residents of the Potong Pasir electoral constituencies voted against the PAP from 1984 to 2011 and those in Hougang have voted for the Workers' Party, since 1991 till today. In both constituencies, the residents have been denied government funding for estate-upgrading programs of their public housing estates (Chua 2000b).

Until today, the prevailing political quietude in Singapore has been read as a direct result of authoritarian repression and the people's fear of punishment. Alternatively, it has been read as widespread "political apathy" among Singaporeans. The latter is partly an ideological effect

---

[9] Ironically, the PAP has a different kind of difficulty in convincing successful individuals to stand for election. This is not only because the commitment in terms of time and effort are considerable but, and more importantly, the loss of face is irreversible if one is dropped as an MP after a short tenure, which is tantamount to a public sign of having been tested and found wanting—in other words, one is a failure.

of liberalism. Within liberal pluralism, politics is active when public contestations on different issues are visible; where such contestations are not seen, by definition, there is "political apathy" or even "no politics." However, even the most severe critic of its authoritarianism would acknowledge that the longevity of the PAP in parliamentary power and government has been underpinned by more than five decades of phenomenal economic growth which has brought massive improvements in the lives of Singaporeans across the board. The palpable political quietude may be said to reflect a general agreement between the governed and the PAP government, a working "citizen-government compact." As argued elsewhere (Chua 1995: 41–3), this is a condition akin to the Gramscian concept of ideological hegemony where the PAP sees itself as providing moral/ideological leadership for Singaporeans and only exercising coercion for the Singaporeans' collective interests. As we shall see, it is within this framework of providing moral/ideological leadership that the PAP has sought to leverage on its status as a duly elected government to not only exercise calibrated repression but also to redefine the meanings of "election" and "rule of law," which differ from those offered by liberal democracy.

Undoubtedly, the absence of an opposition in parliament and tight media control of public opinion have shielded the government and civil service from public scrutiny. However, it has enabled the melding of the PAP government leaders and long-serving civil servants into a "unity of purpose," greatly facilitating the setting and implementing of long-term policies and plans, without the disruptions caused by changes in government.

Chapter 3

LIBERALISM DISAVOWED

[I]f I were in Singapore indefinitely, without having to ask those who are governed whether they like what is being done, then I have not the slightest doubt that I could govern much more effectively in their own interests. That is a fact which the educated understand, but we are all caught in this system which the British...export all over the place, hoping somewhere it will take root. (Prime Minister Lee Kuan Yew 1962)

THE ASCENDANCE OF THE PAP TO parliamentary power was one paved with political repression. After consolidating its stranglehold on the parliament, it relied heavily on its "performance legitimacy," that is, its economic performance to draw continuous electoral support from Singaporeans. Its ability to sustain incremental improvements in the material life of Singaporeans across the board and opportunities for inter-generational upward social mobility through economic growth has been presented as evidence of having discharged the "trust" of the electorate to govern in the latter's best interests. The ideology of trust became increasingly explicit after succession of the founding generation of cabinet ministers by the second generation PAP leaders and the handover of the Prime Minister position from Lee Kuan Yew to Goh Chok Tong. However, by the time Goh took over the Prime Minister-ship in 1991, the PAP had already seen declines in popular electoral support in three successive elections—in 1984, 1989 and 1991. In the face of these setbacks, the new leadership began to search for a new social consensus, or in their preferred terms, a new "social compact." In the process, the PAP government experimented with different ideo-logical formulations in an attempt to institutionalize a communitarian ideology, which involved the redefinition of some political concepts without forfeiting its claim to being an electoral democracy.

Performance Legitimacy

Performance legitimacy sat well with the temperament of the top tier of the first generation PAP leaders who, being lawyers, economists, journalists and academics, were quintessential goal-oriented, instrumental rationalists. General economic growth and employment creation took priority from the beginning of nation building, rapidly absorbing the underemployed and unemployed. Education opportunities in primary and secondary schools in the English language were extensively expanded to improve the "quality" and productivity of the citizens as an industrial workforce. Investments in transport infrastructure reduced traffic gridlocks that sapped national productivity. A very important and tangible material benefit was the ownership of public housing flats for practically the entire nation; its importance to the legitimacy of the PAP government will be discussed in detail in Chapter 5. All these investments were considered "pragmatic"—rational, necessary and unencumbered by political ideology—policies towards sustained economic growth. PAP "pragmatism" thus meant the hegemony of the economy (Chua 1995: 5–78). Political questions were reformulated into technical and/or economic problems which could be solved by the government to contribute to overall economic development. By the mid-1970s, there was a chronic labor shortage, instead of persistent unemployment. By mid-1980 more than 90 percent of the resident population lived in high-rise public housing estates, of which 80 percent had a 99-year lease on their flats. Expansion of education had resulted in palpable inter-generational upward mobility. These "real reforms of benefit to the working class" (Rodan 1989: 66) were essential to the PAP's direct appeal and political penetration into the social base.

Governance was above all else an instrumental transaction. The government would deliver the "good" life in exchange for the trust and votes from the citizens—reciprocity with different tokens. The five-year periodic general election became but an occasion for the PAP to present its "report card" (a favorite metaphor of the PAP leadership) of achievements to the electorate. General elections were (and still are) thus merely referendums to judge the PAP government's ability to "deliver the goods" on economic growth and improved material life, rather than a multi-party political contest. The overall economic success of Singapore and the improvements in the material life of the citizens is by now a well-known tale (Sandhu and Wheatley 1989) and until now, with occasional hiccups, the PAP performance has been generally satisfactory for the majority of the electorate.

To this performance was added another highly legitimatizing element—anti-corruption. Arguably, anti-corruption is a legacy of the expelled left wing of the original party. During the early years of uncomfortable partnership of convenience, Lee Kuan Yew's faction saw at close range the dedication and commitment of the left-wing unionists and student leaders to toil for the working masses. In awe of this self-sacrificing spirit, the British-trained professionals realized that if they were to win the hearts and minds of the new citizens, they would have to be as committed, clean and ascetic, if not more so, than their left-wing partners. Symptomatically, the PAP leaders quit smoking, beer drinking and other bourgeois affectations in public and adopted "white" as the color of the Party uniform; Lee Kuan Yew dropped his English name, Harry, in public.

When the party came to power, it imposed severe punishments for corruption within the civil service, which was rife with petty corruption under the colonial regime.[1] Just before he stepped down from being Prime Minister, Lee Kuan Yew thought that cabinet ministers and top civil servants should be paid a comparable wage to that of their counterparts in the private sector in order to embed anti-corruption at the highest level of government. A formula was computed to peg cabinet ministerial salaries to the top earners in several professions, including bankers. This elevated the salaries of the political office holders to the highest in the world; the Prime Minister's salary was higher in multiples of the President of the United States. This was controversial from the start. Thus, the salary was adjusted downwards, by more than 30 percent after the 2011 general election, when it was a source of expressed discontent among the electorate. The elected president's annual salary which was pegged above the Prime Minister's by protocol was reduced from more than SGD 4 million to SGD 500,000 per annum.

---

[1] For example, my family had a land transportation business. My father paid a small sum of money to many traffic policemen monthly to avoid summons for violation of traffic rules. One day, a plain clothes policeman came, took him to a police station and placed him in a lock-up, without any explanation. At the end of the day, he was told that the police knew that he had been corrupting traffic police. He was not charged with a criminal offence as it was the way business was done. After that, my father simply transferred the increased cost of running the business, due to traffic summons, on to his clients. Under the new PAP government, if he had continued the practice, he would have been jailed.

However, it should be noted that from the founding generation onwards, selective members of successive generations of PAP cabinet ministers have taken large reductions in their private sector professional salaries when they stand for election and take up ministerial responsibilities in response to the "call" of the nation.[2] High salaries may have diminished the respect Singaporeans hold for PAP political office holders (Wong 2013), but self-discipline and incorruptibility became the operating principles and critical symbolic political capital of the PAP, the government and the civil service in a sea of postcolonial states where corruption is endemic and deeply entrenched.

The PAP sees itself as an exemplary model of the formula "Good economic performance + anti-corruption = good government." The political capital accrued from incorruptibility, state capacity and sustained economic growth cannot be underestimated. It has obviously enabled the PAP government to legitimatize its rule. Political capital is continuously being used to finesse government interventions and repressions. Singaporeans are well aware that part of their current comfortable material life has been built on abuses of some of their rights as citizens. They could be said to have quietly acquiesced to this trade-off, thus complicit in the repressions. However, as the successful economy engenders an expansion of successive generations of a progressively better educated middle class, demands for more political voice and an increased interest in democracy and liberal rights have correspondingly expanded. The perceived precariousness of national "survival" at the time of independence has begun to lose its hold on the popular imagination. The ideological efficacy of "economic survivalism" has worn thin and heavy repressive measures, such as detention under the Internal Security Act, have become clumsy instruments of political control, especially now when such repressions are no longer tolerated, let alone condoned, by the Western liberal democracies. It was these changed social domestic and global conditions that led the second generation of PAP leaders to search for a new social compact with the people.

---

[2] In the second generation, Tony Tan was chairman of the Overseas Chinese Banking Corporation and S. Dhanabalan was chairman of the Development Bank of Singapore; in the third generation, Ng Eng Hen was a top cardiac surgeon, Vivian Balakrishnan was a prominent eye surgeon and K. Shanmugam was a senior partner in a major law firm.

Serial Electoral Setbacks in the 1980s

As the governing party of a capitalist society, the PAP recognizes that individualism (defined as self-interest) is essential to drive Singapore's economy. Lee Kuan Yew lauded Singaporeans as being of migrant stock who developed a keen self-centeredness which motivated them to work hard in their struggle to survive and prosper (*Straits Times* 1 May 1981). Encouragement of self-interest is implicitly embedded in the government's insistence that meritocracy must be a fundamental principle of the social distribution of rewards, as any other mode of distribution— such as family, race or other social affiliations—leads inevitably to corruption. This translates into an unwavering ideological "economic individualism" that rewards individuals on ability, diligence and determination to succeed.

The conundrum of meritocracy is that its behavioral manifestations seep into other spheres of social life in myriad ways with potentially socially negative consequences: a materialistic orientation to life with excessive consumerism that accentuates visible class differences and divisions in society; an irresponsible financial attitude with the liberal use of credit facilities; a sense of self-entitlement among the successful that elevates individual desires and demands as rights; and, finally, the tendency of self-importance among the successful who consider themselves the elite of society.[3]

Ironically, of all these tendencies, the PAP has been largely responsible for reinforcing elitism in society. Since Lee Kuan Yew's time, the core belief of the PAP is that it selects and recruits only the "best" into ministerial positions and top civil servants. The "best" are selected very early: a handful of best performers in the annual national pre-university examinations are given scholarships to the elite schools of the world, bonded to return to Singapore and fast-tracked to the top of the civil service or the armed forces. Some of these top servants and military officers are subsequently recruited into the PAP, elected and immediately given a ministerial rank. No PAP politician would deny that the PAP leadership is elitist (Barr 2014), but all PAP leaders caution against the

---

[3] The list of social ills and its attribution to excessive individualism appears to be relatively stable across national boundaries and historical times. They were similar to those offered by the post-1960s conservatives and the 1990s neoconservatives in the US and elsewhere in the West.

negative consequences of a culture of "elitism" in society (Wong 2013). This contradiction has become a source of ideological and practical anxiety for the PAP government as it worries about the "unravelling" of social cohesiveness—the common purpose, which has bound the population and the government in a singular determination to survive as a nation through economic growth.

On hindsight, the first revolt against PAP elitism was registered in the 1984 general election. From the 1980 national census, Lee Kuan Yew observed that university-educated women were placing career before marriage and childbirth in contrast to their less educated counterparts. With his elitist eugenic bias, he saw this as a "thinning" of the "talent" gene pool as the "non-talented" genes propagated unchecked which could result in a potential disaster for Singapore, which is completely dependent on the quality of its workforce. In 1983, the government introduced a "Graduate Mother" policy: tertiary-educated women were given generous tax incentives to increase childbirth; conversely, lesser educated women were given an SGD 10,000 cash grant to their social security fund if they would "stop at two" or less. This blatantly unequal policy flew into a storm of protest, no less from the graduate women whom the policy was meant to benefit.

Lee dismissed the protest offhandedly because "nature is undemocratic." The consequence was immediate. In the 1984 general election, the PAP garnered 63 percent of the popular vote, 12 percent less than the 75 percent it had regularly come to expect from past elections. A post-election survey showed that the result was a venting of deep dissatisfaction with the style of the PAP government (*Straits Times* 19 Apr. 1985), that was framed later as an "arrogance of power, an inflexible bureaucracy, growing elitism, and the denial of consultation and citizen participation in decision making" (Chan 1989: 82). The 1984 election results had opened up a sluice-gate for dammed-up public discontent. The PAP's percentage of the popular vote also failed to reach the 75 percent mark in the next two successive elections—in 1989 and 1991. It lost four seats to two opposition parties in 1991.

PAP leaders were quick to express disappointment and concern after the 1991 general election. Reflecting his distaste for elections, Lee Kuan Yew raised the idea of a "freak election," in which the electorate voted against the PAP with a limited intent to send it a message of discontent but ended up inadvertently electing another party to parliament and thus a government which it did not want. The idea of a freak election assumed that Singaporeans wanted the PAP to stay in power, in spite of some grievances. To prevent freak elections, Lee suggested, the "one person one vote" system should be modified to give "better qualified" and presumably "more rational" individuals greater voting weights, such as the past British practice of giving university graduates an additional vote (*Straits Times* 21 Nov. 1992).

Goh Chok Tong, Lee's successor, asked, "Why when it comes to national leadership, selection is left to the 'spectators' when you never do it this way for a football team or other important job?; when such a process often led to the election of incompetent administrators of state affairs or worse, 'crooks and thieves'?" (*Straits Times* 12 Dec. 1992). Goh's comments were in fact contemptuous of "ordinary" Singapore citizens as voters, in spite of the fact that they had voted for PAP consecutively for five decades. Longevity in power had obviously imprinted on the PAP leadership an egotistical sense of being the "only" party that could possibly govern Singapore for the benefit of the citizens; all other choices were by definition "irrational." Both men's comments projected Singapore society as ideologically "frozen" into a politically and intellectually "immature" population, infantilized and in constant need of elite leaders who could decide what is best for the society.

However, the successive election setbacks for the PAP significantly transformed perceptions of Singaporeans as an electorate. Until 1984, Singaporeans were seemingly unquestioning in their support for the PAP. They were often seen as politically "apathetic" and/or cowed by fear of punishment to vote against the PAP. These (mis)perceptions were spawned by the fact that until then, most of the government's "pragmatic" policies might be said to have had a very tangible material focus which had benefited and were rationally acceptable to the overwhelming majority of Singaporeans.

Furthermore, the absence of public debates was also significantly due to the poverty of communicative spaces for the voicing of public opinions which, until the current Internet age, were limited to a couple of pages daily in each of the pro-government daily newspapers. Under such conditions, the PAP government's common refrain that it had to make "tough but unpopular policies" was a misperception because the policies were indeed popular. It was a misperception, or "myth," that it believed in to its own peril. Once government policy intervention began to wade into less tangible "soft" focus areas that infringed on the private sphere and personal preferences, such as marriage, childbirth and other "lifestyle" or "cultural" issues, Singaporeans were quick to show their disagreement and resistance to government policies through their

votes, showing up cracks in the broad legitimacy of the PAP government. In demonstrating their adeptness in using the ballot box to
express discontent, the three successive election results also called into
doubt the much circulated idea that Singaporeans were politically unquestioning, apathetic and fearful.

In Search of New Ideological Concepts: Confucianism[4]

The new Prime Minister, Goh Chok Tong, began to accept that contemporary Singapore was no longer the Singapore of the 1960s. In
contrast to conditions of privation in the 1960s to the late 1970s, there
was full employment, every child was in school, the entire population
was well housed in government-subsidized flats and an expanding middle class was increasingly visible. Consequently, governance of a socio-
economically differentiated citizenry had increased greatly in complexity.
The ideology of "survivalism" which had restrained demands on the
government was no longer convincing, thanks to the economically successful policies of the PAP government. As one cabinet minister put it,
"We just can't always be telling them to compare their situation with
that of the 50s and ask them to be grateful" (*Straits Times* 19 Sept.
1984). Fearing the loss of social cohesion among an increasingly socially
stratified citizenry, the second-generation PAP leaders realized that a
new social compact/consensus between themselves and the people was
needed.

At the time, the phenomenal high economic growth in East Asia
was attracting political and academic attention. The fast-growing economies of South Korea, Taiwan, Hong Kong and Singapore, and earlier
that of Japan, was dubbed the "Asian Miracle" by the World Bank. This
was a puzzle in search of an answer. The academic explanation turned
out to be quite "simple." Harvard sociologist, Ezra Vogel, looking at
the phenomenal economic rise of Japan in the 1960s and the 1970s
and the concurrent relative decline of the American economy, stated:
"I found myself, like my Japanese friends, wondering what had happened to America." (1979: iiiv). The cause of America's decline was

---

[4] This section is heavily drawn from my earlier book, *Communitarian Ideology and
Democracy in Singapore* (1995: 26–31, 147–68). Quotes from the text are left
unmarked.

supposedly excessive individualism. Vogel's prescription for revitalization was for America to return to "traditional values," like East Asia where traditional values remained operative.

Similarly, British political scientist and then editor of the *China Quarterly* Roderick MacFarquar (1980) explained: "If Western individualism was appropriate for the pioneering period of industrialization, perhaps post-Confucian 'collectivism' is better suited to the age of mass industrialization." MacFarquar's argument was empirically "confirmed" by Lodge and Vogel's (1987) finding that a nation's economic competitiveness is affected by whether it is relatively more communitarian or individualistic. The critique of excessive individualism resonated well with the PAP's anti-liberal individualism. Additionally, the belief that Confucian collectivism was the "essential" value for economic growth in late capitalism was icing on the cake. In 1983, the Minister for Finance Goh Keng Swee, set up the Institute of East Asian Philosophies in Singapore to research the possible link between Confucianism and economic growth. Unsurprisingly, the Institute's very first conference aimed to compare Confucianism and Weber's thesis on protestant ethics and capitalism (Tu 1991).

On the broader ideological front, the necessary ingredients seemed to be ready at hand for the PAP leadership to articulate a new consensus. The incipient individualism among young Singaporeans was said to be part of the "deculturalization brought about by the large-scale movement to education in English." As a consequence, the young had lost their traditional values and acquired "the more spurious fashions of the West." Thus, moral education was introduced to provide the cultural ballast to withstand the stresses of living in a fast-changing society exposed to influences good and bad" (*Straits Times* 15 Mar. 1979). Moral education from primary through secondary schools was to be taught through "religious studies"—Bible Knowledge, Buddhist, Hindu and Islamic Studies—for students who professed these respective religions. The program was to teach the moral precepts of religion, minus the theism. For Chinese students who professed no religion, Confucian ethics would be taught. Confucian scholars were invited by the Ministry of Education to develop the needed teaching materials. Unfortunately, from its inception in 1982, Confucian ethics was not taken up by many Chinese students. In 1989, the exclusively Chinese student enrolment stood at 17.8 percent relative to Buddhist Studies (44.4 percent) and Bible Knowledge (21.4 percent). More importantly, government-funded research found that Religious Studies in schools had led to the intensification of religious fervor and religious difference among students, with potentially untoward consequences in the long term (Kuo, et al. 1988). Ever vigilant about possible religious conflicts in the multi-religious population, the government abolished the Religious Studies curriculum in schools in 1991. A side effect of this entire episode was the excitement Confucianism generated in the overwhelmingly Chinese majority community at large. According to local sociologist Kuo (1989: 24), the government's promotion of Confucianism became a mass campaign for "a moral system of the Chinese population in Singapore." The mass campaign was timely, as even the idea of filial piety had diminished among contemporary Singaporean Chinese. For example, the traditional idea that the greatest unfilial act is not to produce children, especially male descendants, appears to have little moral purchase among the younger Chinese population, who have delayed marriage and child bearing in the pursuit of careers. With the closing of Confucian Studies in schools, all public discussion of Confucian ethics ceased (Kuo 1992). The effort to inject Confucianism among the Chinese turned out to be a massive failure.

However, Confucianism was received quite differently in the political sphere. Stripped of all historically accumulated scholarly subtleties, MacFarquar (1980) summarized Confucian political philosophy thus: government by a benevolent bureaucracy under a virtuous ruler; a leader's benevolent rule that is reciprocated by the loyalty and obedience of his subjects; and benevolence that ensures harmony within stratified and unequal relations between the leader and the led. Similar unequal, hierarchical but harmonious relationships hold within a family—between father and son, husband and wife, and elder and younger family members. Such familial relationships are thus congruous with national sentiment. Habits of disciplined subordination and acceptance of authority fostered at home apply equally well in the factory and the nation. It was as if MacFarquar was describing Lee Kuan Yew's view of himself and of the PAP in general. Lee had always seen himself as a "benevolent" leader who worked tirelessly to improve the lives of Singaporeans. The PAP leaders felt that their incorruptibility and self-sacrifice deserved respect and gratitude from Singaporeans. They considered caricatures, rumors, innuendoes and aspersions on their personal character and behavior, not only disrespectful but also a diminishment of their authority, which should not be tolerated. The PAP government was therefore quick in adopting this version of Confucian political philosophy as the ideological basis to reinterpret its established practices.

Its selection of academically brilliant scholars for leadership positions in government followed the traditional Confucian way of selecting state functionaries through stringent academic examinations. Instead of crediting the ideology of their radical left partners of the 1950s for the idea of high moral behavior in government, the PAP ascribed the absence of corruption at the highest levels to the presence of honorable Confucian men at the helm. The enforcement of an unpopular public policy was rationalized as the Confucian statesmanship of a sage leader, and the PAP's pragmatism was rationalized as reflecting the concern of Confucian philosophy for right living in this world. According to the Confucian idea of good government by "honorable men" (*junzi*), there must be

> rigorous insistence on high standards of personal and public conduct among political leaders and public servants who must do the correct thing because they know it is their duty to do so, not because they fear to be found out doing wrong. (The White Paper 1991: 9)

For Prime Minister Goh Chok Tong, his predecessor Lee Kuan Yew was one such honorable man, a "modern Confucius" (*Straits Times* 24 Apr. 1990). That the PAP leaders should want to hold themselves to the standards of *junzi* behavior was no bad thing. In general, Singaporeans do recognize and respect, albeit sometimes grudgingly, the PAP leaders' incorruptibility and generally good behavior in government. However, respect did not mean unconditional obedience, which should be obvious from the series of electoral setbacks the PAP suffered during the 1980s. Here again, it is worth remembering that elections can be a mechanism for checking the tendency of the dominant single-party state to slip into authoritarianism.

Communitarianism—Resurrecting the Social Democratic Past

Although the mass diffusion of Confucianism and religion-based moral education in schools failed, the perceived need for a new consensus between the PAP government and Singaporeans remained. In 1988, a government committee was established to formulate a new national ideology. In January 1991, a White Paper on Shared Values was tabled in Parliament, "to evolve and anchor a Singaporean identity, incorporating the relevant parts of our varied cultural heritages, and the attitudes and values which have helped us to survive and succeed as a nation." The shared values were "nation before community and society above self, upholding the family as the basic building block of society, resolving major issues through consensus instead of contentions and regard and community support for the individual."[5] That the shared values blatantly privileged the collective over the individual was obviously ideologically predetermined. Nevertheless, the government insisted that the "communitarian" core of these values was distilled from the "traditional" values of the Chinese, Malay and Indian communities and, in this sense, generalized and ideologically elevated to the so-called "Asian Values."

The idea that "Asian Values" are essentially communitarian was picked up by other Southeast Asian political leaders who were indubitably authoritarian, including Malaysia's Mohammad Mahathir and Indonesia's President Suharto, to "explain" the political stability and capitalist economic development in their respective countries. Predictably, this ideological formulation flew into a storm of skepticism and criticism from inside and outside Asia. The criticism mainly focused on two anti-liberal aspects in the communitarian argument, namely, the hierarchical social order in contrast to the equality of individuals and the "obedience" of the governed in contrast to individual self-determination. As these two concepts were essential characteristics of an authoritarian state, the "Asian Values" discourse was criticized as merely a thin veil for authoritarianism.[6] The debate around "Asian Values" abated after 1997, when the Asian Financial Crisis put a stop to the seemingly sustainable rapid economic development in East Asia, which in turn stopped the triumphal touting of Asian values among political leaders and their thought-supporters. Critics were further appeased by the exposure of corruption and the removal of the authoritarian regimes in the rising Asian countries of Taiwan, South Korea and Indonesia. However, instead of retreating, the PAP government continued to emphasize "nation before community, society above self," as its principle of governance.

The emphasis on the "community" and the "social" opened the door for George Yeo, the ideologue of the third generation PAP leaders,

---

[5] "White Paper on Shared Values," presented in Parliament by PM Goh on 3 January 1991 (*Straits Times* 4 Jan. 1991).

[6] There is a large body of literature on the so-called "Asian Values" debate. For a sampling see, Fareed Zakaria, "Culture is Destiny: A Conversation with Lee Kuan Yew," *Foreign Affairs* 73, no. 2 (1994): 109–26; Robison (1996); and Kim (1994).

to resurrect the democratic-socialist origin of the PAP. He argued that the "socialism" that motivated the founding of the PAP should not be forgotten or forsaken in spite of being apparently discredited because of the failure of the socialist economies of communist regimes. Making a classic ideological move, Yeo naturalized the idea of socialism by taking it beyond the historically contingent. He argued, "Socialism will never die, of course, because it springs from the very nature of man as a social animal. At least, the family will always stay social" (*Straits Times* 17 June 1994), thus indirectly connecting socialism back to both Confucianism and one of the shared values, "family as the basic building block of society."

He further redefined the economic redistributive dimension of social democracy. Lee Kuan Yew had always frowned on direct cash transfer, which he argued "saps" the work ethic of the recipients. In any case, three decades of continuous economic growth and full employment for a relatively young population had radically minimized the need for direct cash redistribution.

Nevertheless, social expenditure is an unavoidable function of the state. Yeo conceptualized government social expenditures in the provision of public housing, education and financial assistance to voluntary welfare organizations as "supply-side" socialism, in which state subsidies are made "to maximize the ability of all human beings," that is, human capital investments which in turn contribute to national economic competitiveness (*Straits Times* 17 June 1994). Unlike the old socialism that aimed to replace market capitalism, this "supply-side" socialism is market oriented and supplementary to capitalism. Ideologically this "supply-side" socialism differentiates and distances the PAP from firstly, the failed socialist economies of communist regimes; secondly, from the European, especially the Scandinavian, type of social welfare state; and finally, from neoliberal "supply-side capitalism" where liberals withdraw from their social welfare responsibilities.

However, in spite of the ideological cunning, as income inequalities increased in Singapore in the 2000s, directly redistributive social welfare was ultimately unavoidable, as with all mature capitalist economies. The Minister for Finance, Tharman Shanmugaratnam, proclaimed in 2013: "You still get diversity of views in Cabinet, but the centre of gravity is left-of-centre," and "focused on upgrading the lives and improving the lives of lower income Singaporeans and older folks" (*Straits Times* 19 Apr. 2013). The timing of this leftward shift was telling. With the

globalization and financialization of capitalism in all developed economies, Singapore included, middle-class incomes had been stagnant for
more than a decade; the income of the lower economic strata had declined annually. Overall, wages had not been able to keep up with asset
inflation and the rising cost of living for a very significant portion of
the working population. Moreover, since assets generate higher capital
returns compared to wages earned through labor, the rich asset-owning
class became richer. Thus, overall income inequalities intensified, making
the direct transfer of cash to an increasing number of households inevitable. In 2013, Singapore government transfers of cash and in kind
amounted to 50 percent of the annual income of the bottom 20 percent
of the income strata (*Straits Times* 19 Sept. 2014). In addition, a universal healthcare system was put in place for the first time and a one-
off endowment fund of SGD 8 billion was established to defray the
medical expenses of citizens who were above 65 years of age in 2013,
known as the "Pioneer Generation." These first-generation citizens of
independent Singapore have little savings for their retirement because
they were mainly low-wage earners during their working years. The
hefty funding of these social expenditures, as we shall see, is partially
facilitated by the profits derived from state capitalism.

Redefining the Terms of Democracy

The PAP government's attempt to embed a communitarian ideology
in a world where liberal individualism is hegemonic is symptomatic of
its growing confidence, buoyed by electoral parliamentary legitimacy at
home and international recognition for its spectacular capitalist economic success abroad, in articulating the underpinning logic of its system
of governance. To be consistent with the political logic of "nation before
community, society above self," the PAP government has, in effect,
redefined the conventional liberal understanding of democracy. However,
it insists that such redefinition is necessitated by the particularities of
Singapore's geopolitical context and its need for sustained economic
development and social stability.

Representation/Trusteeship

While accepting election as the process of selecting the ruling party,
the PAP government is against the liberal understanding of election as
"representation." It rejects the idea that an elected individual is obliged

to represent the relatively narrow interests of the constituency which has elected him/her. This is because it assumes that competition among "representatives" of different particularistic "constituencies"—defined either by geographical spatial boundaries or material interests of a social class or the business interest of lobby groups—would inevitably lead to gridlocks in parliamentary proceedings, thus delaying government decisions and actions.

Examples of such gridlocks in contemporary liberal democracies abound. For example, during the Obama presidency, the US federal government was frozen into inactivity because of the ideological intransigence and radical partisanship of the two national political parties. In instances where a coalition government is the regular outcome of multi-party contests, the minority government is regularly held hostage by its smaller coalition parties in exchange for support to continue in government, thus yielding to the latter disproportionate bargaining power in governance, and consequently subverting the idea of majority rule. A prime example is India, where a weak federal government constituted by the Indian Congress Party in coalition with smaller regional parties became beholden to highly corrupt, even criminal regional leaders, and for years perforce regularly gave in to the latter's demands (Prasad 2007).

When gridlock and unwieldy coalitions jeopardize the elected government's ability to enact legislation and implement public policies, they have been destructive of national/collective interests and they have arguably engendered ambivalence towards liberal "representative" politics as a desirable mode of governance. Although the PAP's hegemonic parliamentary majority has not been threatened by radical partisanship or the need to form a coalition government, it is nevertheless terrified by the possibility of a polarization of interests in parliament, which it sees as leading to the fragmentation of Singapore society at large. Consequently, while it accepts that it has to "suffer" elections, it remains unconvinced that a two-party system of government is desirable for Singapore, let alone multi-party and/or proportional representation, given all the imaginable vulnerabilities of a small state.

In practice, there are also limits to the politics of "representation." Even the most liberal representative government cannot constantly turn to its constituency for opinions or conduct a national referendum on every major issue. There will always be occasions in which the elected government has to act according to what it sees as the "national" interest, particularly when the action is against the wishes of the majority of the citizens. This includes the exclusive right of the elected Prime Minister or President to decide to take the nation into war. For example, in 2003 the British Prime Minister, Tony Blair, decided to join US President G.W. Bush in declaring war on Iraq, against the expressed wishes of an overwhelming majority of the British public, with a disastrous, decades-long outcome for the entire Middle East. He argued that he was morally compelled to act because Iraqi President Saddam Hussein had to be stopped before he unleashed weapons of mass destruction on his people and potentially terrorize the world. Blair might be said to have been acting on the assumption of being "entrusted" to act in the "national" interests, the negative consequences notwithstanding.

Co-existing with the definition of election as representation is the democratic idea that regardless of how individual citizens might have voted, how divided the votes were for different contesting political parties and how slim the margin of the winning party, the elected government is obliged to declare itself as a "government for all," without favor for those who voted for it and prejudice against those who did not. All differences are supposedly to be set aside and the result of a general election is to be taken as the "will of the people." The elected government is to govern in the interest of all citizens of the "nation" as a single entity even though empirical evidence might leave one skeptical as to whether this still holds in contemporary liberal democratic countries, let alone in developing nations. In principle, the elected government is "entrusted" by the electorate to govern in the best interests of the latter, a trust that can be withdrawn in the next general election, as in the case of Blair. This is very much part of the liberal conception of democratic government (Locke 1988).[7] In practice, an elected government necessarily operates by following the concepts of both the "representation" of constituency interests and the "trusteeship" of "collective" interests. However, in the contemporary global liberal ideological hegemony, representation has displaced and limited the evocation of trusteeship to exceptional occasions.

In his arrogant self-assuredness that he was governing Singapore in the best interests of Singaporeans, Prime Minister Lee Kuan Yew was unfazed by criticism that his regime was authoritarian. However, Lee's

---

[7] In the British colonial context, trusteeship was fundamental in the debates and transformation of India from a trading partner of the East India Company to become part of the British Empire (Bain 2003).

immediate successor, Prime Minister Goh Chok Tong, faced more intense pressure to ideologically justify the hegemonic single-party dominant state because of post-Cold War global hegemony of pluralistic liberal democracy, a lack of the historical moral authority enjoyed by founding generation leaders, and a demand for alternative voices to be heard. Immediately upon assuming office, Goh began to invoke the idea of election as trusteeship: "I know that my role as a trustee of Singapore is a heavy responsibility. But its heaviness is lightened by your support" (1991). For him, the choice for Singaporeans was stark:

> My purpose is to ask you to ponder over this question: is a democratic system an end to be pursued in its own right, or is it a means to select a government to look after our lives like a good guardian or trustee? If it is the latter, how do we ensure that it returns a good government to serve the people? As we can see from examples around the world, simply observing the form of democracy does not necessarily deliver good governance and results. (Goh 2010)

This idea of elected government as trustees was repeated in the 2015 general electioneering by Prime Minister Lee Hsien Loong:

> We are not the bosses of Singapore, we are not the commanders or the owners of Singapore, we are the trustees and the stewards of Singapore, we are like the *jaga* (Malay for one who is hired to watch over property, like a night-watch). (*Straits Times* 9 Sept. 2015)

The PAP government has categorically chosen the trusteeship of collective interests over the representation of constituency interests as its ideological operating principle. Given the PAP leaders' self-claim of being Confucian *junzi* in government, then their understanding of "trust" is quite different from the liberal understanding.

Chan provides a very succinct distinction between the two conceptualizations: the Confucian conception of trust "refers to the confidence and faith people have in their rulers, and trustworthiness is a virtue by which rulers gain the trust of the people" (2014: 43). This is in contrast to Locke's liberal concept of trust:

> For all power given with trust for attaining an end, being limited by that end, whenever that end is manifestly neglected, or opposed, the trust must necessarily be forfeited, and the power devolve into the hands of those that gave it, and place it anew where they shall think best for their safety and security. (quoted in Chan 2014: 42–3)

Chan suggests that for Confucianism, trust is ethical and "defined without reference to any prior notion of rights" (2014: 43), while for liberalism, trust is juridical, where "people, who possess rights prior to the setup of government choose to entrust some of their rights to the government" (2014: 42).

Given that the PAP has to operate within an elected parliamentary system and that it is ideologically attracted to Confucianism, the PAP leaders' understanding of trust is likely to be a somewhat muddled mixing of the two traditions, with a preference to believe that they have built an "ethical" government based on "moral authority" rather than a limited exchange between themselves and the Singaporean electorate (Yao 2007: 19–22). In practice, the PAP government's slippage into partisanship has on occasion placed its claim to trusteeship in doubt: throughout the 1990s, it punished public housing residents in constituencies that had elected non-PAP MPs by denying them funds for upgrading estate facilities and amenities (Chua 2000b).

Rule of/by Law

The history of the PAP regime is filled with laws that severely restrict conventional liberal freedoms and civil society activities. For example, the genesis of the 1966 Punishment for Vandalism law was to punish members of the left-wing Barisan Sosialis for painting "anti-American aggression" slogans in public spaces during the Vietnam War (Rajah 2012: 74–88). By placing such acts under the vandalism law, the political act was transformed into an act of "mischief" of defacing public property in violation of public interest. However, severe punishments, including mandatory imprisonment and the corporal punishment of caning, are exacted for defacing public property, thus elevating this "mischievous act" to a "serious offence." The state thus exacts severe punishments for acts of political dissent by criminalizing such acts under "apolitical" laws.

The Societies Act was pressed into service to constrain civil society organizations and activities. It disallows mutual associations between political parties and any civil society organizations, keeping civil society organizations out of electoral politics. It also restricts every civil society organization to activities within its declared purposes, proscribing coalition to fight a common cause. Taken together, these conditions of association suppress the possibility of coalition building among oppositional social forces. Furthermore, the Registrar of Societies is vested with the power to refuse to register or to deregister any organization on the presumption that the activities of the organization may have negative consequences on public order (Tan and George 2001).

The government claims that all civil society organizations are subjected to the same constraints of the Societies Act. This is dubious because of the continuing "symbiotic" relationship between the National Trades Union Congress and the PAP, as both a political party and the government. As mentioned in the previous chapter, individuals move in and out of the revolving doors of all three entities, as "labor MPs," union advisors and managers of NTUC cooperatives. Furthermore, leaders of NTUC-affiliated unions are not allowed to join any political party except the PAP, and NTUC-affiliated unions' rank-and-file members are mobilized to campaign during every general election. In principle, all these PAP-NTUC acts are in violation of the Societies Act.

The Public Entertainment Licensing Unit (PELU), housed in the Ministry of Home Affairs, is responsible for granting the license for group activities in public. Giving public speeches is included as "public entertainment," and thus requires a license. The basis for granting/denying a permit is deceptively simple: the police assesses whether the proposed event has the potential to lead to law-and-order problems. In practice, the licensing process severely suppresses the freedom of expression of all dissenting voices, particularly those engaged in political dissent. This led the Secretary General of the Singapore Democratic Party, Chee Soon Juan, to engage in acts of civil disobedience, speaking in public without a license in defiance of the law. For this, he was imprisoned three times for providing public entertainment without permit; the length of his last imprisonment also disqualified him from contesting in the 2006 general election. Similar denials of licenses have also been meted out to other civil society organizations. However, with increasing public pressure for greater freedom of expression and at the behest of some civil society organizations, in 2000, the government designated a small public park, the Hong Lim Park, in the central region of city as a "free speech space." The Park has since been well used by civil society groups to voice collective discontents against the regime and/or celebrate collective desires, such as the annual Pink Dot Day, a carnival for lesbians, gays, bisexuals and transsexuals (LGBTs) and their friends (Chua 2014: 119–22).

Other laws that constrain conventional democratic freedoms include: press laws that constrain the mass media to support the developmental orientations of the government; the Legal Profession Act which keeps lawyers out of commenting on law-making; and religious harmony regulations that are used to keep religion out of politics. Control has been extended to the gazetting of Internet websites as "political" sites in order to prohibit them from receiving foreign financial assistance. Clearly the PAP government has been using laws, extensively and without any qualms, as instruments to suppress dissent and development of alternative bases of political power. Such instrumental use of the legal system regularly abuses individual rights, contrary to liberal expectations that laws are to be used to protect and guarantee the rights of individuals. It has, therefore, been dubbed as a regime of the "rule by law" rather than the "rule of law" (Rajah 2012), which makes the PAP government authoritarian. Yet, the PAP government continues to insist that it governs and is governed by the "rule of law."

In his keynote address to the International Bar Association conference in Singapore in 2007, Lee Kuan Yew suggested that Singapore has kept to the British common law tradition which it inherited as an ex-colony (Lee 2007). However, he argued that the common law tradition had to be adjusted to local "contingencies;" that is, specific laws must be instrumentally used or enacted to assist in guaranteeing the national survival and security of Singapore. Only then should the law be executed fairly and applied equally to not only individuals but also to the government itself. The Singapore judiciary has always endorsed this argument of public order above individual rights. For example, former Chief Justice Yong Pung How commenting on religious beliefs "considered that an administration which perceived the possibility of trouble over religious beliefs but preferred to wait before taking action was 'pathetically naïve' and 'grossly incompetent';" "while religious beliefs merited 'proper protection,' religious acts had to conform to 'the general law relating to public order and social protection';" and "[a]nything running contrary to 'the sovereignty, integrity and unity of Singapore warranted leashing'" (Thio 2004: 107).

Another former Chief Justice, Chan Sek Keong, acknowledges that Lee Kuan Yew's "precepts and values [are] reflected in all the laws," where the "rule of law simply meant the supremacy of the law, without reference to whether the law is just or unjust;" that "the law must apply to all and be above all;" and that it has nothing to do with human rights or democracy (quoted in Hussain 2008). Chief Justice Chan is satisfied that the PAP government has always subjected itself to the laws it enacts. For example, besides the multiple suits brought by PAP ministers against opposition party members, there was one instance in which

Chiam See Tong, the leader of the Singapore Democratic Party, sued two PAP ministers for libel. The cases never went to court because the two ministers apologized unreservedly publicly and paid compensation to Chiam. This incident demonstrates that the PAP is subjected to the same law and is thus evidence that there is "rule of law" in Singapore.

Chief Justice Chan argues that the PAP government's interpretation of the concept of "rule of law" is based on a conceptual foundation that explicitly contests the prevailing liberal understanding and that it is entirely defensible. For him, the separation of power between the government and the judiciary is clear-cut in the Singapore legal system. The Parliament elected by the citizens is the proper and best institution to articulate the societal values as the basis of its laws and the legal system. It possesses the exclusive right to law-making. As long as laws are procedurally enacted in a properly prescribed manner and by Parliament, the judiciary's work is limited to the execution of the duly enacted laws, ensuring that these are applied equally to all, including the government. It is up to the people to change the ruling government if they judge it to be mistaken in articulating the values of society. For him, such are the conditions that have prevailed in Singapore and it is not the place of the judiciary to change the law. Indeed, his argument is not without precedent: "[t]he idea of a judicial body modifying the will of the elected legislature, and therefore the sovereign will of the people whom the legislature represents, has traditionally been rejected as a distortion of the democratic process and the rule of law" (Pech 2004: 87).

The difference between Singapore's "statist" conception and the liberal conception of the judiciary's function has been analyzed from a political-economic perspective. According to Jayasuriya (2007), capitalism in Western Europe was first shaped by the bourgeoisie and subsequently by the rise of working class unionism from the 1920s to the 1980s. The liberal legal system is the result of the efforts of both of these organized social forces to limit the power of the state. In contrast, post-war capitalist development in East Asia has been largely led by activist states with clear industrial policies, which guide and provide administrative and financial assistance to selected capitalist enterprises to ensure their success. Additionally, attempts by the emerging industrial proletariat to organize themselves have been either smashed by the force of the state or incorporated into corporative relations with companies, as in house unions, or into the state project of capitalist nation building. According to Jayasuriya, in East Asia the result is a legal system with several identifiable characteristics:

- emphasis is placed on the performance of public duties rather than the distribution of rights and entitlements;
- legal institutions are designed to "play a *policy implementing* role in that they serve to enforce government objectives and policies;"
- a strong emphasis is "placed on adherence to formal rules, processes and procedures regardless of the fairness of substantive outcomes;" and finally;
- an organic conception of the relations between the state and society, in which individual freedoms have to be "balanced" and sacrificed if necessary in the interest of the society.

In historically specific terms, the last characteristic means that individual freedom needs to be sacrificed for the sake of national economic development. Singapore is an instance in this generalized pattern of state and capitalist development in post-war East Asia.

However, there has been no shortage of liberal criticism, at home and abroad, of the anti-liberal character of the legal system of Singapore. Such criticism is premised on the ahistorical and ideological assumption that with the rise of capitalism in East Asia, "the emergence of institutions will replicate the trajectory travelled by Western European institutions," and that "while these [East Asian] institutional trajectories differ markedly from those of Western European variety, they are merely in transition towards a common institutional end point" (Jayasuriya 2007: 368). Such liberal criticism, however, has had no impact on the PAP government, which consistently dismisses them; foreign critics are especially discounted on the grounds that they are happy to spout pious liberal principles because they have no tangible stake in Singapore's presence or future. To local liberal-minded citizens, the overwhelming popular electoral support at every general election has thus far provided little hope that a more liberal legal regime will emerge anytime in the future.

Conclusion

Although the PAP has remained in parliamentary power since 1959, the political system of Singapore has not been static; it has been evolving. In the critical first decade, the first generation PAP leaders strategically used their "legalized" power to orchestrate, step by step, the elimination of its political opponents and any alternative power bases. When Barisan Sosialis, the only political party that had any hope of constituting a parliamentary opposition to the PAP, boycotted the 1968 general election, it left the PAP to monopolize all parliamentary seats. The potential two-party, Westminster-style parliamentary system was transformed into a PAP-dominated single-party parliament and it has remained so ever since. Even when there are no realistic contenders for power, as it eliminated them, the PAP has retained elections as the minimum necessary political institution to its legitimacy, although electoral rules and procedures are regularly modified to create an uneven playing field to its own advantage.

The other plank of the PAP government's legitimacy has been its relentless pursuit of national economic growth which translates into improving the material life of the people by lifting those in poverty into the middle class. This has secured the sustained popular support of the electorate for the party and reduced the periodic general elections to referendums on the government's economic performance. The ideological consensus grounded in the common pursuit of economic growth began to weaken by the mid-1980s, ironically, precisely because of successful capitalist growth. Capitalist economic growth necessarily feeds on competition among self-interested individuals, encouraging ideological individualism. This is both the cause and consequence of the ideology of meritocracy that is encouraged by the government and embraced by the population. As the much-dreaded belief in "individualism" became evident, the second-generation PAP leaders began to search for ideological concepts for a new social compact between themselves and the people. Religious studies and Confucianism were introduced in schools to inculcate social responsibilities among the students. However, the program was quickly dropped when it was discovered that it had encouraged greater religiosity and enhanced religious differences among the students, with potentially dire future consequences.

Significantly, the brief ideological dalliance with Confucianism led the leaders' self-characterization as "honorable men" (*junzi*)—able and incorruptible individuals who govern in the interests of the governed, in exchange for the latter's respect and trust. The ideas of election and government were then redefined in terms of trust: the vote is an exercise of citizens' trust in their elected officials, as trustees, to govern in the interest of all citizens in contrast to the liberal definition that these elected officials must represent the narrow interest of the constituency that elected them. On a broader ideological level, Confucian collectivism subsequently morphed into a set of "Shared Values," which was supposedly distilled from traditional values of the three Asian races in

Singapore and which emphasized collective welfare over individual rights. More importantly, the ideological communitarian turn enabled the PAP to resurrect its social democratic past as a new "socialism"— a "supply-side" socialism—in the current post-Cold War, post-socialist global order. This reclaiming of its socialist roots is consequential, as we shall see in subsequent chapters, in the ongoing management of both state capitalist investments and the increasing income inequalities characteristic of a mature economy in global capitalism.

What we have in Singapore at the beginning of the twenty-first century is a PAP-dominant, single-party government which ideologically espouses communitarianism, politically continues to maintain the formal features of an electoral democracy, and continues to pursue economic growth, full employment and the improvement of material life for Singaporeans—efficiently, effectively and without corruption. Much to the chagrin of its liberal critics, Singaporeans appear to have become accustomed to the benefits derived from the efficacy of this system for more than five decades (Wong 2015). A 2011 Institute of Public Policy survey found that "efficient government remained the top concern" among Singaporeans.[8] Under this broad ideological and practical umbrella, details of policies and administrative regulations are constantly being adjusted to manage ongoing changes in the politics, economy, society and culture to reflect the government's responsiveness and accountability to an increasingly better educated electorate clamoring for greater input in the running of the nation—responses that are essential for the PAP to continue its single-party hegemony in Singapore.

---

[8] http://lkyspp.nus.edu.sg/ips/research/surveys/ips-perception-of-policies-in-singapore-survey/pops4-ips-post-election-survey-2011 [accessed 20 Oct. 2014].

Chapter 4

DISRUPTING PRIVATE PROPERTY RIGHTS
National Public Housing Program

We have created a property-owning democracy, that's why we have
stability in Singapore. (Lee Kuan Yew quoted in Han, et al. 2011: 201)

SINGAPORE HAS INSUFFICIENT LAND TO accommodate all the necessary
institutions of nationhood—a fact that is demonstrated by Singapore's
need to train its conscript citizen armed forces on borrowed terrains in
friendly countries like neighboring Brunei. Yet, without doubt, contemporary Singaporeans are among the most well-housed urban citizens
in the world. When the PAP was first elected to parliament in 1959,
improving the housing conditions of the newly enfranchised population
was one of the most pressing social issues. The growing population was
living in over-congested shophouses in the city area (Kaye 1960) or
in wood-panel and thatched-roof houses in urban-fringe *kampong* (the
Malay term for "village"), which the colonial government regarded as
unhealthy squatter settlements of poverty and squalor (Loh 2013). The
tangible material benefits derived from decent housing was an efficacious
way to demonstrate the government's commitment to the wellbeing
of the electorate, which would in turn accrue credibility and political
legitimacy for the government (Chua 1997).

Thus, in 1960 a public housing authority, the Housing and Development Board (HDB), was established to replace the grossly under-
funded colonial public housing authority, the Singapore Improvement
Trust (SIT), whose lethargic building program was unable to meet the
demands of the growing population. In contrast, the HDB was given
sweeping powers over all development work related to housing—land

acquisition, resettlement, comprehensive housing estate planning, architectural design, engineering work, the sourcing of building materials and construction firms, the allocation of flats and managing housing, and all other ancillary facilities in housing estates. However, the actual construction of the housing blocks was undertaken by private constructions firms. In its first five years, the HDB built 50,000 flats. Within a decade, the city center was decongested and most of the urban fringe settlements cleared; all the residents were resettled into high-rise flats in public housing estates. By the mid-1970s, the shortage of housing was essentially solved. By the mid-1980s, the HDB had become effectively the monopolistic and universal housing provider for the nation. By the late 1990s, more than 85 percent of the population lived in public housing estates. The national public housing program with its close to universal provision stands as the PAP government's signal achievement, as a testament to its social democratic impulse, and as a foundation of its legitimacy and longevity in parliamentary power.

The National Public Housing Program

The HDB started modestly with the construction of one-room rental flats for the poor—which had little more than sleeping spaces that could hold the minimum of household furniture—in five-storey walk-up building blocks. While the general public environment and health conditions of the public housing estates were definitely vast improvements, it was not entirely certain that living in these minimal flats was much of an improvement over living in urban shophouse rooms or kampong wood-and-thatch houses. Tenants had to share common kitchens where each household was allocated a cooking space. They had also to share toilets, bathrooms and laundry spaces (Hassan 1997). A significant portion of these flats were completed just in time to accommodate the victims of the 1961 kampong Bukit Ho Swee fire, the largest urban conflagration in Singapore's history, which left more than 100,000 people homeless in a single day (Loh 2013).

These one-room rental blocks were thus called emergency flats to signify both the urgency of need and their temporary status. From this beginning, the quality of the flats improved quickly. In 1964, three short years after its establishment, the HDB began to build three-room flats, which referred to two bedrooms and one sitting room in HDB nomenclature. The kitchen and bathroom-cum-toilet were standard provisions that were not included in categorizing the size of the flats.

The housing units became progressively larger until the late 1980s, when the largest unit was a 135 square-meter five-room flat with three bedrooms, a sitting room and a dining room. Because HDB flats were bigger and several times cheaper than flats of equal square footage being sold by private developers, the government instructed the HDB to shrink the sizes of its flats to the standards of private developers.

In 1964, the HDB began selling 99-year leases on the flats to households who were eligible for state-subsidized housing. As we shall see, this leasehold "homeownership" scheme took off very quickly after residents were permitted to use their social security savings to make down payments and pay for mortgages on the flats. As the national economy grew, the sales program kept expanding with periodic revisions of the eligibility rules, bringing an increasingly greater portion of citizens and permanent residents into the 99-year homeownership, reaching 90 percent of the public housing households by the end of the twentieth century. The public housing program has progressed from rental housing for the poor to housing for all but the top 10 to 15 percent of the highest income earners who have no interest in living with the masses. The HDB's success was dependent on two essential factors: the amount of affordable land available to the state and a low interest mortgage system that would be available to all but the lowest income strata.

Nationalization of Land

Land cost is the most prohibitive factor to any government's ability to provide social housing. Without low cost land, no national public housing program is possible. Committed to its vision of social democracy, the PAP government was very aggressive in acquiring privately held land for national development. After the Bukit Ho Swee fire, the colonial 1920 Land Acquisition Ordinance was amended to include a "fire site provision," which enabled the state to acquire land that had been "devastated" by fire at "not more than one-third the vacant site value" because "it would be unfair to the general public if the landlords were to benefit unduly from an appreciation of the land value now freed from encumbrances" (Wong and Yeh 1985: 40). Furthermore, the government would have to provide housing for the affected families. The 1920 Ordinance was eventually replaced by the 1966 Land Acquisition Act, which empowered the state to acquire any land that was deemed necessary in the interest of national development, at the rate of compensation fixed by the statute or the market rate, whichever was

lower (Lee 2016: 17–8). The Act was amended in 1973 to allow the
state to compensate owners of acquired land at the 1973 market value
or the land's value at the date of notification, depending on which was
lower. In determining "market" value, either the existing use or the
zoned use would be used to determine the lower cost to the government. No consideration was to be given to the potential value of the
land for any intensification of use. As every landholding, whether vacant
or developed, was permanently threatened by state acquisition, this
draconian land policy effectively cut down speculation, as intended by
the government.

The PAP government was well aware that its action violated common laws governing property rights which are sacrosanct to liberalism,
and it did not deny the coerciveness of the state in land acquisition.
There was no lack of legal criticism (Koh 1967). The government's stand
was in the straight-speaking official language of the HDB:

> The majority of the acquired private lands comprised dilapidated
> properties or neglected land where squatters had mushroomed. The
> government saw no reason why these owners should enjoy the greatly
> enhanced land values over the years without any effort put in by them.
> (Wong and Yeh 1985: 41)

Former Minister for National Development, the late Teh Cheang Wan,
claimed that the Land Acquisition Act was "the most efficient and effective way of obtaining land" for the urgent need to resettle "a quarter
million people living in degenerated city slums and another one-third of
a million in squatter areas," while "[l]and owners were understandably
aggrieved, but came to accept it when they saw that their land was
being put to good use, in the national interest" (Wong and Yeh 1985:
40–1). The "largesse" of landowners was likely an exaggeration. It is
more likely that the descendants of aggrieved landowners are among
the approximately 30 percent of the electorate that have consistently
voted against the PAP in every general election since 1968. The 1973
compensation rate was not adjusted upwards until 1986, when the
government deemed that it had already sufficient land banked for development purposes, and it was another ten years later before it started
paying market value for all acquisitions.

By 2010, the state had claimed approximately 90 percent of the
nation's land by various means—the colonial regime's transfer of crown
land to Singapore, the radical land acquisition in the 1970s and 1980s,

and extensive land reclamation from the sea. Land had been effectively nationalized. This gave the government great advantages in long-term planning and development of physical infrastructure for transport, public housing, water catchment areas and military installations.

Periodically, the state also releases land parcels to private developers for condominiums or commercial and industrial developments, with variable leases of 30 to 99 years. Such "land sales" are a significant source of state revenue. With land removed from speculation, the national public housing program has further undermined the workings of the housing market in three significant ways:

- The government through the HDB has been able to fix the prices of new flats at an affordable level for 90 percent of the population, with public subsidies gradated according to the size of the new flats.
- Legal conveyance work for all public housing transactions is executed in-house at the HDB. Although the legal profession has lost a lucrative area of legal fees, its loss has resulted in substantial savings for HDB house buyers.
- As explained in the next section, the funding of mortgages for public housing ownership through social security savings creates a closed circuit of financial transaction between the HDB and the social security savings board, thus avoiding the involvement of private commercial financial institutions, including banks, and possibly higher cost of mortgages.

Mortgage Financing System

The rapid rise in homeownership rate has been facilitated by a mortgage system built on the compulsory social security savings of homeowners. As the colonial government neglected to establish a national pension system, the first elected Chief Minister, David Marshall, established a social security system in 1955 called the Central Provident Fund (CPF) (Chan 1984: 69). Wage earners are compelled by statute to save a portion of their monthly wages, which are deducted at the income source. The employer is compelled to match the wage earner's monthly contributions. The sum of these two contributions constitutes the wage earner's tax-exempt social security savings for retirement. The savings are managed by the CPF Board, which pays an annual interest on the savings. The scheme began modestly with a 3 percent contribution from each party.

As the economy grew and incomes rose, the rate also increased steadily to a peak of 25 percent from each party until the mid-1980s recession, when employer contributions were reduced to cut labor costs. Since then, contribution rates for both parties have fluctuated according to the general health of the national economy. Also, the employer's contribution for workers above 50 years of age was progressively reduced, until a marginal percentage for those above 60 was reached (Low and Aw 1997).

Membership in the CPF grew from 180,000 in 1959 to 1,847,000 in 1984 to 3,593,000 in 2014, and savings received increased from SGD 9 million in 1955 to SGD 5,386 million in 1984 to SGD 29,722 million in 2014. A significant portion of this rapidly accumulating capital by the CPF Board is utilized to purchase government bonds at low interest rates for national development programs, including public housing, thus enabling the government to avoid dependency on multilateral financial agencies, such as the World Bank (Low and Aw 1997). The remainder of the funds is placed with the Government Investment Corporation (GIC), Singapore's first sovereign wealth fund, for global investments to garner greater return than the conventional purchasing of foreign bonds and treasury bills. (The importance of the GIC will be discussed in the chapter on state capitalism.)

In 1968, citizens were allowed to make pre-retirement withdrawals from their CPF savings to make down payments and pay monthly mortgages for HDB flats.[1] A closed loop of financial transactions was instituted: wage earners would save for their retirement with the CPF; part of the national CPF savings would provide loans to the HDB; wage earners could buy a flat from the HDB, which would hold the mortgage; the CPF would pay the monthly mortgage on the home-owner's behalf directly to the HDB, at an interest rate pegged at 0.5 percent higher than interest rate it pays on the monthly savings. The entire homeownership program was executed seamlessly between government statutory boards and, most importantly, without the involvement of any commercial financial institutions. With the cost of the housing kept at no more than 30 percent of a household's monthly income,

---

[1] An individual's CPF is unevenly apportioned into three different accounts: ordinary, medisave and special accounts. Only the ordinary account, which constitutes the largest portion, can be used for housing. Housing consumption is about 60 percent of the annual pre-retirement withdrawal from CPF.

homeowners—especially two-income households—were able to pay the monthly mortgage with their high monthly CPF savings without an additional cash outlay. Homeownership, therefore, did not affect the homeowner's normal consumption. Furthermore, throughout the mid-1960s to the mid-1990s, there was no fear of unemployment disrupting one's ability to meet mortgage payments because there was a chronic labor shortage. Under these favorable economic conditions and seamless administrative arrangements, the rate of public-housing homeownership increased exponentially. In 1968, 44 percent of all housing applicants elected to "buy" their flats; 63 percent did so by 1970. This percentage increased to 90 percent by 1986.

Public housing homeownership is encouraged by permitting lease-holders to sell their flats on the open market after five years of residence to another citizen who is eligible for subsidized housing, instead of selling it back to the HDB. Locally, such flats are known as resale flats, and the transactions take place in the resale market. This "resale" process is meant to assist public-housing homeowners with growing families to purchase larger flats as their space demand increases and to enable financially upwardly mobile families to improve their living conditions. This upgrading process simultaneously filters down to lower-income groups and other new entrants—including permanent residents who are ineligible to purchase new subsidized flats directly from the HDB—by making affordable older and smaller flats available in the housing market. These resale flats also reduced the HDB's need to construct small flats which require higher subsidies.

The upgrading process was very active in the first 30 years of the public housing program for three reasons. First, the need to upgrade living spaces was urgent because Singapore was then a developing economy with a large family size and a young population. Second, there were capital gains to be made. The early generations of public housing estates had been built within or near the city area and had over time developed amenities and services not found in new housing estates. The advantages of location and amenities dovetailed with the desires of potential purchasers to avoid the long queuing time for new flats. Consequently, resale flats began to fetch higher prices than new flats. Third, sellers could use the capital gains from their resale flats to purchase a new subsidized flat from the HDB. Each eligible family became entitled to the so-called "two bites of the cherry" but was not permitted to own two public housing units simultaneously.

The cherry metaphor clearly reflects popular awareness that public housing homeownership is a "good deal." The resale process has enabled public housing homeowners to accumulate and increase their wealth, either in the form of a larger property or in cash. This is reflected in the very active resale market. For example, more than 8,000 units of resale flats were transacted in eight consecutive quarters between the beginning of 2008 and the end of 2009.[2] Additionally, in 2014 one-in-ten homeowners sold their flats after the compulsory minimum five-year occupancy period (*Straits Times* 2 Mar. 2015). The volume of resale flats available tends to expand in tandem with widening of the price gap between resale and new flats; "the correlation between volume and the resale price-new price differential is 93%" (Edelstein and Lum 2003: 348). During the 1990s and 2000s, price differential had been very substantial. For example, a five-room flat sold by the HDB for SGD 140,000 could be resold for as high as SGD 630,000 before the 1997 Asian financial crisis. Resale prices for these five-room flats fell to around SGD 430,000 in 2000, when new HDB flats were being sold at between SGD 250,000 and SGD 300,000. The resale process had serious consequences on the affordability of public housing flats over the long term, which will be analyzed later in this chapter.

In terms of the national budget, the selling of public housing flats makes macroeconomic sense. One critical financial difficulty in providing public housing in any country is the wide gap between the high cost of construction and the pittance collected in subsidized rent from socially disadvantaged families. Each cycle of public housing construction becomes a drain on the national wealth. This was the primary reason why state housing construction stopped after two or three cycles in communist countries (Szelenyi 1983), where housing was ideologically considered as a basic necessity to be provided by the state. For the same reason, capitalist governments became progressively unwilling to construct public housing and opted for cash subsidies to the socially needy to enable them to pay market prices for accommodations. In contrast, the HDB has been able to recover a very substantial proportion of the cost of each construction cycle through the sales of the flats. Additional revenue is derived from rent collected for the provision of ancillary

---

[2] http://www.asiaone.com/Business/My+Money/Property/Story/A1Story20110304-266515.html [accessed 13 Oct. 2011].

services, such as parking and land rentals to commercial enterprises in the housing estates. Overall, the government kept its annual subsidy to the HDB to only an estimated 3 percent from the mid-1970s until perhaps the late 1980s. The government subsidy for the HDB was generally below SGD 2 billion annually during the first decade of the twenty-first century (*Straits Times* 25 Sept. 2015). The price for housing the nation has been a very small sum of money to pay for two political capital returns:

- The unstated gratitude of the citizens for improved living conditions and homeownership is undoubtedly reflected in the consistent popular electoral support for the PAP (Chua 1997). This is partly a consequence of homeowners' tendency to be politically conservative and vote for the status quo to protect their property values (Chua 2000a).
- The government's successful monopolization of housing has effectively eliminated all alternative modes of housing, leaving all but rich Singaporeans with no choice but to avail themselves of public housing. This total dependency on the state for a very important necessity of life has turned the citizens into clients of the state, thereby reducing very substantially the political space and force for citizens to negotiate with the government (Chua 2000a). It has, instead, enabled the government to embed different social policies—ranging from disciplining labor to governing family and race—as the conditions of eligibility for public housing, on a captive citizenry.

Proletarianization

When the homeownership scheme was introduced in the 1960s, Singapore had a declining trading economy with high rates of unemployment and underemployment, which were the results of the easy pace of everyday life. With no work and no money, much of daily life was spent with other residents in residential neighborhoods, resulting in a strong sense of an organic community. Renting housing in congested shophouses and kampong afforded a flexible rent payment schedule to accommodate the tenants' irregular employment. Public housing and homeownership greatly facilitated the transformation of this unemployed and underemployed informal workforce into a disciplined industrial proletariat to fill the new jobs created by Singapore's nascent industrialization.

Unlike the flexible rent payment in informal settlements, the failure to make monthly mortgage payments incurs interest and other penalties, including repossession of the flat by the HDB. The monthly mortgage that has to be paid on time can only be met by regular employment. Homeownership thus channelled the working population into the factories, transforming them into an industrial proletariat. In this sense, the public housing estates are "barracks of the working class" (Tremewan 1994: 45–73) but not ones of squalor and material deprivation but spacious, hygienic and well supplied with consumer desirables. Industrial time was naturalized and punctuality elevated into a generalized social virtue, particularly among the post-1960s generations of young and educated people for whom unemployment was unthinkable. Ironically, the first world standard of living in contemporary Singapore has kindled a nostalgia for the more relaxed life of the socially organic kampong and an implicit criticism of the high levels of stress generated by competition at work and the endless consumption of material goods (Chua 1997: 152–67).

Veiling Inequalities

Every public housing estate is comprehensively planned as a town with blocks of flats of varying heights. The blocks were originally built to a height of 4 and 25 storeys. However, since the 2000s new housing blocks of more than 30 storeys have been constructed because of planned increases in population, with an experimental block with 50 storeys. Estates are divided into neighborhoods, which are further divided into smaller precincts of a few blocks.

Each planning level has its specific service provisions. For example, each precinct has a children's playground; each neighborhood has shopping facilities for daily needs; and each town has a town center with a bus interchange terminal, a mass rapid transit train station, a shopping mall, a fresh-produce market, a local fast-food center of small stalls and the town's administrative office. Each town also has primary and secondary schools, sports and swimming facilities, a centrally located prominent mosque, and small temples and churches (Wong and Yeh 1985: 56–112). In short, all towns and their residents are equally served without discrimination.

This evenness of services and amenities homogenizes the daily life experiences of 90 percent of the population living in these towns, making the experience of living in public housing estates the Singaporean "way of life," which reduces the visibility of social and economic inequalities among the residents. The invisibility of class differences has enabled the PAP government to proclaim that it has achieved its goal of making Singapore a home-owning, middle-class society. The homogeneity of everyday life in the public spaces of the housing estate has veiled but not erased class inequalities. In the privacy of its flat, each family lives with its own material excess or deprivation, surfeit or hunger, happiness or depression, according to its own financial circumstances.

Shoring up Family

The social policies that most significantly leverage on the national public housing program are family policies. As discussed above, the PAP government sought to include the idea of the "family as the basic unit of society" in its new communitarian-based social compact with the citizenry. Also George Yeo, the party ideologue, argued that the family is naturally social in his resurrection of the social democratic foundation of the PAP. The heavy emphasis on the institution of the family has been a response to the tendency of individuals to become progressively dislodged from local social institutions, especially those who are globally marketable. Capitalizing on the family as possibly the last "natural" social institution that can hold an individual in place through a complex bundle of emotional ties, mutual responsibilities and obligations, the PAP government has made it, rather than public assistance, the first-line provider of mutual assistance in its social welfare policies. The shift of responsibilities from the state to the family is framed within an ideology of filial piety which, although neo-Confucian in its inspiration, is applied to all Singaporeans. Thus, the law requires children to care for aged parents. The public housing program is a foundational institutional support in the government's family-welfare policy.

For the first three decades of the public housing program, only families were eligible to purchase new subsidized flats as the HDB (and the government) did not want to facilitate the break-up of families. Public housing homeownership has become so conventionally tied to starting a family that young couples reflexively factor it in as a priority item in their marriage plans. Proposals of marriage are often cast in terms of "let's go register for an HDB flat" and betrothed couples often introduce themselves as "already having registered for a flat" (Teo 2011:

1–21). To reinforce the family institution, married couples who choose to live close to their parents are given priority in the allocation of flats and additional cash grants towards purchasing a new or resale flat. However, such pro-family policies have not reversed the steady decline in marriage and childbirth rates. As the number of unmarried people increased, accommodating them in public housing proved politically unavoidable. Since the early 1990s, individuals who are considered past their potential marrying age—males at 40 and females at 35—have been permitted to purchase resale three-room flats, and they have been able to purchase new subsidized two-room flats with generous cash grants from the state since 2013.

Extracting Political Support

While there is no doubt that the overwhelming majority of Singaporeans are grateful for public housing ownership, it has not guaranteed electoral political support for the PAP government in general elections. For example, residents in the Potong Pasir constituency voted for Chiam See Tong, the founder of the Singapore Democratic Party, against the PAP in 1984 in spite of the brand-new flats with a distinctive "ski-slope" roof design. Immediately, an incensed Minister for National Development, Teh Cheang Wan, announced that from then on any public housing estate within an electoral constituency that voted against the PAP would be the last to be served by the HDB. As the PAP's popular electoral support continued to decline, the government increased its retaliatory measures. In 1995 it announced that anti-PAP public housing estates would not be excluded only from the highly subsidized estate upgrading program, but all programs that were already approved would be withdrawn as well. Because the upgrading programs are crucial for maintaining the market value of existing flats, to vote against the PAP is therefore tantamount to voting against one's material self-interest as a homeowner. The public outcry of unfairness was dismissed by the party as "naïve" because such strategic use of government resources by the ruling party was part and parcel of *real politik* (*Straits Times* 29 Dec. 1996).

However, it is significant that such unfair punishment did not deter defiant anti-PAP residents in two particular constituencies from expressing their opposition to PAP policies. The Potong Pasir constituency continued to elect Chiam See Tong from 1984 until 2011. (When he retired, his wife stood in the 2011 general election but lost to the PAP candidate.) The Hougang constituency had consistently elected the incumbent secretary-general of the Workers' Party, Loh Thia Khiang, since 1991. It continued to elect the Workers' Party candidate in the 2011 and 2015 general elections, when Loh moved out of the constituency to contest in the Aljunied Greater Representative Constituency (GRC). In the end, the threat of withholding the upgrading program proved limited and politically costly. The PAP government was compelled to remove the threat after the 2011 general election when it lost, for the first time, the five-member Aljunied GRC to the Workers' Party, albeit upgrading programs in opposition held constituencies are still being provided with much delay and grudgingly.

Economics of Public Housing

Housing as Asset-based Social Security

The PAP government persistently insists that subsidized public housing homeownership is a privilege, not a right or entitlement of citizenship, for three reasons. First, ownership is restricted to Singapore citizens and permanent residents. Second, housing is provided not according to a family's need but according to a family's ability to pay. Third, public housing remains a commodity and a vehicle for private capital gains and accumulation, facilitated by the resale process in a government-regulated market system. The pressure on Singaporeans to use public housing as a vehicle to accumulated capital is a result of the fact that homeownership is tied to one's CPF retirement savings, which can be used to finance the purchase of a flat. However, doing so severely reduces savings available for eventual retirement.

By the early 1980s, local economists began to warn that the hefty CPF withdrawal for housing might leave a large number of Singaporeans without sufficient funds to finance their retirement years (*Singapore Economic Review* 1986: 51–5; Asher 1991; Asher and Nandy 2008). However, with the exception of one brief short dip of prices during the 2008 global recession (Phang 2013: 82), the annual rate of price increase of public housing has consistently outstripped the annual interest accrued to CPF savings. The wealth of the homeowners has thus increased and, presumably, the proceeds of the sale of their flats eventually should be even better able to cover their retirement needs than keeping the CPF savings. Cognizant of the link between homeowner-ship, CPF and retirement needs, Prime Minister Lee Hsien Loong points out to citizens:

> The most important thing we [the PAP government] do for Singa-poreans, of course, is to help every family own a home—the HDB flat. The house is much more than a secure roof over their heads. The house in Singapore is also a major way for us to level up the less successful and to give them a valuable asset and a retirement nest egg. We are using the HDB as a means to give every Singaporean household a stake.... That's why we are making sure that HDB flats are affordable even to lower-income-households. (*Straits Times* 21 Oct. 2011)

The public housing system has silently become an asset-based social security system (Chia 2011; Ronald and Doling 2010).

Strategies for Value Appreciation in Public Housing

Transforming ownership into an asset-based social security system has had serious consequences on the market prices of public housing. If public housing is to be an asset to fund the retirement needs of a nation of homeowners, the prices of HDB flats must not be allowed to fall below their investment values, that is, the HDB selling price. Other-wise, homeowners could end up with negative equity where the cost of their flats exceeds the flats' market value at the time of retirement. This would jeopardize the retiree's ability to fund retirement. Having en-couraged the entire nation to invest in public housing, the government bears the responsibility to ensure that the value of the investments is maintained, if not enhanced; any serious fall in public housing prices would bring financial trouble to homeowners and a political crisis for the ruling government. Thus, the government must assist in maintaining and/or enhancing the values of existing public housing stock, which it does.

The prices of resale flats have been higher than those of new flats. This has been further reinforced by three major government policies. First, as an estate ages, the condition of its flats and the general estate environment will inevitably deteriorate, thus eroding the property values of the flats. In 1990, to support the property values of older flats against all subsequent generations of better designed flats and estates, the government established a highly subsidized estate upgrading scheme to improve the flats, amenities and environment of older estates; citizens only bore 10 to 20 percent of the cost while permanent residents had to bear the full cost of the upgrading (Chua 2003b).

Second, the rising prices of new flats had led to growing skepticism about whether or not new flats were in fact subsidized and suspicions that the government was profiting from the national housing program. To make the subsidy of new flats transparent, the HDB adopted the practice of pricing new flats at a 20 percent market discount below prevailing prices of equivalent resale flats. This discount formula created an unintended vicious cycle of price inflation: rising resale prices raised the prices of new flats; the increased prices of new flats in turn constituted the base for the further increases in prices of resale flats, thus pushing the price of all public housing flats even higher. The prices of resale flats kept inflating by the "20 percent discount" formula. This cycle was disrupted after the 2011 general election, when the affordability of public housing emerged as an election issue.

Third, estate upgrading does not stop the devaluation of existing flats from devaluation as their 99-year leases run out. This requires a radical solution which involves the "creative destruction" of existing flats. Being a small island nation, there is persistent pressure on state planners, including the HDB, to maximize the carrying capacity of every square inch of land in order to accommodate an expanding population, including the large number of foreign laborers needed to sustain economic growth. Thus, in 2001 the plot ratio was increased by a multiple of three from the existing density in anticipation of intensification of land use in future redevelopment (URA 2001).[3] To intensify land use in public housing estates, the HDB initiated the Selective En-bloc Redevelopment Scheme (SERS) in 1995. The scheme targeted for redevelopment selected older estates with 4- to 12-storey housing blocks, which had been developed during the 1960s and 1970s in the city and its immediate vicinity. Between 2012 and 2015, about 350 blocks in 78 locations were demolished.[4] In the largest SERS exercise, 3,480 flats

---

[3] In 2011, a White Paper on Population radically revised the projection to an eventual population of 6.3 million, when already one in four persons was a non-Singaporean. This led to a push-back by the citizens who voted heavily against the PAP during the election that year, giving it only 60 percent of the total popular vote, the lowest support in the party's history.

[4] http://www.hdb.gov.sg/fi10/fi10329p.nsf/w/eSERSCompleted?OpenDocument [accessed 15 Oct. 2011].

and shops in 31 blocks, some of which were more than 50 years old, were slated for demolition. As public housing is built on state land, the state reserves the right to repossess the land and compensate the 99-year leaseholders of the affected flats. While the level of compensation may be subject to negotiation, the right to repossession is not.

Under SERS, new 30- to 40-storey blocks are constructed in the vicinity of the blocks targeted for demolition. Affected households are then relocated into these new blocks, to minimize disruptions to their neighborhood routines as much as possible. Homeowners are compensated at the prevailing market prices for old flats. With the 20 percent market discount formula, this compensation is more than the amount needed to finance their new 99-year lease flats; any remainder is profit. With such favorable conditions, few affected families have protested being moved as noted by the Minister for National Development, Khaw Boon Wan:

> With every new HDB town becoming more modern and better de-
> signed, there is a need to ensure that the older towns do not end up
> too far behind. They [affected households] will get a new modern
> flat with a fresh 99-year lease, with greenery on their doorstep, and
> panoramic views of the city and surrounding areas. I am sure they
> will find this attractive and exciting. (quoted from the *Straits Times*
> 28 June 2014)

His sentiments are echoed by a 74-year-old resident: "My neighbors and I are all really happy. Why wouldn't you want a new flat?" Those who lament having to move are comforted; saying "at least we [long term neighbors] can all move together and won't be alone" (quotes from the *Straits Times* 28 June 2014). SERS thus appears to be a perfect solution to the problem of declining values of existing flats with progressively shortening leases.

The combined effects of the above policies have practically guaranteed public housing homeownership as a fail-safe investment for all citizens, except those too poor to buy even the smallest public housing flat. Thus, despite its insistence that subsidized public housing is a privilege of citizenship, for the citizens it has become an unspoken right of citizenship that the government/HDB is obliged to provide for all but rich Singaporeans. Ironically, the same factors, which guarantee private capital gains for existing public housing homeowners, have also created a systemic inflationary pressure that causes public housing prices to rise inexorably, with serious repercussions on their affordability for first time entrants into the market. This contradiction has serious political consequences for the PAP government.

Political Perils of the State-Regulated Market

The 1997 Asian regional financial crisis followed by the SARS epidemic in 2002–03 created financial uncertainties which led to a slowing down of public housing purchases and disrupted the 50-year-long increase in prices for both new and resale public housing flats. The HDB found itself holding 17,500 completed unsold flats at the end of 2002. Unable to reduce the prices of these flats without deflating the entire public housing market, it reduced the supply of new flats. The HDB thus switched from building ahead of demand, trusting that demand would always be there, to building to order only when 70 percent of a block was pre-sold. Although the backlog was sold by 2005, the HDB continued to slow down construction of new flats, sharply reducing supply when economic conditions had changed for the better.

Due to Singapore's very stable domestic condition, foreign direct investments (FDI) continued to flow into the country. Between 2006 and 2008, the total FDI grew from SGD 370 to SGD 496 billion.[5] To meet the increased demand for workers created by this capital inflow, the government had to allow a massive inflow of immigrants. Between 2005 and 2011, the population increased from 4 million to 5.18 million, of which one in four was an immigrant.[6] The government vigorously defended the sharp increase of foreign labor because "for every one foreign worker employed ... 1.5 local jobs were created" (*Straits Times* 22 Apr. 2011). The increase in population inevitably intensified demand for housing. This combined with the reduced supply of new flats led to an acute housing price inflation during the latter half of the 2000s as reflected by this very rough estimate from the following citizen:

> In 1981, I earned $800 plus as a fresh graduate. At that time, one of my colleagues bought a five-room HDB flat for $35,000. Now, a graduates' pay has risen about four times but HDB flat prices have risen more than 11 times. (*Straits Times* 21 Oct. 2011)

---

[5] Singapore Statistics, "Foreign Direct Investments in Singapore by Country/Region, 2005–2009," http://www.singstat.gov.sg/stats/themes/economy/biz/foreigninvestment. pdf [accessed 3 Nov. 2011].

[6] *Monthly Digest of Statistics*, Singapore, October 2011: 16, http://www.singstat.gov. sg/pubn/reference/mdsoct11.pdf [accessed 31 Oct. 2011].

The mismatch between the rapid inflation of housing prices and the tepid rates of income increase was common knowledge and caused widespread anxiety regarding the affordability of public housing for future generations.

The supply and prices of resale flats were affected by three different factors. First, a standing regulation restricted permanent residents to purchasing only resale flats. In 2012, 20 percent of all resale flats were bought by permanent residents, intensifying the competition for resale flats between Singapore citizens and permanent residents. Second, to house the new migrant workers, new regulations were introduced to permit homeowners to rent out an entire flat to generate a live stream of income rather than sell the flat. Third, at the same time, higher income public housing households were deterred from buying private residences because "private home prices had surged 60%" between mid-2009 and mid-2013 (*Straits Times* 1 July 2014).

All three factors combined to reduce the supply of resale flats in the market, leading to rapid price inflation. The resale price index rose 86 percent in six years from 2005 to 2012. For example, "the median price of a resale five-room flat in Ang Mo Kio (an older estate) increased from SGD 327,000 to SGD 609,000. This increase of SGD 282,000 was more than four times the median annual income of resident households" (Phang 2013: 81–2). In addition to a reduced supply of resale flats, the prices of new flats also increased in tandem with the prices of resale flats due to the above-mentioned 20 percent market discount price formula. Thus, the spiral of price increases of both the new and resale public housing flats kept spinning upwards, making the purchase of public housing increasingly difficult for a middle class whose income had been stagnant for a decade and a working class which had suffered declines in real wages.

By 2009, the government realized that the rapid inflation of public housing prices would become a political issue in the forthcoming 2011 general election, so it took some small steps to address the affordability issue. It substantially increased "additional housing grants" to first-time homeowners to offset the rising cost—up to SGD 60,000 for households with a monthly income below SGD 1,500, which was more than half of the price of a new two-bedroom public housing flat (*Straits Times* 19 June 2013)—and lengthened the payment period for 20- and 25-year mortgages to 30 years. Considering the fact that homeowners generally buy their flats in their mid-30s, paying off a 30-year mortgage would bring them to the current statutory retirement of 62 years old; homeownership was (and is) indeed for life. However, these minor adjustments were insufficient to quell Singaporeans' multiple discontents—the influx of immigrants, competition for public services and the rising cost of living, which prominently included housing costs. The 2011 May election delivered the PAP the worst election results in its more than 60 years in power. It lost six parliamentary seats instead of the usual one or two and garnered only 60 percent of the popular vote. Given that the promise of affordable public housing to all citizens had been absolutely fundamental to its legitimacy and longevity, the PAP government immediately undertook more radical measures to regain its political ground.

The new Minister for National Development, Khaw Boon Wan, first, increased the number of housing units built, from 9,000 in 2009 to 25,000 in 2011. By 2014, more than 50,000 new housing units were placed on the market, involving both ahead-of-demand and build-to-order schemes. First-time homeowners were counseled publicly to delay their purchase of a flat and wait for the new supply. Second, he removed the inflationary 20 percent market discount formula that linked the prices of new flats to the resale flats. Prices of new subsidized flats were set by the HDB, and affordability was facilitated through generous cash grants from the state to new homeowners to bring about a slow but tolerable decline in prevailing prices of resale flats. Third, he ended the practice of the HDB providing valuation for flats ahead of an actual resale transaction because buyers and sellers used this valuation as the base price from which they would negotiate an additional cash payment, locally called the Cash-over-Valuation (COV), which was borne by the buyer. The COV could add 5 to 7 percent to the valuation. Finally, the government gave public housing grants to lower middle-class households that needed to upgrade their housing in addition to the grants given to first-time homeowners. For example, two low-income single persons applying for an SGD 75,000 flat with one-bedroom and one sitting room could receive up to an SGD 60,000 grant (*Straits Times* 31 July 2013). The cost for these subsidies from 2005 to 2013 was SGD 1 billion.

Changes in the public housing sector regulations have made an impact on the smaller private housing market. To reduce speculation across both public and private housing sectors, the amount of down payment was sharply increased from 10 to 30 percent for the purchase of second and subsequent properties. Additional stamp duty was also imposed on property purchases—15 percent levy on all foreigners, 5 percent on permanent residents buying their first flat and 7 percent on Singaporeans purchasing second and subsequent properties. Because the cost of private condominiums is usually in the millions, these additional levies add up to very hefty sums, which deters property investments. The greatest dampening effect is the limit imposed on personal debt of Singaporeans. In 2013, the total debt of an individual, including existing mortgages, car loans and credit cards, was capped so that it could not exceed 60 percent of their monthly income. Banks were not permitted to make loans beyond this total debt-servicing ratio. The combined effect of these financial regulations had a chilling effect on housing sales. In the private condominium sector, sales in the first quarter of 2014 dropped more than 50 percent from the same period in the previous year (*Straits Times* 1 July 2014).

Of greater political symbolic significance were the additional constraints placed on permanent residents as their presence in the resale market had become a lightning rod for public anger. The new restrictions on permanent residents included: (1) not being permitted to purchase a resale flat for the first three years of residency; (2) having to dispose of all other properties, including those in their country of origin, within six months of purchase; and (3) obtaining permission to rent out the flat from the HDB every year for a limit of five years rather than every three years. Considering permanent residents owned only 5 percent of the total public housing stock of nearly one million units, and they were only renting out slightly more than 2,000 flats, these constraints had a marginal impact on the housing market. However, politically, they served to inform the citizens that undeserved privileges for permanent residents had been removed (*Straits Times* 26 July 2012). Reinforcing this point, the annual growth of immigrant arrivals was reduced from a high of 19 percent in 2008 to 4.1 percent in 2011. To adjust for the economic effect of this sharp reduction of the labor force, the government speeded up its economic restructuring program by enhancing financial support to industries which sought increased productivity through technology.

By mid-2013, the prices of all properties, public and private, began to inch lower by average of 1 percent every quarter for four consecutive quarters (*Straits Times* 2 July 2014) and continued to fall for the next four quarters. According to the Minister for National Development, his ultimate aim was to bring the prices of new flats to "about four times the annual median income of its applicants—30 percent lower than the current 5.5 times" (*Straits Times* 13 Apr. 2013). It would appear that the government had wrested back control over the prices of the public housing sector and reoccupied its place as the price-setter for the entire housing market, for now. Instead of touting "public housing as asset," Prime Minister Lee Hsien Loong re-emphasized public housing as a necessity for the long term, rather than for quick turnaround for profit.[7] By the 2015 general election, public housing affordability disappeared as a political issue and the PAP won a landslide victory, recovering its popular electoral support to close to 70 percent.

Monetizing Housing Asset for Retirement

If public housing flats are the main asset to fund the retirement needs of homeowners, the latter must be able to monetize the capital that is invested and accumulated in their flats. The most direct way is, of course, to sell the existing flat. Retirees can then either downgrade to a smaller flat or, if possible, move in with their adult children and keep the profit for retirement needs. An alternative to selling is the "lease/ buy back" scheme in which homeowners sell back to the HDB all but 30 years of the remaining lease in return for a monthly income, without having to vacate the flat. As homeowners are most likely to buy a 99-year lease flat in their early 30s, there will still be more than 60 years left in the lease when they retire at 62. Keeping the last 30 years of the lease would enable the homeowner to age-in-place for the remaining years of his/her life. Both sales schemes have not been popular since their initiation in the early 2010s because they are not as lucrative as renting out a flat.

Rental regulations of public housing flats have evolved over time. At the outset, public housing homeowners were disallowed from owning additional property to prevent speculation. By the mid-1980s, as household wealth grew, the government lifted the injunction and permitted public housing homeowners to invest in private property. However, they

---

[7] Lee Hsien Loong, "2010 National Rally Speech," http://stars.nhb.gov.sg/stars/ public/viewHTML.jsp?pdfno=20100914001 [accessed 3 Nov. 2011].

had to continue to reside in their public housing flats. Since the early 2000s, homeowners have been permitted to rent out either unused bedrooms or their entire flat in order to accommodate the sharp increase of foreign labor. By 2014, about 44,000 rooms and 40,000 whole flats in HDB estates were rented out. Among those who rented out an entire flat were aged homeowners who moved in with their children, an arrangement encouraged by the government's pro-family policy, as it relieved the government of long-term financial responsibility for these senior citizens. Others moved into their own private properties; more than 45,000 or approximately 4 percent of public housing homeowners own private property (*Straits Times* 12 June 2014). In either mode, they have all become landlords with public housing flats.

Conclusion: Permanent Balancing Act

The social democracy of the early PAP caused it to be committed to the universal provision of affordable public housing. To this end, it nationalized land and encouraged the entire nation to avail itself of subsidized public housing by drawing on its social security savings. Every public housing flat thus holds the retirement capital of its owner and must be monetized eventually to provide for the latter's retirement years. For this reason, administrative rules and regulations have been introduced to ensure that the prices of existing public housing units are protected and increased. Using the same rules and regulations, Singaporeans have strategized to improve their capital accumulation through public housing homeownership, which has inflated the cost of public housing and raised concerns about its affordability to future generations of new homeowners. When affordability becomes a political issue, counter-measures have been taken to cool the inflationary housing market, but these measures have not been allowed to cause prevailing prices to drop to levels that would destroy the national capital formation embodied in the entire public housing stock or to jeopardize the financial interests and the retirement funding of existing homeowners. Thus, when cooling measures begin to threaten the interests of existing homeowners, other measures are taken to prevent the market from falling precipitously. Such measures include cutting the supply of available housing units and easing housing mortgages and loans. The need to balance the financial burden of new entrants to the public housing market and protecting the investments of existing homeowners is understood by Singaporeans.

The universal public housing program is thus double-edged. On the one hand, it garners political support for the PAP government, reflected by the successive electoral victories since the 1960s, when HDB was established (Chua 1997). On the other hand, having encouraged Singaporeans to invest in their public housing flats, the PAP government is obliged to bear the responsibility of ensuring the security of the investment. It is thus engaged permanently in balancing a set of contradictory demands:

- supplying sufficient new flats and keeping them affordable for first-time homeowners and low-income families without turning public housing into a welfare entitlement;
- preventing an oversupply of new flats that might hurt market values of existing and resale flats; and
- increasing property values of existing flats and resale prices to ensure that retirees have sufficient funds for retirement while closely watching the buildup of inflationary bubbles that might jeopardize the affordability of resale prices to potential buyers.

To use a favorite metaphor of the government, the management of these tightly balanced demands is like a marathon race without an end. Failure to maintain a balance of the competing demands through periodic intervention in the market will incur a political cost. In sum, the housing market sector is severely circumscribed and controlled by actions of the government/state, instead of a free market and a minimal state.

All governments endorse the ideas that every citizen is entitled to "decent" housing. However, the history of housing provision is strewn with failures. Singapore is one of the few success stories in the universal provision of housing, going way beyond the conventional demand for minimum social housing provision as welfare for the needy. When the PAP government embarked on selling public housing in 1964, it was without precedent, without a model to emulate. In fashioning its own system, the sacrosanct liberal value of private property has been displaced by the national interest; the private interest of landowners was sacrificed for the collective wellbeing of the entire nation. Periodic policy intervention is necessary to redirect market forces towards price stability. This ensures affordability on the one hand and protects the investments of the existing homeowners on the other. The collective welfare requires constraints to be placed on the market. While adequate housing for the nation remains an unachievable goal under a free market ideology and liberal democratic capitalism, the universal provision of a necessary good stands as an important emblem of the PAP's ideological claim to being communitarian/socialist. Politically, it has enabled the PAP government to leverage on the political capital accrued from the housing provision to enact various social policies that are potential political problems, like family support, immigration and, as we shall see in a later chapter, race relations.

Chapter 5

DISRUPTING FREE MARKET
State Capitalism and
Social Distribution

From the outside, Singapore under the PAP government appears to be a champion of free market capitalism. The government began inviting foreign multinational enterprises from independence in 1965, nothing short of ideological heresy at a time when such enterprises were regarded as a continuation of economic colonization in newly independent post-colonial nations. It established a "one-stop" bureaucracy that cut all red tape and provided generous tax incentives, including an extended tax-free period, to assist foreign enterprises to get started. It tamed labor unions under the state-controlled National Trades Union Congress (NTUC), and redirected them towards a tripartite (state-enterprise-union) collaboration for peaceful labor relations that prevented disruption of production. With all these measures in place, it practically guaranteed profits to foreign enterprises in Singapore. Today, Singapore continues to compete for foreign direct investments, albeit from only highly capital-intensive advanced technology industries, such as pharmaceuticals and biotechnologies, instead of low wage, low technology, labor-intensive consumer manufacturers of the 1960s and 1970s. However, alongside this multinational corporation-driven industrialization is the simultaneous development of a string of state-owned enterprises (SOEs). Established initially to develop the local economy and serve the citizens, many of these SOEs have become global companies in their own right and contributed very significantly to national wealth formation. The SOEs have been reorganized and consolidated under a single holding company, Temasek Holdings, one of the two Singapore government sovereign wealth funds (SWFs), the other being the Government Investment Corporation (GIC). In addition to making long-term investments in the global enterprises in the financialized global economy, Temasek Holdings Private Limited (henceforth Temasek or Temasek Holdings) also invests in local private enterprises which have potential to regionalize and/or globalize their businesses.

SOEs are conventionally seen as money-losing endeavors which survive only from a constant injection of state funding because they are inefficiently managed by state bureaucrats who have a penchant for corruption. One reason why SOEs have such negative characteristics is their origin. They are commonly enterprises that were coercively nationalized by a new government, such as colonizer-owned enterprises nationalized by post-colonial states or private enterprises nationalized by post-revolution communist regimes. In both cases, the tendency was to appoint ranking state bureaucrats and/or party members who were unlikely to have the requisite business skills, knowledge and experiences to managerial positions in the nationalized enterprises. Such appointments imparted to the appointed a sense of "entitlement" to the positions which often translated into an "entitlement" to wealth, including through corrupt means. A typical example is the Indonesian military control over nationalized enterprises since independence in which corruption remains an ongoing issue (Human Rights Watch 2010). Another is the current state of SOEs in the economic transition of China and Vietnam where corruption is endemic, and the prevailing issue is how to shed unproductive SOEs and transform the others into profitable enterprises (Wen and Xu 1997; Fforde and de Vylder 1996).

SWFs, and to a lesser extent SOEs, face general criticism of a lack of transparency in investment strategies, sources of funds and the extent of government involvement in investment decisions (Rodan 2004: 48–81; Balin 2009). With immense cash reserves for global investments, SWFs have become increasingly significant players in global financial capitalism. In 2012, it was estimated that SGD 4.62 trillion of assets were under the management of SWFs, a 50 percent increase from SGD 3.05 trillion in 2008 (Solebo 2012). *Global Insight*'s SWF Tracker reported that at the rate global SWFs were growing, their economic output would exceed that of the US by 2015 and that of the European Union (EU) by 2016; thus, they would quickly appropriate the positions of "new financial power brokers" and "[usurp] central banks as the international capital providers of the last resort" (Hopkins 2008). This rather "alarmist" projection is reflective of the concerns among developed nations regarding SWFs.

A central issue of concern is how SWF-owning nations might use their investments to further their political interests, which could affect the security of the investment receiving nations (Gow 2008; Truman 2010). This concern is particularly acute when "the universe of SWFs may be said to be dominated by three classes of countries: seven Arab oil exporters (Abu Dhabi, Algeria, Dubai, Kuwait, Libya, Qatar, Saudi Arabia), two non-Arab oil exporters (Norway, Russia) and three emergent East Asian economies (China, Hong Kong and Singapore)" (Cohen 2009: 716). With the exception of Norway, there is a general absence of SWFs in the West. For example, Preston (2010) lamented Britain's missed opportunity in the 1980s to establish an SWF to invest surpluses made from North Sea oil and gas. The proposal for doing so was dismissed by the Tories in power. Price Water House Coopers estimated that earnings from an SWF established then could have forked out GBP 450 billion to tide over Britain's economic woes during the 2008 financial crisis. This absence of SWFs occurs because as vehicles of the state-as-capitalist-entrepreneur SWFs violate the three cardinal demands of liberal capitalism: private ownership of capital, the free market and minimal state. Suspicion of SWFs in the West is illustrated by German legislations reported readiness to veto any takeover by SWFs of national firms that could be seen as a threat to "public order or security" (Gow 2008). Undoubtedly a significant ideological bias lies behind these expressed concerns of Western developed nations. The controversies surrounding the sale of the British private firm, Peninsular and Oriental Steam Navigation Company (P&O) to state-owned Dubai Ports World (DPW), illustrate this. With the takeover, the management of six American ports, formerly carried out by P&O, would be overseen by DPW. Some American political figures objected to the sale on the grounds that seaports are strategic industries; the sale of P&O would give a foreign country control over these six seaports, which could jeopardize national security. As if P&O is not a foreign firm and Britain not a foreign country!

Aware of political sensitivities most SWFs have avoided investment practices that could be perceived as threats to the national security of the host country, including avoiding holding majority stakes, waiving shareholder voting rights, and/or refraining from investing in companies belonging to countries which have direct conflicts of political interests with the investing party (Balin 2009). However, this was not always the case. Temasek Holdings, a Singaporean SWF, got into serious controversy with two major regional investments. The first was the substantial share Temasek held in Indosat, Indonesia's second largest telecommunications company, through its other vehicles, SingTel and ST Telemedia. In 2008, the Indonesian Business Competition Supervisory Commission charged that Temasek had breached Indonesian anti-trust laws; after some protest, Temasek relinquished its entire stake in the company to Qatar Telecom, with the apparent consent of the Indonesian government but the objection of the Commission.[1] The second was the purchasing of Shin Corporation of Thailand in 2006, using Thai registered companies in which Temasek had controlling shares and/or decision-making power. The family of then Thai Prime Minister, Thaksin Shinawatra, who sold the company, was able to escape paying any tax on the sale. This provided the opening for the political opponents of the controversial Prime Minister to mount public protests and demonstrations which eventually led to a bloodless coup that ended Thaksin's political career and created political instability in Thailand for the next decade. As of 2016, the country is still under military rule. Perhaps after these two experiences, Yeung (2011) suggests that the Singapore SWFs will go to great lengths to avoid suspicion and political backlash from host nations, especially the immediate neighbors. Regardless, regulatory procedures and mechanisms to oversee SWF investment activities to assuage the anxieties of receiving nations have been established. In 2008, an International Working Group on SWFs coordinated by the IMF established the so-called "Santiago Principles" of 24 guidelines with the overarching aim of achieving the "shared goal of maintaining a stable and open investment environment" globally.[2] Adherence to the principles is voluntary (Cohen 2009: 724).

Attitudes towards SWFs seem to have changed after the 2008 global recession generated by the US sub-prime mortgage crisis. SWFs from the Middle East and Asia played a very significant role in stabilizing the global economy by taking sizeable stakes in US and European

---

[1] http://news.asiaone.com/News/the+Straits+Times/Story/A1Story20080624-72494.html [accessed 15 Feb. 2014].

[2] International Working Group of Sovereign Wealth Funds. http://www.iwg-swf.org/pubs/eng/santiagoprinciples.pdf [accessed 15 Feb. 2014].

financial institutions, estimated at USD 69 billion (*The Economist* 17 Jan. 2008), saving many insolvent financial establishments from bankruptcy. However in the process, SWFs reportedly suffered heavy losses. As a consequence, SWFs have come to be viewed more positively, even courted by both public and private sectors. In 2012, British Prime Minister David Cameron thought that Chinese SWFs might be potential investors in Britain's plans to semi-privatize its road transport system, which would involve repairing the road system's ailing infrastructure and building needed new roads (Watt 2012). This was an about-face from protectionist obstructions that Chinese SWFs often receive from Western governments (Gow 2008; Truman 2010; Cohen 2009). Also, the UN appealed to SWFs to invest in some African states, where investments are high-risk and wrought with corruption (Cognato 2008: 33). At the 2009 Asia Pacific Economic Community (APEC) summit held in Singapore, a panel of representatives from Kuwait, Singapore, China and Norway defended SWFs as a "source of stability" in the global financial market because they look to long-term investments rather than act as short-term investors in the "frenzied chase of high yields" (Chew 2009). The representatives also cautioned against the stands of national governments as they hinder the economic recovery of markets experiencing greater risk. It is clear that the SWFs have an abiding interest to profit from global capitalism, not to destroy it.

In contrast to the negative image/reality of SOEs as coercively nationalized inefficient money losing enterprises managed by political appointees, Singapore SOEs and SWFs are directly established by the PAP government,

- run by wage-earning professional managers with the government maintaining oversight to ensure the SOEs and SWFs perform well;
- disciplined by market; and
- allowed to stay in business only if they are profitable.

The SOEs and SWFs constitute the two pillars of state capitalism in Singapore. Their annual profits contribute very significantly, first, to the depth of the national wealth, which fosters the stability of the Singapore currency against speculation and avoids intervention by multilateral international financial institutions, such as the IMF; and, second, to the government's annual revenue, expenditure, and social redistribution. Politically, the extensive direct and indirect employment opportunities they provide engender political conservatism among professional middle-class Singaporeans and general political stability.

Initiating Industrialization

Throughout the colonial period, the British never veered away from maintaining trade as the main economic activity for Singapore (Wong 1991: 49). By the late 1940s, it was clear that *entrepôt* trade was no longer a viable source of economic growth to sustain the post-war high rate of population growth. Trade was to receive one last gasp during the 1950 Korean War, as prices of primary commodities soared. However, "[t]he boom was too short-lived to restore much faith in the *entrepôt* trade as the basis for future development and prosperity" (Cheng 1991: 187). When the PAP was elected in 1959 in a self-governing Singapore, the first Finance Minister, Goh Keng Swee, was convinced that the British's *laissez-faire* policies "had led Singapore to a dead end, with little economic growth, massive unemployment, wretched housing, and inadequate education" (Goh 1976: 84).

The PAP sought advice on economic growth on two occasions in those early years after independence. In 1959, the PAP engaged Canadian F.J. Lyle under the Colombo Plan; in 1961, a World Bank/UN appointed mission led by Albert Winsemius, "a former director-general for industrialization in the Netherlands" (Schein 1996: 32) was consulted. Both Lyle and Winsemius had the same advice—industrialize. Winsemius submitted a set of "recommendations for a ten-year industrialization programme as well as a crash programme to alleviate the immediate unemployment problem" (Cheng 1991: 189). However, the prevailing economic condition was not encouraging for industrialization. Local capitalists were overwhelmingly traders who were "accustomed to short-term risks and quick profit" and lacking not only in industrial know-how but also in "willingness to embark on long-term projects" (Cheng 1991: 190). The leaders of the Chinese Chamber of Commerce, among whom were those most successful in trade, would not be persuaded to embark on industrial investments (Visscher 2007: 186–7, 191–4). The government thus turned to foreign capital, enticing foreign companies to set up shop with institutional support and attractive tax incentives. Where foreign capital was not available because the "initial capital required is too large for private investors and in projects which are still experimental in nature" (Ow 1976: 169), it had to draw from the state treasury to invest its own capital to develop SOEs.

Initially, in line with the prevailing economic wisdom, the industrialization program focused primarily on "import substitution," encouraging industries which were already selling products locally to set up manufacturing in Singapore to supply the larger Malaysian market. Political separation in 1965 meant the loss of the Malaysian market. However, it brought forth a new vision with an expanded horizon. The Minister for Foreign Affairs declared Singapore as a "global city" (Rajaratnam 1972), a full three decades before sociologist Saskia Sassen (1991) made the concept of the "global city" a conventional idea. The world was to be its hinterland and market for its industrial products and services. With this re-orientation, the PAP government adopted the export-oriented industrialization strategy that had rapidly transformed the war-devastated Japanese economy into one of the largest world economies and subsequently also led to the rapid economic development of Taiwan, Hong Kong and South Korea. The rapid and sustained annual double-digit growth generated through this industrialization strategy in these East Asian economies was hailed as an "East Asian miracle" by the World Bank (1993).

By the mid-1970s, with industrialization, Singapore was already experiencing permanent shortage of labor. By the mid-1980s, its per capita income had risen sharply to levels exceeding many European countries. With the severe constraint on labor supply and rising wages, Singapore was no longer able to compete with the other Asian countries which had embarked on similar export-oriented industrialization.[3] The PAP government began to cast away low-end, labor-intensive manufacturing to the regional neighbors. It compelled the manufacturers that remained to increase capital investment and move up the technological ladder. From then on, the Singapore economy has continued to evolve in response to changes in regional and global economic conditions. For example, after the 1997 Asian Regional Financial Crisis, the government started the process of making Singapore into a global financial center. To entice global financial firms, it placed a significant quantum of the national reserve to be managed by these firms. It also allowed

---

[3] By the early 1980s, the "export-oriented industrialization" strategy had become a "model" for all developing countries. China, with its endless supply of cheap labor power quickly emerged as the "factory of the world" and, in 20 years became the second largest economies of global capitalism. In retrospect, as Lee Kuan Yew put it: "Suppose, China had never gone communist in 1949, suppose the Nationalist government had worked with the Americans—China would be the great power in Asia—not Japan, not Korea, not Hong Kong, not Singapore. Because China isolated itself, development took place on the periphery of Asia first" (*Der Spiegel* 14 Aug. 2005).

large statutory boards, such as the Housing and Development Board, to float its own bonds in order to initiate and establish a bond market locally. By the beginning of the twenty-first century, Singapore's economy was decidedly post-industrial, with 80 percent in services and only 20 percent in industry. While it still competes and attracts foreign direct investments, it has also become a global capital-exporting nation through its SWFs.

State-owned Enterprises

Obviously, SOEs have played a role in the industrialization of Singapore. There were broadly three routes by which the SOEs were established. The routes involved the government

- partnering with private investment to develop new industries;
- expanding companies that provided services required by the new national armed forces into SOEs; and
- transforming the statutory boards of the colonial regime, which provided public services such as utilities, telecommunications, transportation and infrastructure, into SOEs.

These formation processes were critical to the ability of the SOEs to grow and transform themselves into global enterprises.

The Economic Development Board as Generator of State Enterprises

The two international consultants had independently suggested that the government should "go out after the business, not sit at home and wait for it to come in" (quoted in Cheng 1991: 188). Among the various industry promotion agencies established, the most important was the Economic Development Board (EDB), established in 1961. It was helmed by civil servants appointed by the Minister for Finance and tasked to attract foreign investment for the manufacturing sector. As "a one-stop shop investment agency" (Cheng 1991: 190), it provided adequate, affordable and efficient infrastructure and public services (such as liaising between investors and all relevant government agencies, granting a variety of generous tax incentives and grants), staff-training programs, professional consultation and it assisted potential investors in finding premises, investment partners, downstream or upstream contractors and labor supply. The EDB radically reduced the start-up time to get production up and running. Within its first decade, it began to encounter difficulties in coordinating and managing the activities and potential conflicts between its different divisions. Retaining its role as the pivotal state agent in attracting foreign investment, it spun off many of its initial functions into independent entities. To "sell" Singapore as an investment location, the EDB established a one-person honorary representative in New York and San Francisco in 1965 and official representatives in Hong Kong in 1966. By 1972 it had investment promotion centers in London, Stockholm, Frankfurt, Zurich, Chicago and Tokyo; by 1973 there were investment promotion centers in Paris and Osaka and in 1975 there was one in Houston (EDB 1991: 32). With the generous tax incentives, the array of assistance provided by the EDB and a cooperative and disciplined workforce under the PAP-affiliated National Trades Union Congress, foreign investors came. The number of foreign enterprise leaped from 165 in 1965 to 3,739 in 1976 (Schein 1996).

The EDB was willing to co-invest in new enterprises which required large capital or carried high risk. This co-investment strategy has had more impact on domestic enterprises than foreign investments. For example, it made direct investment in the National Iron and Steel Mills Ltd, the first local factory to convert scrap metal from ship-breaking into construction bars. In 1988, it spearheaded an international direct investments program to help local private companies and SOEs undertake overseas investments which would provide vital linkages and spin-off benefits to the Singapore economy. The program provides attractive tax exemptions on surpluses acquired from overseas ventures, while capital losses can be fully written off for tax purposes. Between 1988 and 1992, a total of 61 companies participated, the majority being SOEs, with approximately SGD 2 billion invested overseas excluding investments in Indonesia and Malaysia, the two immediate neighbors. With its co-investment activities, its 2009/10 annual report showed that the EDB had amassed approximately SGD 11.8 billion in fixed assets and SGD 12.5 billion in estimated returns from investments in industries such as info-communications and media, energy and bio-medical manufacturing.

Among the spun-off independent entities, two stand out. First is the industrial infrastructure project, undertaken in 1961, to develop an area of barren hills and swamps in the western part of the island into an industrial estate. Within ten years, more than 3,000 hectares were developed as a self-sufficient town with factories, a harbor, transportation, communications, housing and social amenities. In 1968, the

Jurong Industrial Estate was transferred to a new corporation, the Jurong Town Corporation (JTC). The JTC is now a state-owned independent developer of industrial infrastructure and industrial parks in various parts of the world. Second, the EDB's financial functions were bundled together to establish the Development Bank of Singapore (DBS), which subsequently expanded into a fully licensed commercial bank. In 1998, the DBS acquired the Post Office Savings Bank, an institution started by the colonial government in 1877, to provide low-cost banking services to its customers, greatly expanding its domestic market. The rebranded DBS Bank is currently the largest bank in Southeast Asia by asset. It further acquired two private banks in Hong Kong in 1999 and 2001 to constitute the DBS (HK), which extended its presence into China, as the latter opened up its financial market. In 2000, changes in the government's banking regulations after the 1997 Asian regional financial crisis compelled the DBS to relinquish its property arm, DBS Land, to be merged with another state-owned property development company, Pidemco Land, to form CapitaLand. CapitaLand grew to become a global property company with vast investments in Singapore, China and to a lesser extent, Australia and Europe; its 2013 financial year revenue was more than SGD 3.9 billion and, after tax profit, approximately SGD 850 million.[4]

Spin-offs from the Defense Industry

The withdrawal of the British armed forces in the late 1960s left behind a naval base and approximately 10,000 displaced workers. The PAP government established the Sembawang Shipyard to take over the base and absorb the workers. In 1998, it absorbed some other SOEs to form the current Sembcorp, a multinational corporation with worldwide operations in shipbuilding, energy, waste-management and infrastructure industries. Illustrative is its wholly-owned subsidiary, Sembcorp Power, that owns and operates the following:

- power plants in Singapore;
- an energy-from-waste operation in Singapore;
- a biomass station in the UK; and
- wind power assets in China.

---

[4] http://news.capitaland.com.phoenix.zhtml?c=130462&p=irol-fundSnapshot [accessed 12 Apr. 2014]

It co-owns and operates the following:

- a 490-megawatt power and desalination facility in Salalah, Oman;
- the Thermal Powertech Corporation India Limited (TPCIL);
- a 1,320-megawatt power facility in Krishnapatnam, SPSR Nellore District, Andhra Pradesh, India; and
- an 893-megawatt power and desalination facility in Fujairah, the United Arabs Emirates.

It also co-owns the largest co-generation plant in Shanghai, the Shanghai Cao Jing Cogeneration Plant and a 746-megawatt combined-cycle gas turbine power plant, Phu My 3, in Vietnam.[5] The Singapore state holds 49.5 percent of Sembcorp shares. Its 2013 financial year turnover was SGD 10.8 billion with a net profit of SGD 820 million.[6]

The British withdrawal also speeded up the development of the Singapore Armed Forces (SAF). Like all armed forces, the SAF generated its own demands for industrial services. In 1967, Chartered Industries was established as a wholly owned state enterprise to produce ammunition. As the SAF expanded, the Chartered Industries group of companies also grew.[7] Singapore Shipbuilding and Engineering was established in 1968 to build vessels for the Singapore Navy; in 1969 Singapore Electronic and Engineering Limited emerged out of the workshops and staff of the departing British Royal Navy to provide services and maintenance of electronics and communications equipment, including aviation electronics, for the SAF; in 1971, Singapore Automotive Engineering started with servicing but subsequently it also designed SAF vehicles; in 1973, Ordnance Development and Engineering and Allied Ordnance Company developed artillery, field guns and other weaponry; in 1975 and 1977, Singapore Aerospace Maintenance Company and Singapore Aero-Engine Overhaul were established; and finally, in 1978, Unicorn International was established to market the products and services offered by the entire stable of defense-related companies. All these companies were to run as corporate enterprises and compete with private companies to sell their services to the SAF. This was formalized in the 1987 Singapore Defense Industries Charter which declared that

---

[5] http://www.sembcorppower.com/aboutus.aspx [accessed 5 Dec. 2016].

[6] http://www.sembcorp.com/en/about-quick-facts.aspx [accessed 15 Apr. 2014].

[7] Details on the evolution of Chartered Industries to the present Singapore Technologies is drawn from http://infopedia.nl.sg/articles/SIP_1042_2011-03-19.html [accessed 5 Apr. 2014].

the defense industries must commercialize and market their services to non-defense-related industries to maintain their economic viability and sustainability. The less defense-sensitive companies were immediately transformed into commercial enterprises through public listing on the local stock exchange, with Singapore Technology, the holding company, retaining 51 percent of the shares. All these spin-off companies began to independently pursue their respective business expansions, including taking equity in other existing companies in the private sector, often in completely unrelated businesses. As the group of companies multiplied, they were progressively placed under a common holding company, Sheng-Li ("victory" in Mandarin), to better co-ordinate activities and businesses. In 1990, in a major restructuring exercise, all the defense-generated companies and the holding company, Sheng-Li, were re-grouped, renamed and rebranded as Singapore Technologies (ST), which was in turn placed under Temasek Holdings in 1994. It remained operational as an independent corporation until 2004, when all its assets were transferred to and managed directly by Temasek, which lists ST Engineering and ST Telemedia in its stable of companies.

An SOE which is from a different political legacy needs to be mentioned. Malayan Airways, established in 1947 was renamed the Malaysian Airways in 1963 after the formation of Malaysia. With political separation, Malaysian Airways was renamed Malaysian-Singapore Airways. In 1972, it split into Malaysian Airways and Singapore Airlines (SIA) to become the national carriers of their respective countries. SIA has since grown into one of the few profitable national carriers in the world and a leader in the commercial aviation industry whose practices are studied and emulated by others, such as Emirates Airlines. SIA is now an investment company in other international airlines, such as Virgin Atlantic, and it has established subsidiaries in the budget airline industry with Tiger Air and Scoot, a long distance budget air service. In its 2015 financial year report, its revenue was in excess of SGD 15.5 billion and profits were SGD 4.1 billion.[8]

De-linking Regulation and Supply of Utilities

The third route to establishing the Singapore SOEs was to transform the statutory boards inherited from the British colonial regime. These

---

[8] https://www.singaporeair.com/saar5/pdf/Investor-Relations/Annual-Report/annual report1415.pdf [accessed 5 Dec. 2016].

statutory boards provided public services in utilities, telecommunications, transportation and infrastructure. They included the Currency Board, Singapore Harbour Board, Singapore Improvement Trust, Public Utilities Board, Singapore Telephone Board and Central Provident Fund (CPF). Of these, the Currency Board and the CPF remain unchanged while the Singapore Improvement Trust was replaced by the Housing and Development Board. The other three boards—Harbour, Utilities and Telephone—all underwent major transformations to emerge as SOEs with significant global investment portfolios. Each was divided into a regulatory authority of the service and an enterprise that supplies the service. The Singapore Telephone Board was divided into the Telecommunication Authority of Singapore and Singapore Telecommunications Limited, or SingTel, in 1992. The Public Utilities Board continues to supply water to the nation but its electricity and gas supply business was hived off to form Singapore Power, an energy company, in 1995. The Singapore Harbour Board became the Port of Authority of Singapore in 1964. Between 1996 and 1997, it was restructured into the Maritime and Port Authority of Singapore, a regulatory body, and the Port of Singapore Authority (PSA) Corporation, a corporate enterprise, which was in turn restructured in 2003 as the PSA International Private Limited, the holding company of the PSA group of companies.

Delinking the regulatory body from a "commercialized" service provider enables the government to distance itself from the business side of service provision, the better to avoid the common practice of providing the essential services as state-subsidized "necessities." The enterprise provides its service on a commercial basis, although its profit margin in the domestic market is subject to restraint by the respective regulatory authority. Families who are unable to meet the commercial prices of essential services are assisted by the government to pay for their consumption. For example, on 1 April 2014, 800,000 households who lived in public housing flats received between SGD 45 and SGD 65 each from the government, totaling SGD 45 million (*Straits Times* 1 Apr. 2014). Natural monopolies are thus converted into profit-minded SOEs which are free to seek opportunities and grow their business abroad without direct government supervision and eventually transform themselves into multinational companies. For example,

- SingTel currently owns 100 percent of Optus, the second largest telecommunications company in Australia and close to 40 percent of Bharti Airtel of India, which according to its official website operates in 20 countries in Asia and Africa;

- Singapore Power is a 51 percent majority shareholder of SPAusNet, which provides energy-related services in the state of Victoria, Australia; and
- PSA International Private Limited is a leading operator of port services globally, which according to the company's official website has investments across 16 countries in Asia, Europe and America.

The companies that were hived off from the EDB, the hydra-like growth of the defense industries and the enterprises that grew out of statutory boards that supplied essential services to the nation, have all been transformed into multinational enterprises. Once an enterprise was notably successful, that is, stable and profitable, they were "corporatized" through public listing on the local stock exchange, during which the government sold off a portion of its shares for very substantial capital gains but continued to hold the controlling shares. Corporatization enabled the state to retain control while simultaneously deepening the market discipline of the companies as they now had to be accountable to private investors. As a successful corporation grew too big for the very limited domestic market it was compelled to push its products and services, including taking direct investments in related enterprises, to other countries, that is, to globalize (Low 2003: 141). The government took a further step to coordinate the activities of the successfully corporatized SOEs by placing them under a single holding company, Temasek Holdings. In addition to oversight of the SOEs, Temasek Holdings reorganized the surplus profits amassed by the SOEs into a separate SWF for direct global investments, extending further Singapore-state's presence in global capitalism. The SOEs have transformed Singapore from an economy that was dependent on foreign capital investment to one that is exporting capital to both emerging and developed economies worldwide.

Singapore's Sovereign Wealth Funds

The Singapore government has two SWFs: the Singapore Government Investment Company, which is officially known as the GIC, and Temasek Holdings. The capital for these two SWFs is distinctively different. The GIC is funded directly from the national reserve and is purely an investment fund, while Temasek is funded by profits derived from SOEs. With very substantial war chests to invest in financial markets, the two SWFs place the Singapore state squarely in the global capitalist market, against the liberal injunction for privatization of state enterprises and free market. Of the two, there is a relative absence of information on the GIC; thus, detailed discussion will be restricted to Temasek Holdings which, in any case, better illustrates the more complex role of SWFs in Singapore state capitalism.

Singapore Government Investment Corporation

Until 1981 the national reserve, derived from each year's annual budget surplus and the very high rates of CPF savings of every wage earner, was managed by the Monetary Authority of Singapore (MAS), the nation's central bank. Goh Keng Swee, the first Finance Minister, realized that the annual large surplus would continue with regularity. He argued that the conventional investment of the surplus in foreign government bonds with very low but secure interest, while appropriate for "economies in chronic deficit," was too conservative and unsuitable for the healthy economic growth of Singapore. The Singapore Government Investment Corporation Private Limited (SGIC), later renamed the Government Investment Corporation Private Limited (GIC), was thus established on 22 May 1981 as a non-listed, wholly state-owned company. Its objectives were to (1) absorb accumulated surpluses to avoid inflationary pressure in times of domestic growth and (2) to pursue investment interests abroad to garner greater profits for the rapidly accumulating foreign reserves. However, in 2006, Prime Minister Lee Kuan Yew as the Chairman of the GIC faced criticism that its investment returns were too low relative to the returns generated by private fund managers. He stated that "my cardinal objective for GIC was not to maximise returns but to protect the value of our savings and earn a fair return on capital" (quoted in Clark and Monk 2010: 438). Indeed, as a reserve investment corporation, the GIC has to preserve the savings of the citizens, which consequently explains the GIC's relatively conservative investment attitude. According to Yeung, it prefers to "invest in small stakes of typically below 0.5 percent [of a company] and avoid direct intervention in management" (2011: 645). Nevertheless, beginning with a modest SGD 2 million start-up capital, the GIC had an estimated SGD 320 billion investment chest by 2014.[9]

---

[9] http://www.swfinstitute.org/swfs/government-of-singapore-investment-corporation/ [accessed 23 Apr. 2014].

The relative absence of information on the GIC is a deliberate government policy. In 2013, the SGIC was renamed GIC Private Limited to enable the company to claim for itself the right not to disclose details of its business activities publicly. To reiterate its former Chairman, Lee Kuan Yew: "We are a special investment fund. The ultimate shareholders are the electorate. It is not in the People's interests, in the nation's interest, to detail our assets and their yearly returns" (quoted in Rodan 2004: 64). The current Prime Minister Lee Hsien Loong elaborates: since the GIC constitutes a very significant portion of the national reserve, publishing detailed information about its investments abroad would reveal information regarding the reserve and this would enable currency speculators to "assess their chances and plan their attacks [on the Singapore currency] and this is not the public interest" (Rodan 2004: 64). Although the lack of transparency did not seem to be an issue for the business community and the citizenry (Rodan 2004: 73), the GIC started to report publicly its major investments through press releases beginning in 2008 (*Straits Times* 13 Mar. 2014).

However, the question of the GIC's rate of profit relative to the interest paid to Singaporean workers has been a persistent public issue as the GIC invests the accumulated CPF savings of the citizens. It is common knowledge that the annual investment returns rate of the GIC exceeds the annual interest rate paid to CPF savings; by implication the government is making gains off the savings of Singapore workers/citizens. The government's explanation for the different rates is that the GIC bears market risks in its investments, while CPF subscribers are guaranteed an annual interest that has been significantly higher than bank interest on private savings (as of 2014, 3 percent versus less than 1 percent). This remains unconvincing to skeptics. There has, therefore, been a quiet but persistent demand for the government to "return" more money to Singaporeans by paying higher interests and/or allowing for an earlier and higher draw-down of the CPF.[10] Public dissatisfaction came to a head in mid-2014, when blogger Roy Ngerng was sued by Prime Minister Lee Hsien Loong for allegedly accusing the latter

---

[10] The policy decision to retain a significant amount of an individual's total savings in the CPF after retirement in order to provide him/her with a monthly stipend throughout old age has also caused resentment, particularly among lower-income retirees who are in immediate need of money for daily living.

of corruption, in his capacity as Chairman of the GIC (*Straits Times* 4 June 2014). Ngerng was found guilty of defaming the Prime Minister and ordered to pay SGD 150,000 in damages, which he will do in small instalments until 2033.[11] However, this incident led the government to admit that greater flexibility on the management of CPF savings may be possible. A CPF Advisory Panel was convened in 2015. One of the Panel's recommendations was to allow CPF members, especially those in the lower-income strata with immediate financial needs, to withdraw a lump sum of no more than 20 percent in their savings upon retirement, although this would affect the long-term payout from the savings during retirement years.[12] The immediacy of the government's response to a long simmering public unhappiness was, perhaps, a reflection of the historic low of popular electoral support for the PAP in the 2011 general election, at 60 percent.

Temasek Holdings

In 1974, 36 SOEs were transferred from the Ministry of Finance to Temasek Holdings, with a capital input worth SGD 345 million. The initial motivation was to consolidate capital, improve coordination of investments and pursue profit-making opportunities more efficiently with a large cash reserve. According to its former Chairman, S. Dhanabalan, a former cabinet minister and former chairman of the DBS Bank, the mode of management was not direct control of the companies under Temasek's stable: "There was no central figure directing and making decisions for everybody.... The Government's main interest was to make sure the right people were in charge and after that the management was to chart its own course."[13] He likened Temasek to an intelligence-collection central unit that was to monitor investment activities and collate information on government-linked investment projects with the purpose of updating the Ministry of Finance and Cabinet on state monies. Nevertheless, he conceded that state officials do insist on a

---

[11] http://www.straitstimes.com/singapore/courts-crime/blogger-roy-ngerng-to-pay-150000-in-damages-to-pm-lee-in-instalments-lawyer [accessed 16 Mar. 2016].
[12] http://www.mom.gov.sg/Documents/employment-practices/cpf-advisory-panel-report-executive-summary.pdf [accessed 15 Aug. 2016].
[13] All Dhanabalan's statements are from his media interview on the 25th Anniversary of Temasek Holdings (*Straits Times* 25 June 1999).

pro-active leadership, reinforced by the right to veto any business pro-position made by representatives of any of the 36 companies, to ensure that it was in the national interest.

In the early years, Temasek quickly acquired a public image of "an all-pervasive government which cannot stay away when there is profit to be made."[14] However, Chairman Dhanabalan points out that there was no compulsion nor necessity for companies within its stable to be everywhere, "no need for us to be in the travel business, no need for us to be selling televisions or VCRs. We got into these things basically because we had very energetic, aggressive management.... Every oppor-tunity they saw, they went in."[15] This aggressive expansion began to encroach into and draw grievances from the local small- and medium-enterprise community. Thus, from the mid-1980s onwards, Temasek began to divest itself of companies in industries in which the state had no particular strategic interests. It also began to reduce its stake in several large successful companies. For example, in November 1985, it sold 48.4 million of the 100 million shares issued by the SIA "one of the most successful local corporations [that] constituted as much as five percent of Singapore's GDF in its peak" (Yeung 2004: 46). The divestment enabled Temasek to streamline and consolidate its resources to invest more strategically for greater returns. By 1999,

> ...the market capitalization of first-tier public listed GLCs (govern-ment-linked companies) controlled by Temasek Holdings alone was SGD 88 billion or 25 percent of total market capitalization of the Stock Exchange of Singapore. The share of Temasek Holdings in these GLCs amounted to SGD 47 billion or 13 percent of the total market capitalization. (Yeung 2004: 46)

Until then, Temasek's portfolio was largely concentrated in Singapore.

It was not until the 2001 economic review, headed by then-Deputy Prime Minister Lee Hsien Loong that a more clearly defined direction for Temasek was articulated. A new charter committed it to

> ...concentrate on two categories of companies: those domestic busi-nesses deemed strategic enough to warrant government involvement,

---

[14] Ibid.
[15] Ibid.

for example, those that involve control over critical resources such as water, power and gas grids, airport and seaport facilities, and public goods like broadcasting, subsidised healthcare, education and housing and assorted amenities; and those with the potential for regional or international growth. (Rodan 2004: 69)

Hence, Temasek "will divest businesses which are no longer relevant or have no international growth potential." Its mission is stated thus: "holds and manages the Singapore Government's investment in companies, for the long term benefit of Singapore," nurtures "successful and vibrant international businesses from its stable of companies … to broaden and deepen Singapore's economic base," and "shape strategic developments, including consolidations, mergers, acquisitions, rationalization or collaborations as appropriate, to build significant international or regional businesses."[16]

With the new orientation, Temasek successfully scaled up and transformed many of the enterprises within its portfolio from the national to regional and international levels, such as SingTel and PSA Holdings. At the same time, it also established itself as an independent investor that is interested in long-term sustainable returns rather than short-term equity gains in both foreign global enterprises and local non-government-linked companies with international growth potentials. Investments range across these sectors: financial services; telecommunications and media; transportation and logistics; real estate; infrastructure, industrial and engineering; energy and resources; technology; life sciences and consumer and lifestyle.[17] Temasek rode the wave of rising capitalism in Asia, and by 2009, it had achieved a balance of one-third investments in Singapore, one-third in Asia and the remaining third in Organization for Economic Cooperation and Development (OECD) countries with an increasing exposure in emerging economies.[18]

---

[16] Temasek Charter 2002. Singapore: Temasek Holdings.

[17] www.temasek.com.sg [accessed 14 Apr. 2014].

[18] Temasek has attributed much of its successful globalization to the appointment of Ho Ching as an Executive Director in 2002 and as the Chief Executive Officer in 2005 (Temasek Press Release 6 Feb. 2009). As Ho Ching is the wife of the incumbent Prime Minister Lee Hsien Loong, her appointment was not without public controversy.

Looking at the institutional history of Temasek, one could say that it had become an SWF through evolution rather than a conscious decision from the start (Yeung 2011). This is partly reflected in the changing role of the government in the running of the companies within its portfolio. When the SOEs were first placed under Temasek in 1974, according to former Chairman Dhanabalan,

> [T]he composition of our Board and management comprised mostly civil servants. Nominations to the boards of our companies were managed by the government Directorship and Consultancy Appointments Council or DCAC. As Temasek developed to become a more active shareholder, both the Board and management changed to include more private sector investment expertise and experience. By the mid-1990s, the DCAC had relinquished its responsibility for nominating board members to Temasek's portfolio companies. In 2002, we were at the cusp of accelerating this change as we began to place greater emphasis on sound governance and strong boards as salient features of the relationship with our portfolio companies.[19]

In addition, to increase transparency, it began to publish the annual report, the *Temasek Review*. In view of all the earlier mentioned skepticism and speculations that surrounded SWFs, Temasek is at pains to insist on its independence from political interference, although the present and immediate past chairman are former PAP government cabinet ministers. In the words of its CEO, Ho Ching,

> In many countries, if you are owned by the government, you are directed by the government or the politicians. In this case, we are not... we have put out information on the relationships in our *Temasek Review*, well before the debate on Sovereign Wealth Funds began.[20]

Notably, Temasek ranks very highly on the Linaburg-Maduell Transparency Index, developed by the SWF Institute.

With the shift towards global capitalism, Temasek's internationalized portfolio includes direct investments in the newly corporatized Bank of China, Industrial and Commercial Bank of China, China Construction

---

[19] Remarks by S. Dhanabalan, Chairman of Temasek Holdings, Temasek Charter Media Roundtable, 25 Aug. 2009.
[20] Ho Ching, Temasek Charter 2009 Media Roundtable, Key Questions and Answers, 25 Aug. 2009.

Bank Corporation and the established global financial enterprises—Standard Chartered Bank and the AIA Group Limited in the US. In communications, media and technology, Temasek invested in Bharti Airtel Limited in India. In energy and resources, it invests in companies in the US and China, and its PSA International Private Limited operates various ports globally. Between 2004 and 2013, the portfolio value of Temasek Holdings rose rapidly from SGD 90 billion to SGD 215 billion; its assets rose from SGD 180.8 billion to SGD 317.4 billion; and its revenue rose from SGD 56.5 billion to SGD 83.8 billion.

Institutionalizing State Capitalism

Singapore demonstrates that profit-driven SOEs can be successful so long as the enterprises are disciplined by market forces, professionally managed and resistant to political and bureaucratic administrative corruption. The accumulated surplus in profits of the SOEs can in turn be aggregated and channeled as the investment capital of SWFs to finance subsequent cycles of state investments and capital accumulation. The capital gains, dividends and interests generated by the SOEs and the SWFs constitute part of the national wealth which remains in the public coffer to be used to finance the governance of the nation. This has been built into the national budget system of the PAP government since 1991. The annual net dividends and interests from state capitalist investments have since been divided into two equal halves: 50 percent goes to reinvestment that grows the SOEs and the national reserve while the other 50 percent is a revenue stream in the national budget as a subvention to the cost of governance, thus enabling the government to provide greater social benefits without increasing the tax burden of the citizenry.

The continuous augmenting of the national reserve with a portion of the annual profit from the state capitalist sector is an important factor in securing and protecting the long-term financial stability and resilience of the Singapore economy (Shih 2009; Yeung 2004). It strengthens and stabilizes the national currency, shields it from potential speculative attacks in the constantly fluctuating international currency market and "insures" the domestic economy against financial crisis and interventions from multilateral institutions, which could result in "gradual erosion of national sovereignty." For example, some neighboring governments were forced to accept IMF-imposed economic restructuring in exchange for loans, during the 1997 Asian Regional Financial Crisis (Clark and

Monk 2010: 431).[21] During the crisis, Thai, Indonesian and Malaysian currencies were all under speculative attack but the Singapore dollar was left alone. From July 1997 to January 1998, the decline of the Singapore dollar against the US dollar was offset by its appreciation against the currencies of other ASEAN countries. Consequently, "Singapore's nominal and real effective exchange rates were relatively stable both before and during the crisis" (Ngiam 2000: 5).

Furthermore, the government reduced business costs with rebates on property and rental taxes and costs of public utilities; sped up development projects; and stabilized the property market by suspending land sales and deferring stamp duties on uncompleted properties. All these measures "helped prevent more bankruptcies and an increase in non-performing loans" (Ngiam 2000: 17). To prevent erosion of national competitiveness, in addition to a 10 percent cut in the employer's monthly contribution to their employee's compulsory social security fund, the CPF, real wages were cut by 5 to 8 percent, and a 10 percent rebate on corporate tax was provided for 1999. With these, the unit business cost of the manufacturing sector dropped sharply. At the household level, rebates on maintenance charges were given to the 90 percent of the population who lived in public housing flats. For homeowners who became unemployed, mortgage rescheduling, including suspension of payment, was provided if necessary. The aggregated effect was a short-lived crisis. Unemployment, which hit a high of 4.5 percent in December 1998, dropped to 2.9 percent one year later and the economy recovered by the second quarter of 1999. The government was able to forego revenues during the crisis because of the deep national reserve stored in the state capitalist sector and the cash supplement it provided to cover shortfalls in the national revenue.

In 2008, the formula for drawing down the profits of state investments was recalibrated in anticipation of increased developmental and social expenditure in education and other human capital investments, healthcare for an aging population and social welfare benefits in the face

---

[21] During the 1997 Asian Financial Crisis, the IMF-imposed economic restructuring was devastating to the Korean economy and the emerging economies of Indonesia and Thailand. Malaysia was able to escape the same devastation when then Prime Minister, Mahathir Mohammad imposed capital control and fixed the exchange rate between Malaysia currency and the US dollar.

of a widening income inequality. Under the new formula, according to Finance Minister Tharman Shanmugaratnam, returns from government investments would be based on

> (1) total returns, including capital gains; (2) long-term expected returns (based on an investment horizon of 20 years), instead of year-to-year returns; and (3) real returns, rather than nominal returns, so that we preserve the purchasing power of our reserves and, 50 percent of this recalibrated state income is to be allocated as part of the annual national revenue. Reflecting the different sources of capital formation of the two SWFs, the new formula was applied with immediate effect on GIC and investments by the Monetary Authority of Singapore. The older formula of 50 percent of interest and dividend was retained for Temasek Holdings, because "Temasek's investment strategy is still evolving, having begun a major effort to diversify its investments geographically as well as sectorally in 2002".[22]

However, from the budget year 2015, the same formula was applied to both. Since then, rough estimates of the combined annual contributions of the GIC, MAS and Temasek have ranged between 12 percent and 15 percent of the government's annual operating budget. With this supplement, the government has been able to fund several major social spending initiatives. In 2014, an SGD 8 billion "Pioneer Generation" fund was established to assist healthcare and other social needs of those who were born before 1949 and had not benefitted from the prosperity of national economic development. In 2015, a deficit budget of SGD 6.5 billion was projected, with a significant social distribution to the aged and the socially disadvantaged, in addition to skills development for workers and infrastructure enhancement. In 2016, due to the greater social expenditure there would have been a shortfall in the SGD 68 billion annual expenditure had there not been an SGD 14.5 billion infusion from state investments which turned the budget around to an anticipated surplus in excess of SGD 3 billion. The overall effect of this financial contribution from the state capitalist sector has been the reduction of the tax burden of the citizenry. It contributes directly to the social welfare provisions for the low-income and other socially disadvantaged populations. The social transfers have contributed to keep

---

[22] Minister for Finance, Tharman Shanmugaratnam, Constitution of Singapore (Amendment) Bill, Parliamentary Proceedings 20 Oct. 2008.

wages and the general labor cost lower than the persistently tight labor market would bear.

Politically, with its extensive networks of investment in local enterprises, the state capitalist sector has provided direct and indirect employment to a sizeable number of people (many of whom are at the top of their fields) in a wide range of professions such as law, finance and trade. According to Rodan and Hughes (2014: 33–5), these beneficiaries constitute a "state capitalist class," which shares the "material and ideological interests" of state bureaucrats and political leaders. The result is strong elite cohesion which explains why the rising middle class in Singapore has had little incentive or interest in constituting itself as a force for political change, frustrating the liberal expectations that a rising middle class would lead to demand for greater liberal democracy. The direct and indirect financial benefits for a wide spectrum of the citizenry that result from Singapore's role as a state-capitalist entrepreneur constitute good reasons for Singaporeans to support state-capitalism over free-market capitalism.

Conclusion

The development of state capitalism in Singapore was a consequence of the historical contingencies of decolonization and political independence. At the time, industrial capital was sorely lacking. Consequently, the state had to finance many of the industries that were essential to the nation-building process, from creating employment to providing essential services to the building of a defense force. After more than five decades of economic growth and the integration of Singapore's economy in global capitalism, the initial nation-building rationale for establishing the SOEs has been transcended. The continuing expansion of the state capitalist sector and the way the resulting profits are utilized have possibly a deeper underlying ideological foundation. Founded as a social democratic political party, the PAP had a serious commitment to certain socialist economic practices. However, given the Cold War geopolitical context of the 1950s and 1960s, it chose capitalist development as the road necessary for the material "survival" of the island-nation and its newly enfranchised citizens. Nevertheless, it did not completely forego its "social democratic" beliefs in exchange for a liberal minimalist state and a free market economy of private enterprises. Instead, it redefined the social democratic ideology to delineate a space for the state in the economy.

According to the first Minister for Finance, Goh Keng Swee:

Democratic socialist economic policies range from direct participation in industry to the supply of infrastructure facilities by statutory authorities, and to laying down clear guidelines to the private sector as to what they could and should do. (1976: 84)

He further asserted that, "[i]t is one of the fundamental tenets of socialism that the state should own a good part of the national wealth, particularly what is called the means of production," and "let us not forget that the ultimate objective of this whole industrialization is not to provide fortunes for a fortunate few but to raise the standard of living of the entire working class" (Goh 1972: 210).

Following through on these beliefs, the PAP government has continued to have "direct participation in industry" and to "own a good part of the national wealth" through SOEs and SWFs. The national wealth has grown beyond the confines of the country's island territory into the financialized space of global capitalism. Finally, the SOEs and SWFs are technically owned by the citizens of Singapore rather than "the fortunate few," and their contributions to the national revenue have contributed to "raise the standard of living of the entire [perhaps, not all] working class" (Goh 1972: 210).

Politically, the high visibility of successful state capitalism and its contribution to national revenue are important elements of the government's overall economic performance, which the PAP presents routinely to the Singapore electorate as one of the primary reasons why it deserves to be re-elected in each successive election. So far, this appears to be convincing as the PAP continues to be elected to parliament; as recently as 2015, it won close to 70 percent of the popular votes nationwide. Internationally, in spite of the state's visible presence in the local and global economy and the PAP government's explicit disavowal of political liberalism, in 2011 the IMF appointed Singapore's incumbent Minister for Finance, Tharman Shanmugaratnam, as the Chair of the IMF Financial Committee, the policy steering committee, reflecting the symbolic capital that has accrued to the Little Red Dot.

Chapter 6

GOVERNING RACE
State Multiracialism and Social Stability

With the increasing global flows of legal and undocumented migrants across national boundaries, most countries are demographically multi-ethnic, multi-religious and multicultural. The management of the multicultural differences has become part of routine governance. Liberal democratic states try assiduously to avoid the concept of "race" because of its easy slippage into "racism," replacing it with the supposedly less emotively charged "ethnicity" (Lentin and Titley 2012: 132). Nevertheless, social injustice based on ethnicity is still affectively labeled as "racism" and not "ethnic-ism." Differences between ethnic groups are often neutralized through the idea of multiculturalism, which extends beyond socially ascribed ethnicity/race to embrace differences of all self-proclaimed minority groups constituted through voluntary affiliations (Gunew 2004: 7), such as feminists, LGBTs and vegans. For critics like Joppke and Lukes, the expansion which transforms "multiculturalism" into a dispersed terrain is the "piracy of minority discourse" by lifestyle groups (1999: 13). For the present purpose, the analytic focus will be restricted to socially ascribed differences of ethnicity or race. Furthermore, given that "race" is the term used both in the Singapore constitution and by the government and the everyday conversation of Singaporeans, the term, "race," rather than "ethnicity" will be used in this chapter.

Liberal democratic management of ethnicity in multicultural settings may be placed on a continuum. At one end, the civic rights and obligations of citizenship are the primary concerns of the state while all matters of culture, including ethnic cultures, are left to the private sphere. American sociologist Nathan Glazer suggests, "Let us agree that ethnic and racial affiliation should be as voluntary as religious affiliation and of as little concern to the state and public authority" (1997: 159).[1] Individuals as citizens are separated from their ethnic identities and histories of their ethnic communities, "which might contradict the abstract form of citizenship" (Lowe 1996: 2). This is, in a strict sense, a defensible liberal democratic principle of race-blind governance. In practice, it is of course impossible to ignore ethnic cultural differences in governance. Most liberal democracies pragmatically accommodate everyday differences (Favell 1998: 262) as long as they "do not touch upon the core values of the majority society, such exemptions are trivial and routinely granted, because no majority society interests are involved" (Jokppe and Lukes 1999: 13). Examples are

> ...allowing Hindus...to scatter the ashes of their dead in rivers, even to submerge corpses off the coast; allowing the Jewish and Muslim method of not stunning animals before slaughtering them, and... exempting turban-wearing Sikhs from the legal duty of wearing crash helmets on motorbikes. (Jokppe and Lukes 1999: 13)

Such pragmatic ad hoc managing of difference displaces the demand for multiculturalism as official policy. At the other end of the continuum is the adoption of multiculturalism as official policy, as in Canada and Australia, in recognition of not only the multi-ethnic composition of the citizenry but also the historical injustices suffered by the different minority ethnic groups in the hands of the White-Anglo majority. Notably, none of the three practices—citizenship, pragmatism and multiculturalism—has quelled the persistent demand by minority ethnic groups for recognition, historical redress and compensation.

Contradictions in Liberal Multiculturalism

According to Canadian philosopher and liberal multiculturalist, Will Kymlicka, multicultural policies emerged in the West in the aftermath

---

[1] For Glazer (1997: 147), the rise of multiculturalism, "is the price America is paying for its inability or unwillingness to incorporate into its society African Americans, in the same way and to the same degree it has incorporated so many groups."

of Nazism and the Holocaust of World War II, to reject White supremacy.[2] He argues that acceptance of multiculturalism as public policy
by the majority populations in the West is premised on "the hope and
expectation that liberal democratic values will grow over time and take
firm root across ethnic, racial, and religious lines, with both majority
and minority groups" (2007: 94). Liberal multiculturalism is based on
two fundamental tenets:

- the liberal conception of respect for difference is dependent on a
  conception of "dignity" of the individual that is common to everyone and is reciprocally respected between individuals as equals; and
- the liberal assumption that differences are always negotiable
  rationally, thus liberal multiculturalism "demands both dominant
  and historically subordinate groups to engage in new practices,
  to enter new relationships and to embrace new concepts and discourses, all of which profoundly transform people's identities and
  practices" (Kymlicka 2007: 99).

Each of these premises has its own logical and practical contradictions. Regarding the first premise, Taylor points out, "[The] principle of
equal respect requires that we treat people in a difference-blind fashion,"
however, in respecting difference "we have to recognize and even foster
particularity." Logically, taking the "recognition of difference" seriously
is to "violate the principle of nondiscrimination," while taking the "difference-blind rule" seriously would be open to the criticism of "forcing
people into a homogenous mold that is untrue to them" (1995: 43).
Practically, there is a further consequence:

> ...the supposedly neutral set of difference-blind principles of the poli-
> tics of equal dignity is in fact a reflection of one hegemonic culture...
> the supposedly fair and difference-blind society is not only inhuman
> (by suppressing identities) but also, in a subtle and unconscious way,
> itself discriminatory. (Taylor 1995: 43)

It is due to this tendency to discriminate against, even suppress, minority
cultures that ethnic minorities demand recognition and legal guarantees
of their cultural survival, which in turn leads to push-back by political

---

[2] Whereas liberal multiculturalism in the West is premised on the rejection of White
supremacy, in postcolonial Asia and Africa liberalism is associated precisely with
Western White cultural supremacy. To reject one is to reject both simultaneously.

conservatives who call for the "reinscription" of the values and norms of the majority people. For example, the late Samuel Huntington (2004) called for the reinscription of Anglo-Protestant Creed in the social, political and cultural life of the US.

Regarding the negotiation of difference, a conundrum emerges immediately for a liberal multiculturalist "at precisely the point at which it [difference] matters most to its strongly committed members" (Fish 1997: 379), as in the case of Muslims in Europe. There are three exhaustive scenarios at such contact points. First, a liberal multiculturalist might immediately denounce the interlocutor who refuses to negotiate as "irrational." This shows the superficiality of the liberal multiculturalist's commitment to respect difference—a position Fish pejoratively labels as "boutique multiculturalism." Second, the liberal multiculturalist might accept that the interlocutor has good reasons to not negotiate certain differences because to do so would compromise his/her sense of self. However, the liberal multiculturalist is unable to take the next step, which is to agree with the interlocutor's point of view. Ultimately, s/he would likely reject it, thus actually remaining monocultural. Finally, if the liberal multiculturalist were to accept the interlocutor's point of view and go over to the side of the interlocutor, then the liberal would also become a monoculturalist, erasing difference and commitment to multiculturalism. Confronted with these logical and practical conundrums, the coerciveness of liberal multiculturalism makes its appearance.

According to Kymlicka, "to ensure that multicultural policies and institutions cannot be captured and misused for illiberal purposes" (2007: 94), minorities who are given "group rights" will "have no legal capacity to restrict individual freedoms in the name of maintaining cultural authenticity, religious orthodoxy, or racial purity" (2007: 91). In short, individual rights must trump group cultural rights. Embedded in this prioritizing of individual rights is an "exit" clause in liberal multiculturalism: an individual's membership in a cultural group is premised on one's individual rights and interests being preserved. Once the cost of membership is to one's disadvantage or beyond one's willingness to bear, one is free to leave the group. Membership can therefore be no more than a "free ride" for personal gains. The exit clause thus poses a perennial threat to group stability and solidarity. To the extent that membership in a group is voluntary, leaving the group would likely be accepted without penalty. However, this is not so for involuntary ascribed membership in an ethnic/religious group. First, individuals in ascribed groups are also socialized into a culture—a way of life—that is "foundational" to their subjectivity. Rejection and/or escape from the group would likely cause a crisis of subjectivity and identity, psychically and socially, especially when an individual is unable to join the mainstream majority culture. Second, faced with a perceived or real threat to group solidarity, such groups might impose sanctions on individuals who wish to leave their groups. These sanctions range from mild disapprobation to social excommunication to the extreme case of death, such as tribal "honor" killings. Given the potentially high costs for both a group and individuals leaving the group, exit from ascribed ethnic groups, if undertaken, is often taken quietly with minimal publicity.

Since the end of the twentieth century, individual-freedom-first liberal multiculturalism in and outside the West has faced challenges from the global presence of Islamic communities, which are "parallel" societies (Lentin and Titley 2012: 125) that hold values which are diametrically opposed to liberalism. Taking Britain as an example, Kundnani argues that "Muslims occupy this special role within the crisis [of multiculturalism] discourse," among the many other groups deemed "alien," such as African communities, who are caught up in it as well (Kundnani 2012: 158). Three major leaders of Europe—David Cameron, former Prime Minister of Britain; Angela Merkel, Chancellor of Germany; and Nicolas Sarkozy, former President of France—announced the failure or "death" of multiculturalism (Back and Sinha 2012: 140) in Europe, within a period of a few months in late 2010 and early 2011. The same three political leaders began to call for the re-emphasis on immigrants learning the "national" values and "national" cultures of their host nations; for the Muslims, this could only have meant White-Christian values. In view of the apparent abandonment of the so-called "multicultural experiment" in Europe and the strengthening of anti-immigration right-wing nationalist political parties, Kymlicka's claim that the majority in the West has accepted multiculturalism would now appear to be too sanguine.

Recall here, Gray's critique that the asocial liberal individual is but a conceptual fiction as it is "without history or ethnicity, denuded of the special attachments that in the real human world give us the particular identities we have" (1995: 5). Culture is reduced to being an individual's right and volition to choose and practice rather than being a milieu in which one is socialized and which shapes an individual's biography, identity and subjectivity. Furthermore, within liberalism only individuals can bear "natural," inalienable rights; groups are not similarly endowed. Liberalism has no conception of "group rights." Given these constraints, liberal multiculturalism is ill-equipped to deal with any group which holds that its core values are not negotiable lest the identity and solidarity of the group become seriously compromised. Faced with a multiracial population, the PAP government has disavowed liberal multiculturalism and managed the political pragmatics of governing race through a conceptual framework which places group rights at the center of official multiracialism; the term "race" has been officially retained intentionally to better emphasize the differences between the three visible groups—ethnic Chinese, Malays and Indians.

Assembling a Multiracial Singaporean Nation

At the time of political independence, Singapore had approximately 75 percent ethnic Chinese, 17 percent "Malays," and 7 percent South Asians, as well as a small residual category of the "rest" that included local-born Eurasians and other mainly White individuals. It was thus an ethnic Chinese majority nation in the Malay world of archipelagic Southeast Asia, where Islam is the religion of the majority and variations of the Malay language constitute the indigenous lingua franca. In this geopolitical context, combined with the presence of Communist China in close geographical proximity, establishing Singapore as a "Chinese" nation would not have been accepted with equanimity by the "Malay Muslim" world. The demographic reality of a multiracial population of immigrant stock was thus re-scripted as a defining "national" character, and the Constitution of Singapore declared the new state a "multiracial nation" with equality for all races. This was a departure from the conventional European understanding of a nation being supposedly constituted by one single ethnic group sharing one language, one history and even one "blood." Furthermore, unlike Western liberal democratic societies, which institute multiculturalism as a response to discriminated minority groups clamoring for redress and recognition, in Singapore it was a conscious ideological decision to develop constitutional or state "multiracialism" as an instrument of social and political administration (Chua 2003a).

Singapore citizenship was granted without erasing the individual's "race origin." Everyone was racialized, without exception. Ethnic cultural differences among the citizenry were radically simplified to four racial groups—Chinese, Malays, Indian and Others (colloquially abbreviated as CMIO). No consistent criteria were used in defining the three major racial groups. Each racial category was a discursive and administrative category which used only a single element—social, cultural or geographical—to simplify and homogenize the complex ethnic, linguistic and religious differences that it represented. The different spoken languages by ethnic Chinese from different provinces of southern China—for example, Hokkien with sub-provincial languages such as Hokchew and Hinghua, from Fujian province, and Cantonese and Teochew from Guangdong province—were declared as "dialects" and, from the early 1970s, banned in all broadcast media and official transactions. Mandarin was adopted as the only official race language for all ethnic Chinese. As a result, fluency in the "dialects" has declined in each new generation. Communication across generations between children who speak no Chinese language other than Mandarin and the parents and grandparents who do not speak Mandarin was seriously disrupted. By the late twentieth century, the dialects had all but disappeared in public places. The ethnic Chinese was renamed *Huaren* (华人) in Mandarin, and the Mandarin language was renamed *Huayu* (华语) in contrast to *guoyu* (国语), the "national" language in Taiwan and *putonghua* (普通话), the "common" language in China. Henceforth, ethnic Chinese Singaporeans will be referred to as Huaren in this chapter.

Javanese and Boyanese from Java, Minangkabau from West Sumatra, Bugis from Sulawesi and Malays from Riau and Peninsula Malaya were reduced to the single category of Malay, defined as "someone who is Malay, Javanese, Boyanese, Bugis, Arab or any other person who is generally accepted as a member of the Malay community by the community" (Rahim 1998: 18; Kahn 2006: 15–23; Nasir and Aljunied 2009: 23–36). Furthermore, the PAP government adopted the mid-nineteenth century British colonial practice of fusing Malay ethnicity with Islam (Kadir 2004: 359; Rahim 1998: 17–9). As a result, all Malays are constitutionally Malay-Muslim. All non-Muslims from the Malay world, such as the descendants of Bataks from Sumatra, who are Christians, are excluded from the Malay-Muslim community. In deference to their regional origins, Malays were recognized constitutionally as the indigenous people of the new state. This came with some privileges: Malay was made the national language with English, Mandarin and Tamil as the other official languages; a prominent site for a mosque in every public housing estate was provided, while edifices of other religions had to compete by tender for sites made available by the land authority; and, Islam would be the only religion in the secular state with direct parliamentary representation in the person of the Minister for Malay and Muslim Affairs, who concurrently would hold another ministerial portfolio.

As South Asians are adherents of a number of religions—Buddhism, Christianity, Islam and Hinduism—religion could not serve as a homogenizing element. Regional linguistic differences among them are equally varied, if not more so, than those among the Huaren. Consequently, geography was used to constitute the "Indian" race. All Singaporean citizens who were from South Asia—India, and later East and West Pakistan, and Sri Lanka—were grouped as Indians. Tamil, the south Indian language spoken by the majority of Indians in Singapore, was imposed as the official Indian language. However, in recent years, other South Asian languages, such as Bengali, Hindi and Urdu, have been accepted as mother tongues for different "Indian" students.

The instrumental use of different convenient elements—language, religion and geography—as the basis of organizing the three race groups shows clearly that the race categories were politically constructed to derive the constitutive components of "multiracialism" as both a national character and a national ideology. Here, the smallest group, the Indians, played a critical symbolic and substantive role in rendering Singapore as a multiracial society. Without them Singapore's racial composition and politics would be one of the majority/dominant Huaren and the minority/subordinate Malays with all its untoward implications, instead of racial equality in a constitutional multiracial nation. Of course, the logic of equality of race groups, which ascribes group membership and emphasizes group solidarity, will impose constraints on individual cultural practices. It is, thus, potentially contradictory to the guarantees of liberal freedoms and rights of citizenship in the other parts of Singapore's constitution. However, before examining the contradictory demands generated by the routine pragmatics of governing race by the PAP government, it is necessary to distinguish state multiracialism from liberal multiculturalism.

Multiracialism is not Multiculturalism

To the extent that every Singaporean is officially ascribed as belonging to a particular "race," every Singaporean is subject to prescribed behavioral constraints imposed by the respective race culture. The common perception is that Islamic beliefs and doctrines subject the Malay

Muslims to greater level of constraints than the Huaren and Indians. This is because some of the constraints are highly visible, such as the sartorial demand for modesty (symbolically signified by the headdress for women); the injunctions against the consumption of pork and alcohol; and the expectation that Muslims should eat only halal food (food prepared according to Islamic religious regulations). The behavioral constraints imposed by the cultural practices of an individual's race can best be conceptualized as the "cost" that one has to bear for membership in his or her race-community, which imparts some elements of identity to oneself (Chua 2005). Homing in on such constraints, many Singaporean and foreign critics argue that ascribing race to citizens creates essentialized mono-racial/cultural silos into which each citizen is confined. Such simplistic critiques of state multiracialism overextend the reach and force of race and culture and underestimates the complexity of the cultural terrain of contemporary Singapore society.

At the individual level, culture may be conceived as a process of the lifelong accumulation of layer upon layer, a palimpsest, of learning and acquisition of knowledge and practices; the individual is unavoidably a complex "multicultural" subject. The "race culture" may be the foundational layer acquired primarily within the family and it may have greater impact than subsequent layers in the individual's subject formation. Nevertheless, the totality of an individual's everyday cultural practices readily and necessarily exceeds the prescribed boundaries of the race culture. For example, in contemporary Singapore, to function effectively requires an understanding of capitalism as a set of relatively coherent practices. Likewise, making a living requires formal education in the English language to transform oneself into a productive human resource in a competitive labor market and to discipline oneself to meet the requirements of wage earning in order to reap its consumerist rewards. Understanding and engaging in the practice of capitalism on a daily basis constitute a far greater influence in the life of all Singaporeans than do their particular race-based traditional beliefs and practices. Also, these common demands often displace the cultural values of one's race if a conflict arises between the two. At the societal level, multiracialism is only a limited segment of the larger culture sphere in practice. Indeed, the government's constant exhortation for Singaporeans is to expand the "common ground" among themselves rather than to focus on their cultural differences.

Against the inevitable teleology of individual and society becoming multicultural, confinement of an individual within a "mono-race culture" silo would have to be either the result of a conscious and voluntary ideological decision of the individual or one of coercive confinement against his/her will. In Singapore, race culture injunctions are not stringently observed. For example, Malay/Muslim women retain the freedom to choose whether to wear headdress and whether to marry under Muslim (*shariah*) or civil law. Young Sikh men may choose not to wear a turban and dressing in ethnic Chinese clothes has all but disappeared for Chinese men. With the exception of having to learn one's so-called "mother tongue" as a second language in primary and secondary schools, individuals have not been officially confined rigidly to their respective race-cultures under state multiracialism. Politically such confinement would be difficult to enforce. For example, as we will see later, compulsory learning of one's mother tongue in school has been progressively relaxed as a result of resistance and political resentment, particularly from Huaren parents.

Contemporary Singaporeans generally embrace two modes of what we might call "everyday" or "vernacular" multiculturalism. The first is the self-reference to "Singaporean" culture as a *rojak*—mixed—culture. (*Rojak* is a Malay work referring to a local dish made with a mixture of fresh fruits and cooked vegetables coated with a heavy shrimp-based sauce and crushed peanuts.) Here, "multi" means mixing, as in the idea of cultural hybridity in liberal multiculturalism, sometimes hyperbolically elevated as "cosmopolitanism" (Duruz and Khoo 2015: 1–25). Second, most Singaporeans know and respect, without necessarily understanding, the different practices among the three racial groups, such as Muslims do not eat pork, a dried bay leaf pinned on the door signifies a Hindu household and Huaren burn ritual offerings by roadsides and trees. If there is any compulsion to abide by such "traditional" cultural practices, which constitute a shrinking part of the culture of Singaporean everyday life, it is imposed by the race-groups themselves, not by law. Here, "multi" is merely numerical, meaning many and separate cultures. There is no demand for Singaporeans in general to have a deep understanding of each other's race-cultures (Lai 1995); only a high degree of tolerance is required to maintain generalized racial-cultural harmony.

Haunted by past instances of racial violence and the geopolitical embedding of Singapore in the Malay world, state multiracialism in Singapore is therefore not about the politics of culture but about the politics of race. It is not about regulating individual cultural practices but about monitoring and policing the boundaries and contact points between races. In instances where race and religion are mutually impli-cated, state multiracialism unavoidably extends into regulating religion. The ascription/inscription of race on every Singaporean is a "collateral" necessity that gives "race" social materiality as objects of governance.

Race-Group-Culture Equality

Central to the governance of multiracialism in Singapore is the formal equality of race groups. Two areas of immediate policy-making concern after independence were religion and language, which are closely tied to race. Administratively all the major religious festivals are national holidays.

- Ramadan and the Haj are Islamic holidays largely for Malays and other Muslims;
- Deepavali (Festival of Lights) is a Hindu holiday exclusively for Indian Hindus although polytheistic Huaren devotees can be found worshipping in Hindu temples despite the fact that Hinduism does not accept converts;
- Vesak Day is a Buddhist holiday for Indian and Huaren followers of Buddha;
- Christmas and Good Friday are Christian holidays for Indian and Huaren Christians; and,
- the first two days of the Lunar New Year are Huaren holidays.

A mix of religious and race-based festivals is pragmatically used to approximate equal allocation of national holidays to CMIO. Beyond public holidays, race-culture and religious festivals are left to the respec-tive communities.

Before independence, all three races had their own community-funded schools, alongside English-language schools funded by the colo-nial government or White missionaries. *Huawen* (华文) or Mandarin schools were by far the most ubiquitous (Gwee 1969). In the late 1950s, there were a series of strikes, examination boycotts and confron-tations with the police by Huawen secondary school students against the colonial government's intention to conscript them for the insurgency war against the Malayan Communist Party (Huang 2006). A govern-ment committee was convened to examine the education system and recommended that (1) all children receive a "multilingual" education regardless of their medium of instruction; and (2) a common and nationally-oriented curriculum be developed to help build a "united nation." The recommendation for a national multilingual education was implemented as the bilingual national education system. English would become the students' "first language" in school while their race languages would be their "second language."[3] However, in cases of cross-racial marriages, the parents could opt for either of their languages as a child's second language (Purushotam 1997).

Primacy of the English Language

Upon assuming political power in 1959, the PAP government instituted English as the language of public administration, commerce and industry as it would provide the most direct and efficient path towards gaining technological and scientific knowledge that is essential to a modern economy. The government rapidly expanded the number of state-funded English-language schools, where the three official Asian languages were taught as mother tongues. By the early 1970s, the obvious economic advantages of English-language proficiency in the rapidly expanding employment market led parents to enroll their children in these government-funded schools. The immediate consequence was the collapse of the non-English schools. The Huawen school system atrophied, and the Malay and Tamil schools all but disappeared. The government then seized the opportunity to institute the national education system in which English was permanently installed as the language of instruction in all education institutions.

The primacy of the English language is reinforced by the government's ideological emphasis on open competition in the economy. Just as internationally Singapore must compete with other countries, at home individuals must compete with each other. Financial success or failure of an individual is to depend on a combination of one's effort and natural aptitude; that is, "meritocracy" is the basis of economic and social order. Since English is a foreign tongue for every Asian Singaporean, it reduces everyone, in abstraction, to a culturally equal starting point for "fair" competition, without prejudice. Facility in English, thus, reinforces the ideology of "meritocracy."

---

[3] *White Paper on Education Policy*, Cmd.15 of 1956, Legislative Assembly Sessional Paper, Singapore 1956. Race languages are officially called "mother tongues." However, this is a misnomer because a child's mother tongue is determined by patrilineal descent of the child.

Historically in fact English was not an Asian race-neutral language in Singapore. Indians were the first non-white population in Singapore to acquire a high proficiency in English. For many contemporary Indian families, English has been the home language for generations. During the colonial days, there was a palpable over-representation of Indians in professional positions such as doctors, lawyers, school principals and teachers. As most Huaren children went to community-funded Mandarin-language schools, they were not in competition for those positions. However, once English-language education was provided for all Singapore children, Indian over-representation was reduced. Comprising more than 75 percent of the population, normal statistical distribution has placed the Huaren in the majority of all professions.[4] Against the history of their privileged access, this statistical norm has been frequently misrecognized as evidence of racial discrimination against Indians in contemporary Singapore. This perception can, perhaps, be countered by a persistent over representation of Indians in politics, including in the ministerial ranks of the PAP government.

As English became increasingly the language in school, at home, at work and in public places, there was unavoidably a progressive general decline in competency in the three official Asian languages. Parenthetically, before formal education became a national phenomenon, most Huaren and Indians could manage simple communication in what is called *pasar* Malay (that is, a variety of Malay spoken in the marketplace or the street). The general decline of competence in Malay is reflected in the lamentable situation that an overwhelming majority of non-Malay Singaporeans do not take the trouble to understand the national anthem which is in Malay, the national language. The compulsory learning of their respective "mother tongues" is made compulsory for all primary and secondary students to supposedly improve the situation. This bilingual policy is further rationalized by the dubious argument that the second language will instill in the students "traditional" Asian values as "cultural ballast" against the insidious "Westernization" of

---

[4] In the Sri Lankan situation, Tamils were privileged over the Sinhalese during the British colonial days. Arguably, and over simplifying the issue, had the independent government adopted the same strategy of retaining English language as the official language, the privileges of Tamils would have been eliminated in the same way as in Singapore.

Singaporeans that inevitably comes with English-language education. Beyond schools, the race languages are to be boosted by annual month-long public campaigns dedicated to the use of each language. The success of these efforts to maintain the three official Asian languages has been limited at best, as we shall see in the case of Mandarin.

The greatly expanded national education system has spawned a new and rapidly expanded tertiary-educated, English-speaking middle class in the last five decades. As social and cultural advantages are transferred across generations, children of this new middle class are clearly advantaged over those from non-English speaking, working-class families; consequently, social stratification has progressively rigidified. By the mid-1990s, the government itself raised the very possibility of an emergent "permanent underclass" among the non-English educated, regardless of race. By the beginning of the twenty-first century, it had to admit that "simple" meritocracy was no longer working and a "compassionate" meritocracy was needed. Morally, people who have attained success should be more socially responsible towards those who have achieved less. As a practical measure, the government would invest in early childhood education to try to equalize the educational starting point of all children. However, the ideology of meritocracy remains undiminished. Indeed, meritocracy may be said to have hardened into an element in Singaporean identity formation, as a self-congratulatory justification for success for individual Singaporeans and for the nation.

Governing Race: Racial Harmony as a Public Good

English has effectively become the lingua franca in contemporary Singapore, so it could be argued that the English language has assisted in the emergence of a nation, above and beyond race. This is reflected in the way the language critically inserts a division between issues viewed from a "national" perspective and issues viewed from a "racial" perspective in the national discourse. The national perspective is always articulated in English and is regarded as framing issues in terms of "society as a whole." On the other hand, issues posed in one of the race-languages are seen as representing the narrow interest of that particular race, which may contradict the national interest. This division aligns the national perspective and racial perspectives in an unequal hierarchical structure, where the national perspective is set above the racial perspective with their respective particular interests. This structural arrangement gives the state a very high degree of autonomy relative to the race groups.

As the government maneuvers in and around policing the boundaries of the race groups in the name of the nation and national interests, it claims to be a neutral umpire that fairly and equitably adjudicates disputes and allocates resources among the races (Vasu 2012; Brown 1996). This structural arrangement prevents the state from being captured by any race group, regardless of its size vis-à-vis other race groups. The logic is simple: if the state were to allow one race group to use its race as a basis for making political claims, then it would have to allow the other race groups to do the same. Consequently, whether or not a race-based demand made by a respective race group was accepted and acted on by the government would depend on (1) whether the demand could be granted to all race groups equally; and (2) whether to grant all groups the same demand would enhance or detract from national interests. With state multiracialism, the PAP government has simultaneously strengthened the race group identity while reducing the likelihood of race being mobilized as a political resource.

The premier national interest with reference to race is "racial harmony." Peaceful coexistence among the races stands not only as a sign of tolerance of race differences among Singaporeans but also the successful maintenance of social and political stability essential to economic growth. Thus, "racial harmony as a public good" serves as the overarching concept that rationalizes and justifies the practical policing of contacts between the races in order to intervene when signs of racial antagonism are perceived. Fear of disrupting racial harmony has rendered race, and by extension religion, as politically sensitive issues that preferably should not to be discussed publicly. Public voicing of grievances involving race-related religious issues are quickly suppressed. Individuals and/ or organizations are chastised, even criminalized as "racial chauvinists" and/or "religious zealots" who threaten harmony. A slew of legislations and institutions have been established to ensure racial and religious harmony. These include the Presidential Council for Minority Rights, the Presidential Council for Religious Harmony and the Maintenance of Religious Harmony Act.

Ironically, in spite of the suppression of the public voicing of race-related issues, racializing everyone makes potential racial conflict endemic in society. This is, however, instrumental to the social control of race. For control to be necessary, race must be given a very high public visibility to signify deep divisions that are supposedly permanently inscribed on the national social and political body. Past race riots are invoked at every opportunity by government agencies as evidence to remind the population of the threat of racial violence. Examples include the 1950 violence between the White and the Malay communities when the Singapore court ruled in favor of returning Maria Hertogh, a Java-born, Dutch-Eurasian girl, who was left to the care of a Malay woman during the Japanese Occupation, to the European parents after the war (Aljunied 2009), and the 1964 violent clashes between the Chinese and Malay communities on Prophet Mohammad's Birthday when the Muslim parade was disrupted by some Chinese who allegedly insulted and threw objects at the marchers. Since then the parade has been discontinued. The need to be vigilant against the potential of racial conflict is a constant theme in public speeches by political and race-community leaders.

While in principle state multiracialism demands race equality, in practice, however, the maintenance of racial harmony does not, indeed cannot, mean equality of races at all times and across the entire terrain of public administration and policies. Under the general idea that racial harmony is morally and socially desirable, specific instances of administrative intervention may in fact advantage or disadvantage particular race group. As will be demonstrated below, different principles and strategies are used to govern different races. When overt discrimination for or against a specific race group is exercised administratively, it is politically defensible only when it can be demonstrably shown to be necessary and to contribute to the imperative of maintenance of racial harmony as a public good. Such is the modus operandi of state multiracialism in Singapore.

Governing Chinese: Dismantling Community Power Structure

On the eve of political independence, the Huaren community had the greatest capacity to mobilize its members, both in terms of their number and financial resources, of all the CMIO race groups. Throughout the colonial period, the Huaren community had taken care of their own affairs through an extensive network of clan associations, organized either under the same surname, same province/village/county of origin, same language or same trade. Membership and social solidarity were maintained through annual religious and ancestral rituals (Chang and Yi 2005). The networks of associations provided welfare for the needy, set up schools, ran free medical clinics and paid the funeral costs of homeless sojourners from China. Some of the bigger clan associations became very wealthy through landholdings, which they donated generously for building education institutions, ranging from the primary to tertiary levels. For example, the Ngee Ann Kongsi (the pan-Teochiu clan association) donated land for the Ngee Ann Polytechnic and the Hokkien Huay Kwan (the umbrella organization of all from Hokkien Province) provided land for Nanyang University, now Nanyang Technological University. Currently, they also lease out land for commercial developments, such as the Ngee Ann City shopping center in a prime location on Orchard Road, to replenish the wealth of the association.

As these clan associations were generally helmed by businessmen, from small enterprise owners to tycoons of large trading companies to plantation owners and exporters of raw materials, the clan associations were intimately connected to the local economy (Leong 2007). At the apex of this loosely integrated network was the Singapore Chinese Chamber of Commerce (SCCC), established in 1906 as the umbrella association of the Huaren business community. "Traditionally, one first had to be a clan and dialect group leader before one could become a player in the leadership of the Chamber" (Visscher 2002: 320), and those who spoke English might "also participate in colonial representative bodies such as the Chinese Advisory Board, the Municipal Council or the Legislative Council" (Visscher 2002: 321). The SCCC was undoubtedly the unofficial representative of community interests and fully capable of galvanizing and mobilizing the Huaren population to any cause. During the decolonization period, in anticipation of the new nation the SCCC took the lead in negotiating three issues with the colonial government that preoccupied the community: citizenship, preservation of the Huaren language and education, and a multilingual legislature (Visscher 2002: 320).

Concern with language and education was emphatically demonstrated in the establishment of the only Mandarin-medium university outside of China and Taiwan. With the beginning of the Cold War, travel to Communist China was proscribed by the anti-communist colonial regime, which cut off the possibility of a tertiary education in mainland China for the vast number of high school graduates from Singapore's extensive network of Mandarin schools. Only a trickle of students went to universities in Taiwan. Spearheaded by the rubber tycoon, Tan Luck Sye, the Hokkien Huay Kwan donated the land for a university in Singapore. The entire Huaren population was mobilized to make large or small financial contributions; trishaw riders and itinerant hawkers contributed their income of the day. Being an active member of the university council was either an aspiration or/and an affirmation of having risen to "the highest level leaders" of the Huaren community (Visscher 2002: 321). Nanyang Da Shue (南洋大学) or Nanyang University, fondly referred to as Nantah, was established in 1955 to provide tertiary education for Mandarin-educated students in the Southeast Asian Huaren diaspora, particularly Singapore and Malaya.

Given their power and influence at the apex of the Huaren community, some SCCC leaders naturally attempted to harness and mobilize this political base to run for public office in the new nation. Thus, in the 1955 election for self-government, some leaders formed the Democratic Party. Formally, there was no connection between the Democratic Party and the SCCC, as some SCCC leaders were not in favor of the Chamber being dragged into party politics. However, the financial backers and the candidates of the Democratic Party were obviously SCCC management committee members, leading it to be dubbed the "millionaire party." The Party and its candidates did not have any electioneering organization on the ground and were counting entirely on the fact that they were leaders of the Huaren community to win votes. However, the political atmosphere was infused with left-wing sentiments during decolonization. The Democratic Party of the wealthy was seen as politically conservative and won only two seats out of 20 contested (Visscher 2007: 105–10). The election was won by the Labor Front, led by David Marshall.

From 1959 when it formed the first fully elected parliament to the early years of political independence, the PAP government had to seek the assistance of the SCCC in getting support from the Huaren community. This was particularly critical in the referendum for merger with Malaya, which was strenuously opposed by the Barisan Sosialis. Unable to stop the referendum, Barisan began to encourage voters to cast blank votes. To get SCCC leaders to support its merger proposal, the PAP government assured them that all Huaren with long-term residence in Singapore would automatically become full citizens of the merged Malaya. This support of the leaders helped the PAP government to win the day. In the same year, the political force of the SCCC was again demonstrated with the discovery of mass graves of Huaren who were massacred during the Japanese Occupation. The Chamber undertook the exhumation of the graves and galvanized the community to demand apologies and financial reparation from the Japanese government, with threats of boycotting Japanese products. Lee Kuan Yew, who had just been in office for less than three years and on unstable political footing had to address a mass rally at the Padang, the open field in front of the city hall. The issue was "settled" with the PAP government persuading the Japanese government to provide SGD 50 million, half grant and half loan, to Singapore, as atonement, short of an apology to the people of Singapore. The Chamber was pressured by the Prime Minister to accept the deal and not to make further demands which might hurt the much-needed Japanese investment for the new nation (Blackburn and Hack 2012: 164). In addition, a monument for the massacred, "Memorial to the Civilian Victims of the Japanese Occupation 1942–1945," was completed in 1967 at a prominent site in the city center, with equal financial contributions from the Chamber and the Singapore government.

The PAP government faced far greater difficulty in its dealing with Nantah. From the start, Lee Kuan Yew was wary of its establishment. He warned repeatedly:

> Let us never forget that Singapore is part of Southeast Asia; that we are in the center of a Malaysian people....Our geographical and ethnological positions are realities we must face. If Nanyang [University] becomes a symbol of Chinese excellence and of supremacy of Chinese scholarship and learning, then verily we will aggravate the position of the overseas Chinese in all the other places in Southeast Asia. (quoted in Hong and Huang 2008: 121)

To avoid this, Nantah had to evolve into a "Malaysian" university that catered to all races and not to Huaren exclusively. Besides the regional concern, the PAP had always believed that the politicization of Chinese education was "another 'sinister' communist attempt to feed on the dissatisfaction of the Chinese educated so as to create agitation and tension for political mileage" (Hong and Huang 2008: 90). It claimed that communists had hijacked the Chinese language issue to rally the Huaren population to its cause. With students drawn mainly from the Huawen middle-schools which had a history of active political mobilization during the 1950s, the student body was palpably left-wing, as evidenced by the students' open support for the breakaway Barisan and the fact that some Huaren Nantah graduates stood as party candidates in the 1963 general election. The entangled history of Nantah and the PAP government has been well documented (Hong and Huang 2008: 109–36); suffice it to say that the government moved to finally shut Nantah down in 1980 by merging it with the then University of Singapore to form the National University of Singapore, an English-medium institution. The current Nanyang Technological University occupies the site of the old Nantah, which has morphed into the "Nantah spirit."

The closure of Nantah, along with the eventual reduction of several Mandarin newspapers to a single newspaper under the monopolistic pro-government Singapore Press Holdings (see Chapter 2), were both a symptom and an outcome of the struggle between the PAP government trying to consolidate its rule and the Huaren community being an alternative political base, which the PAP regarded as a force that could frustrate and threaten its effort and ability to govern. Over the years, the PAP government slowly but surely dismantled the Huaren political base and hierarchical community power structure through a combination of direct repressive intervention, such as the above-mentioned closure of Huaren cultural institutions, and indirectly, as an unintended consequence of its single-minded drive for national economic development. In this struggle, the PAP government had to, and eventually did, triumph at all costs.

In terms of national development, it can be argued that the negligence of the British colonial administration to see to the welfare of the Huaren community resulted in the community's development as an organized political force. As the elected government, the PAP government took direct responsibility for the daily life of the citizens. It created education opportunities, generated employment, and provided public housing, healthcare and basic social welfare. The successful execution of these responsibilities seriously impacted three identifiable elements of the Huaren community power structure.

First, the rapid expansion of government-funded, English-language schools unintentionally undermined enrolment in Mandarin-language schools. By the early 1980s, the network of schools that were part of the Huaren community structure was all but gone.

Second, the expansion of public housing, healthcare and welfare services by the government displaced and replaced the traditional role of the clan associations in the provision of these much-needed social services. The disappearance of Huawen schools and the decline of the significance of clan associations severely weakened the foundation of the community structure. The PAP in turn actively incorporated the proprietors of small- and medium-size enterprises into various grassroots level community organizations, for example, placing these proprietors on the management committees of government-controlled community centers, which redirected their leadership aspirations and abilities to national rather than race-centered organizations (Seah 1973).

Third, the Huaren trading business community was left out of the successful industrialized economy that is built on multinational corporations and direct government investments. Although the PAP government did make the effort to encourage SCCC members to start and develop industries as the way to the future, it received little response (Visscher 2008). Throughout the first two decades of rapid economic development, the economic power of the Huaren business community and the SCCC declined rapidly. It was not until the mid-1980s economic recession that the government once again turned its development attention to encourage and promote small- and medium-size enterprises, which had continued to provide the largest share of employment for Singaporeans (Chalmers 1992). By then, the SCCC, now known as the Singapore Chinese Chamber of Commerce and Industry (SCCCI) was largely relevant only to its members. With the economic rise of China, it has become a junior partner in government initiatives for doing business with China.

In sum, in the contest for power and influence over the Huaren community, the PAP government had one great advantage, namely, the successful execution of responsibilities towards the welfare of the population. State provisions brought individuals directly under the government's control as citizens, displacing their dependency on their respective race communities. The result was the simultaneous dismantling and enervation of the race-community power structure that made the population dependent on the government and directed citizens' attention, if not their loyalty, away from their race communities towards the government. The government's capacity to successfully provide the necessities of the population's everyday life produced salubrious consequences for itself. It can thus be said that the Huaren have all been absorbed, in varying degrees, into the Singapore nation.

However, disappointments and frustrations remain deeply felt by those in the community who care about the Huaren language and culture, which have been minoritized, that is, reduced to the status of the other two race languages—Malay and Tamil. Such feelings are often quite publicly expressed when the opportunity is available. As recently as mid-2014, on the occasion of the seventy-fifth anniversary of the Chung Cheng High School, one of the most activist schools during the 1950s, Prime Minister Lee Hsien Loong repeated the government's commitment to help Singaporeans master their mother tongue, although he conceded that the students are unlikely to recover the high standard of the 1950s. This was rebuffed by an editorial in the local newspaper, *Lianhe Zaobao*, which reiterated that the bilingual policy had "turned the use of Mandarin and dialects into a zero-sum game," and the result was "a divide between the dialect-speaking pioneer generation and their mainly English-speaking grandchildren, leading to the loss of traditional Chinese values and hastening the Westernization of society." The Prime Minister's Office (PMO) immediately argued that (1) the newspaper was being "extreme" because "similar shifts in values and attitudes are taking place even in China, Hong Kong and Taiwan;" (2) the bilingual policy was meant to counter rather than aid this shift in traditional values; and (3) "dialects have not been expunged" (*Straits Times* 11 July 2014). However, if dialects are still alive, it is in spite of the government not because of it. They are kept alive by those who failed to succeed in the highly competitive English-first school system. In recent years, some clan associations have started dialect conversational groups for individuals to maintain their fluency in these dialects and for the young to learn them.

The mild response from the PMO to the provocations by *Lianhe Zaobao* is a reflection of the times. In the 1970s, the editor would likely have been charged with "Chinese chauvinism" and detained under the Sedition Act or the Internal Security Act; recall here the jailing of the editors of *Nanyang Siang Pao* recounted in Chapter 2. In the 1990s, the editor could have been similarly chastised for being a "Chinese chauvinist," as in the case of Tang Liang Hong, a Workers' Party candidate in the 1997 general election. He was "accused of being an anti-Christian Chinese-language chauvinist who was a threat to ethnic [racial] peace," for asking, metaphorically, "why the Chinese-educated majority were the ones 'carrying the sedan-chair'" (Mauzy and Milne 2002: 153, 134), for the English-speaking minority. Tang was subsequently sued by the entire team of the PAP leaders for defamation and he chose self-exile in Australia rather than stand trial. From Lee Kuan Yew to Goh Chok Tong to Lee Hsien Loong, the government's use of "legalized" coercion appeared to have "softened" significantly.

The precipitous decline of Mandarin competency in schools has not gone unnoticed by the government. Of all the compulsory mother-tongue/second-language learning requirements, learning Mandarin by Huaren students has attracted the loudest and persistent public complaint. Overly sympathetic English-speaking parents who are incompetent in the language complain persistently about their children's "difficulties" in learning Mandarin ideographic characters and rote recitation of idioms. This has led to the progressive downgrading of learning Mandarin in school from a single standard level of learning for all students to the current three levels of learning offered, namely:

- Chinese Language 1—Mandarin is learned as a "first" language equal to English;
- Chinese Language 2—Mandarin is learned as a second language; and
- Chinese Language B—competency in Mandarin is limited to speaking; competency in reading and writing are not required.

Thus, sadly, the overwhelming majority population's competency in its race language is rapidly diminishing.

This deteriorating situation compelled the Ministry of Education to establish a Centre for Chinese Language in mid-2009 to improve the teaching of Mandarin. The government's effort was supplemented by an SGD 15 million Chinese Language and Culture Fund, jointly established by the Singapore Federation of Chinese Clan Associations and the SCCCI, to promote the learning of Mandarin and Huaren culture (*Straits Times* 5 Dec. 2006). Whether or not these institutional efforts will succeed in reversing the downward spiral of Mandarin learning is highly doubtful. They are more likely to end up as expensive symbolic gestures than concrete steps towards stemming the tide of declining Mandarin competency (*Sunday Times* 7 Sept. 2008). The government appears to have accepted this foregone conclusion and has limited its goal to producing a few hundred truly English-Mandarin bilinguals and bicultural individuals in each cohort of students to meet the need for inter-governmental relations and business transactions with China.

Governing Malays

Questioning Malay-Muslim National Loyalty

As a minority population, the Malay-Muslim community may not constitute a powerful political base within independent Singapore. However, the regional Malay world continues to haunt Singapore's political leadership. This fear is occasionally stoked by Malay politicians in the region. For example, Malaysian Malay politicians regularly claim that Singaporean Malays are politically "lesser" than their ethnic brethren in Malaysia, where Malays have political supremacy. The acrimonious separation still rankles. The late Indonesian President Habibe reminded and taunted Singapore as being only a "little red dot" in the sea of (Islamic) green. For the PAP government, this sparring across regional national boundaries raises a question of national loyalties of the Malay/ Muslim citizens.

The conscript-based Singapore Armed Forces (SAF) was instituted in 1968 (Tan Tai Yong 2001: 287). However, until today, conscripted Malay youth are, with few exceptions, sent to the police force or civil defense units rather than the military (*Straits Times* 23 Nov. 2013); the first Malay brigadier-general in the army was appointed in 2009. The government has not denied this long-standing practice. None other than Lee Kuan Yew has publicly justified it saying, "It would be very tricky business for the SAF to put a Malay officer who was very religious and who had family ties in Malaysia, in charge of a machine-gun unit" (*Straits Times* 8 Feb. 2001). The Malay community's retort:

> And as you said, there is always a possibility that the riots can spill over into Singapore and because of that, the Malays, as long as there are riots and the possibility of riots and as long as the communal conflicts in Malaysia and Indonesia are always there, then we will never be accepted and we will always be discriminated against, especially in the SAF. (*Straits Times* 11 Mar. 2000)

Lee's reply:

> So, we are all prisoners of circumstances. I sympathize with you. I know it's unfair. You're held hostage by events to which you have not contributed. But is it our imagination? Is it unreal? No. If there's an enormous disturbance in Malaysia, we are going to be affected. If there's an enormous disturbance in Indonesia, especially in Batam and the Riau Islands [Indonesia's territory closest to Singapore], we are going to be affected. It's a fact of life. We have to face the real world and the real world is unfair and unkind. It cannot be helped. (*Straits Times* 11 Mar. 2000)

After half a century of nationhood, the national loyalty of Malay/Muslim Singaporeans remains a political issue. They are supposed to accept, under protest, this blatant discrimination as a geopolitical reality and as one of the costs of citizenship. Parenthetically, it should be noted that Lee's belief that "geography is destiny" was also the reason for his concern with the establishment of Nantah as an ethnic Chinese institution, which might have contributed to its eventual closure.

In the aftermath of the 11 September 2001 bombing of the World Trade Center in New York City and the rise of terrorism in the name of Islam, the Malay Muslim loyalty question has extended to the issue of fundamentalist Islam. Being in a region with the world's largest Muslim population, Singapore is unavoidably caught up in vigilance against "Islamic" terrorism. In December 2001, a cell of 15 Jemaah Islamiah members, a network of Muslim radicals working throughout Southeast Asia and allegedly affiliated to Al-Qaeda, was uncovered.[5] Thirteen people were detained without trial under the Internal Security Act for allegedly planning to terrorize Americans in Singapore. Following their arrests, Zulfikar Mohamad Shariff, the president of the *Fateha*, a Muslim youth organization, claimed in its Internet website that Osama bin Laden, the Al-Qaeda leader, was a better Muslim than the Malay PAP MPs. He was immediately publicly isolated by a frenzy of chastisements from government ministers, Malay MPs, Malay community leaders and other citizens in the social and mainstream media. Within a few days he exiled himself to Australia. In mid-2016, while on a home visit, he was detained in Singapore under the Internal Security Act for posting pro-Islamic State messages with the intent of radicalizing Singaporean Malays (*Straits Times* 29 July 2016). The two incidents involving albeit a fringe minority might be symptomatic of, on the one hand, Malay-Muslim community discontent and, on the other, of an internal security risk for the government.

Spatial Management of the Community

Although constituting approximately only 18 percent of the total population, the residential spatial concentration of the Malay-Muslim population can provide them with a physical territory, a "home turf." For any racial group, the home turf is a valuable political material resource worth defending, including using it as a base to retreat to or from which to launch attacks on other groups in the event of conflict. In the electoral political system, spatial concentration also constitutes a vote bank which can be mobilized to successfully elect the group's own race candidates. From a political point of view, such racial spatial concentration should be dismantled to minimize the potential for racial

---

[5] Several plans of terrorist acts were allegedly also uncovered; see the *Straits Times* series on terror in Southeast Asia, during the month of January 2002.

conflict. Prior to the total urban transformation of Singapore, there were several exclusively Malay kampong in the East and West coasts of Singapore, but the nation's rapid urbanization resulted in these kampong being completely dismantled and their populations redistributed and rehoused in public housing estates by the mid-1980s. However, it was observed that Malays continued to favor several housing estates close to their previous kampong resulting in a higher concentration of Malays in these estates than the national percentage.

In 1989, fearing the reestablishment of Malay enclaves, the PAP government instituted a quota system to distribute race groups in housing estates. The percentage of each race group in every housing estate would approximate the composition of the national population— 75 percent Chinese, 17 percent Malays and 8 percent Indians. As the Huaren constitute more than 75 percent of the population, they inevitably constitute the numerical majority in every housing estate and housing block. Consequently, the quota system has had little effect on them. On the other hand, the approximately 8 percent of Indians, internally divided by a dichotomous economic division, is unlikely to be able to organize any significant spatial residential concentration. The consequences of the quota system are likely to have the greatest impact on the sizeable Malay-Muslim community (Sin 2002a; 2002b). For example, take a Malay family who intends to sell its flat. It will not be able to accept offers from a Huaren or Indian buyer if the latter's respective quota in the block is already filled. It is thus compelled to sell to another Malay family. Given the generally weaker financial position of Malays, this means that the family might have to accept a lower price than what a potential Huaren or Indian buyer might be willing and able to pay.

Regathering

In contrast to spatial dispersion, continuing concerns with the imagined/imaginable endemic regional security problem of race violence has brought the Malay-Muslim population under direct government control through a centralized hierarchical administrative structure. First, in 1966 several British colonial administrative regulations which covered the Muslim community were consolidated into the Administration of Muslims Act. Second, in spite of Singapore being formally a secular state, a separate Ministry of Muslim Affairs was established. The cabinet-level Minister for Muslim Affairs is at the apex of the hierarchical administrative structure of the Malay-Muslim community. Under his purview is the statutory board, the Majlis Ugama Islam Singapura (MUIS, the Islamic Religious Council of Singapore), a religious bureaucracy that oversees the management of all mosques in Singapore. Under MUIS is the office of the Mufti, the supreme religious leader who is appointed by the Minister and who oversees religious rulings pertaining to Islamic Law. Islamic Law is administered by the Shariah Court, whose jurisdiction is limited to adjudicating Muslim family and religious affairs, including a separate Registry of Muslim Marriages. In the early 1980s, the persistently high number of economically disadvantaged Malays led the Malay PAP MPs, in collaboration with other Muslim community organizations, to obtain government financial support to establish the Majlis Pendidikan Anak-Anak Islam (MENDAKI, Council on Education for Muslim Children), as an organization dedicated to helping Malay children from lower income families who were falling behind in their education. Progressively, the activities of MENDAKI have expanded to include welfare provisions for adults and needy families, so much so that issues of social welfare and activities of community voluntary organizations are now loosely coordinated by MENDAKI, with Malay MPs continuing to be important in its management.

In accord with the logic of race group equality, the Huaren have set up the Chinese Development Assistance Council (CDAC) and the Indians, the Singapore Indian Development Agency (SINDA). The three organizations have come to be called "community self-help" organizations because each organization is funded by voluntary contributions from all working individuals in their respective race groups, through a small deduction from the individual's monthly CPF savings. Drawing every working person into helping these organizations might renew one's sense of belonging and responsibility in securing the continuity of one's respective race community. As these organizations are only supplementary providers to the overall social welfare needs of the country, which far exceeds their capacity to deliver, they are of greater symbolic political value than substantive assistance.

To those outside the Malay-Muslim community, the hierarchy of Malay-Muslim organizations appears to operate in unison when promoting community cohesion and interests, from the Minister for Muslim Affairs to the small community welfare organizations. Generally these organizations have refrained from airing intra-community differences which could weaken the community's collective bargaining position vis-à-vis the other race groups and/or the government (Kadir 2004: 364–9).

However, considerable differences of opinion appeared in 2003, when a new organization, the Association of Muslim Professionals (AMP), was established. In its inaugural conference, the AMP leadership publicly criticized the centralized governing structure of Malay-Muslim organizations, with Malay PAP MPs at the center. It charged that the Malay MPs had been less than able to fully represent the interests of the community because, being members of the government, they were bound to place national interests ahead of particularistic community interests. One central issue, discussed below, was the Malay PAP MPs' admission of not publicly discussing Muslim women's right to wear the *tudung* (headdress worn by Muslim women), preferring a "continuing dialogue" with the government behind closed doors.

The AMP therefore called for an alternative non-partisan collective community leadership structure that could better represent Malay-Muslim interests (National Convention of Singapore Malay/Muslim Professionals 1990; Kadir 2004). The proposal was summarily dismissed by the government, which immediately framed it as a threat to racial harmony, arguing that it would lead the Huaren and Indian communities to do the same and eventually undermine the government's ability to govern race. The AMP was further charged with straying into politics, which is proscribed by the Societies Act, which then raised the possibility of the AMP's deregistration. However, Prime Minister Goh Chok Tong made a counter-offer: the AMP would receive funding under the same formula as MENDAKI if the AMP would channel its energy in the same direction as MENDAKI. The AMP accepted the offer. The political challenge from an organic community force was thus diffused and absorbed into an existing government-directed program (Ismail 2014: 54–5).

Other miscellaneous issues continue to simmer between the government and Malay Muslims, leading many Singaporeans to see the community as disproportionately burdened with "problems" (Rahim 1998; Li 1989), some of which are related to religion. Under the Shariah law, Muslims are permitted to marry at a younger age than under the civil code. In addition, parents can petition the Shariah court to further reduce the marriage age of their children. Such teenage families are often very unstable, frequently resulting in divorce. In education, the under achievement of students studying in the *madrasah* (independent Islamic religious schools) has led to the addition of the secular national education curriculum to the religious curriculum of the madrasah

(Hussin 2003). Madrasah which do not achieve a minimum standard of achievement for their students in national examinations are threatened with closure. A yet-to-be-resolved issue is the wearing of the tudung. The Ministry of Education does not permit students in government schools to wear the headdress (*Straits Times* 1 Feb. 2003). This has driven some Malay parents to send their daughters to madrasah. Muslim female members of government-employed uniformed groups, such as the police and nurses, are similarly prohibited from wearing the tudung. Malay PAP MPs claim that they have consistently supported the right to wear the tudung but have not made public their sentiments in the interest of racial harmony. However, public debate on the issue has become more frequent. For example, a major debate on Malay-Muslim nurses' right to wear the tudung erupted on the Internet, in mainstream press and in parliament in October 2013 with the government agreeing to continue discussion to find a satisfactory resolution. Since then, there has been no publicly announced progress on the issue.

Governing Indians

As previously mentioned, the "Indian" race group was defined by the convenience of geography. It is thus a group that contains many "minorities within a minority," in addition to the divisions of class, religion and a plethora of languages. As the smallest visible race group of no more than 8 percent of the population, the "Indian" community may be said to have benefited from "equality" of race as it is, in principle, elevated and treated as equal to the other two larger race groups in terms of meritocratic education and employment opportunities, mother-tongue learning, religious public holidays and self-help community organizations. Indeed, successful middle-class "Indians" are often inclined to state publicly their appreciation of these benefits from state multiracialism. There has not been any significant "Indian" incident or publicly noted collective demand since independence and no Indian-specific government management strategy can be clearly identified.

Group Representation Constituency

Ideally, multiracialism should not spill into electoral politics, where one-person/one-vote applies and election outcomes should be determined by issues at hand and the choice of the best candidate for the job, regardless of race. In reality, as every electoral constituency in the nation will have an overwhelming majority of Huaren, the possibility of the parliament being constituted exclusively by Huaren MPs is always there. Excluding Malays completely from parliament would be regionally unsettling. Furthermore, it would undermine state multiracialism. Although thus far there has been no evidence that Singaporeans have voted strictly along race lines, there is of course no guarantee that they will not do so in the future. To avoid this imaginable possibility, the PAP government introduced a Group Representation Constituency (GRC) in 1988, as one of the so-called innovations to the conventional election system to supposedly better suit the local conditions.

A GRC is constituted by combining a number of electoral constituencies to form a larger contested unit. Each contesting political party has to field a team of candidates for all the constituencies. The team that receives the highest aggregate votes wins all the parliamentary seats of the GRC. The foundational rationale for the GRC is to ensure parliamentary representation of the non-Huaren race groups—Malay, Indian and Others, particularly Eurasians (Mauzy and Milne 2002: 145–6). The first GRCs were made up of three constituencies and at least one member of each contesting team had to be non-Huaren. However, subsequently, another rationale for the GRC was added. To enhance the direct responsibilities of an MP to the electorate, the elected team is constituted as members of a town council, with the task of managing municipal concerns of the public housing estates within the GRC. As a result, the number of constituencies in a GRC was expanded to five or six, with one or more non-Huaren candidates. By the 2006 general election, there were nine GRCs with five electoral constituencies and five GRCs with six constituencies; only nine constituencies remained single-seat. This intensified public complaints that the GRC system disadvantaged opposition political parties, as they might not have the financial means to pay the hefty deposit required for a team of electoral candidates. In response to the complaints, during the 2015 general election, the size of some GRCs was reduced and the number of single-seat constituencies was increased.

The GRC system has "denatured" the democratic electoral process in two significant ways. First, it has effectively changed the one-person/one-vote rule. A single vote may now be read as a vote for all the candidates in a contesting slate and thus in effect comprise several votes. Alternatively, each vote may be said to being diluted in proportion to the number of candidates in each slate. Either way, one no longer votes for a particular candidate of one's choice. Second, ironically, in guaranteeing representation for the non-Huaren population, the GRC system also ensures a permanent overwhelming Huaren majority in parliament. In principle, a permanent parliamentary majority of an identifiable group makes a mockery of democracy. However, the PAP argues that it is a realist, if not an entirely laudable, solution to an imaginable all-Huaren parliament. The "innovation" to electoral procedures has permanently inserted race into electoral politics, violating liberal democratic injunction for race blindness.

Conclusion: Social Productivity of State Multiracialism

In Singapore, state multiracialism conceptually and substantively covers a very limited cultural terrain. With racial harmony as its overriding concern, it is concerned with the behavior of individuals only when they disrupt, or are seen as disrupting, racial harmony, such as making disparaging statements against a particular race and/or religion. Beyond requiring each child to learn his/her own race language, the Singapore government does not get involved with the actual substance of race cultures. Many of the cultural behavioral constraints on individuals are imposed by the race cultures themselves and are not a consequence of state multiracialism. While it would be preferable if Singaporeans had a deeper understanding of other races' cultural and religious practices, this is not essential to maintaining racial peace. Tolerance of cultural differences is sufficient. For example, it is good enough that Malay-Muslims and Christians walk around the burnt offerings placed at the roadsides by Huaren, rather than disturb the offerings to vent their disbelief and disrespect. The actual everyday cultural "hybridity" of Singaporeans (Poon 2009) is not and should not be the business of the state, although the government is not beyond capitalizing on Singaporean vernacular multiculturalism as evidence of its achievement in producing "racial harmony."

For state multiracialism to be effective, it must be able to demonstrate social utility, like all public administration strategies. The first thing to note is its production of a national identity. Under state multiracialism, every Singaporean has an identity made up of race (Huaren, Malay, Indian or Others) and nation (Singaporean). The two identities have their separate discursive and practical spaces. The dual identity markers have not prevented the emergence of a Singaporean national identity, albeit it is one that is constantly in search of substantive content. Ironically, this may be in part because the national identity has been facilitated by the extensive use of the English language, which cannot be "racially" claimed by Singaporeans of any race. Nevertheless, survey after survey has found that the young identify themselves as Singaporeans before identifying themselves racially (Vasu 2012). National interests are held as primary and if necessary they must dominate race-interests. National interests have not been collapsed into or captured by the interests of a specific race. Responsibilities to the nation override those to race-groups and are exacted from all citizens through the rhetoric and maintenance of racial harmony.

The dominance of national identity over race-identity is very clearly demonstrated, perhaps unfortunately, in an emerging anti-foreigner tendency among Singaporeans. Since the mid-1970s, migrants from the PRC, Southeast Asia and South Asia have continuously fed Singapore's need for labor. They are racially similar to the CMI of Singaporeans, yet there are scant signs of affinity let alone identification with them as co-ethnic or co-racial individuals; Singaporean Huaren are frequently disparaging about the new mainland Chinese migrants in their midst. The 750,000 low-wage CMI migrant workers are being kept on temporary work permits by the state and excluded by Singaporeans as "outsiders." In instances where one of these "foreigners" belittles a local practice, they are publicly chastised by nationalist Singaporeans. For example, when an Australian-Chinese wrote rudely against the noise generated by Malay weddings in the ground floor of the public housing blocks close to her residence, she was roundly chastised on the Internet and the press and fired from her job for being "racist" and anti-Singaporean by one of the units of pro-government NTUC; she returned to Australia. Similarly, a complaint by a PRC Chinese family against the smell of a Singapore-Indian neighbor's curry cooking spawned a national "share-a-curry day." In these instances, a sense of nationalist belonging, of being "Singaporean," has taken hold, and citizenship is privileged over possible race. These instances where national identity is expressed do not mean the erasure of the race marker on individual Singaporeans, who fairly quickly revert to their race-identity and race-culture-behavior among themselves.

Second, there has been no racial violence in Singapore since 1969. This, however, can be and is often construed negatively. The idea of "maintaining racial harmony" has exaggerated the potential for race riots, suppressed public discussion of race and religion and criminalized the so-called "racial chauvinists" under the Sedition Act. In all these areas, the government has acted preemptively to head off imagined/imaginable troubles. While historical instances can be referenced repeatedly, presumed events can never be shown to have taken place, so there is no evidence that maintaining racial harmony has actually prevented acts of racial violence in Singapore. Singaporeans have understandably grown increasingly skeptical of preemptory policies and regulations as the necessary cost to be paid for racial harmony and the credibility of the PAP government's argument might be wearing a little thin.

Third, Singaporeans who are most supportive of state multiracialism are those who perceive and are concerned that their race-language and culture are being eroded by the ascendancy of English as the lingua franca and their race-values weakened by an ever-expanding self-serving individualism of modern/Western "liberal" values. State multiracialism assures them of the continuity and security of their race-cultural identity, at both the individual and group levels. State-sponsored activities— public celebrations of race-religion-based festivals, establishments of race-self-help organizations and the GRC electoral system—have contributed to reinforcing the sense of race-group solidarity. Citizens who are anxious about "deracination" are thus drawn voluntarily to collaborate with the government's efforts on all these fronts. Indeed, even the tertiary English-educated Singaporeans, who consider themselves modern multicultural cosmopolitans and are thus above and beyond race-cultures (*Straits Times* 28 Feb. 2001), will not necessarily discard their dual identity. Having separate national and race identities arguably provide an additional element in the cultural tool-kit of all Singaporeans in their transactions within Asia, as each identity has its strategic utility. At the most general level, the ideological and practical success of state multiracialism is reflected in the self-congratulatory ease with which Singaporeans readily describe their island-nation as a "multiracial nation" where the races have lived in harmony for the past half century.

If the PAP government had instituted constitutional or state multiracialism out of political necessity in the 1960s, it has ended up with a master narrative for governance. Emphasizing equality of race groups makes the maintenance of racial harmony a fundamental administrative focus of governance. Taking the reasonable assumption that "racial harmony" as a desired good for which Singaporeans are willing to pay a certain political and social price in exchange, state interventions to "prevent" the politicization of race are seen as justifiable, even as they exact a cost from individuals of different race groups with different policies and regulations. In this, the PAP government has moved away from the liberal democratic principle of equality for individuals to governance through the equality of groups in the area of race relations, thus avoiding the entangled problems involved in recognizing differences between groups while maintaining the rights of individuals in liberal multiculturalism.

Chapter 7

CULTURAL LIBERALIZATION WITHOUT LIBERALISM

FIFTY YEARS OF CONTINUOUS CAPITALIST ECONOMIC growth generated by continuous investments in physical infrastructure and human capital, especially the continuous expansion and upgrading of the education system, have radically transformed Singapore society. The changes in Singapore society tend to be neglected in political analyses which remain fixated on the lingering authoritarianism inherited from the Lee Kuan Yew era and the unchanging one-party dominant parliamentary structure. This fixation has perpetuated many outdated assumptions regarding Singaporeans as citizens and their relationship with the hegemonic PAP government.

More specifically, like all wielders of power, the PAP is reluctant to lose its hegemonic power. However, the educated Singapore citizenry is also in no hurry to displace the PAP from its politically commanding position. In such a context, the general election, in spite of the very weak contests put up by other political parties, remains the most significant, if not the only, instrument for Singaporeans to negotiate with the government. The slew of policy changes and about-turns after the 2011 general election, in which the PAP received its lowest popular support, makes this abundantly clear. It had to concede to the demands of the electorate and undertake the changes or risk further erosion of its popular electoral ground. This is to say that the PAP government will do the "popular" thing, if the citizens' demands can be construed as reasonable within the general framework of governance. While the fundamentals of the one-party dominant parliament are unlikely to change in the foreseeable future, it would still be fruitful to examine the challenges/demands thrown up by the citizenry and the social cultural changes undertaken by the PAP government, whose successive generations of leaders have opened up or liberalized the social cultural sphere.

Changing Generations: Shifting Balance between the Leaders and the Governed

The Founding Generation

In the immediate postwar period, the levels of formal education and literacy in the entire population were very low. The first-generation British university-educated PAP leaders were highly privileged individuals who could naturally claim leadership on account of their superior English education. Thus, as soon as they joined forces with the less educated radical unionists who had been educated in local Chinese-medium schools, these university graduates were able to occupy leadership positions in the PAP, although the unionists were the organic leaders with a mass support base. In the ensuing political struggle between the two factions, the radical left was strategically outmaneuvered, with the leaders branded, condemned and imprisoned as "(pro)communist." Given the international Cold War atmosphere, the severe repression of alleged communists under the first-generation PAP leaders was completely overlooked by Western capitalist democracies. Indeed, the reconfigured "moderate" faction of the PAP government under Lee Kuan Yew was in good company in Southeast Asia, which saw the emergence of a fraternity of authoritarian leaders and governments, whose repressive excesses drew no political moral condemnation from the so-called free world. Once these repressive measures had effectively removed the political opposition of the left, the PAP government went about building the economy to the benefit of a relatively homogenously poor population with little popular resistance. This accounts for Lee Kuan Yew's constant political refrain that his generation of political leadership had a very strong compact with the first-generation Singapore citizens in their common struggle in nation building.

The excessive anxiety over survival as a small island-nation resulted in the frequent evocations of sometimes real, sometimes imagined/ imaginable threats to the national interest involving economic viability, security in the face of regional antagonism, racial (communal) conflict, and above all, communism (Yao 2007). Ideologically, the national interest became a trope for social control and political repression, especially during the Lee Kuan Yew regime. To the extent that all the threats to the national interest (minus communism) are permanent features embedded in the external and domestic existential conditions of Singapore, the anxiety has never gone away. It has remained very much the preoccupation of successive generations of PAP leaders until today. Under the pressure to survive, the PAP changed some aspects of its social democratic ideology. The idea of the "social" was rendered as a demand for unity of purpose in nation building. In practice, this translated into an emphasis of the "national"—the "collective"—over individuals. Social democratic anti-liberalism was thus reformulated with a positive tone as communitarianism.

By the late 1980s, global conditions had changed radically. The Cold War was no more. Excesses of repression in any nation were no longer tolerated by world opinion. The West, especially the European Union, was quick to impose diplomatic and trade sanctions against offending governments; for example, the more than two decades of sanctions against Myanmar starting in 1990. Meanwhile, the Singapore economy had become highly integrated into global capitalism. Currently, with its widely recognized successful economic development, Singapore is being given increasing recognition, participation and voice in global forums. A place in these forums is critical to Singapore's survival. According to the current Minister for Law and former Minister for Foreign Affairs, K. Shanmugam, officers in the Foreign Ministry are taught: "If you are not at the table, you could end up being on the menu" (*Straits Times* 6 Aug. 2013). Such international recognition is double-edged. To maintain this highly valued recognition, the PAP government has to show the world that it is a responsible political player; thus, its ability to exercise repression has been severely curtailed. Unlike in the past, it is less able to act with impunity to imprison anyone without evidence that can be presented publicly, if not in open court. After the dubious detention of 22 individuals under the Internal Security Act for the so-called "Marxist Conspiracy" in 1987, the PAP government has been more circumspect at political repression than in the past. Since then, with the exception of the detention of self-radicalized individuals or cell members of Islamic fundamentalist groups, there have been no political detainees in detention without trial.

Towards the tail end of Lee Kuan Yew's rule, his unrelenting top-down, leader-knows-best politics was already losing popular support. From 1984 onwards, the PAP's popular support at general elections kept slipping, dropping from 77.7 percent in 1980 to 64.8 percent in 1984 to 63.2 percent in 1988 to 61 percent in 1991. The sharp drop of support in 1984 was undoubtedly largely because the government, following Lee Kuan Yew's eugenic views, introduced the "Graduate Mother" policy. The policy caused a mini-social revolt which showed up in the election results. The electorate had made itself heard and felt. When the new parliament convened, the new cabinet retreated from the "Graduate Mother" policy.

In retrospect, the 1984 general election was a decisive moment in the relationship between the PAP government and the electorate. The record of economic growth and improvement of citizens' material life, hitherto felt by Singaporeans as collateral benefits of political acquiescence, was no longer enough to keep the citizenry docile. The general election provided a timely opportunity for the citizens to vent their dissatisfaction with the "arrogance of power, an inflexible bureaucracy, growing elitism, and the denial of consultation and citizen participation in decision-making" (Chan 1989: 82). This unexpected push back raised in Lee Kuan Yew the fear of what he called a "freak election," in which the electorate in reaction against the PAP might "inadvertently" vote in opposition parties who would be incapable of running the government and economy. Ironically, Lee's response to the election result was an acknowledgement that the electorate retains the power to remove the PAP from government, lest it forget, after hitherto more than 30 years of unbroken rule.

The Second Generation

In 1991, the Prime Minister's position was passed on to Goh Chok Tong. The presumptive leadership of the founding generation could not be passed on to the succeeding generations of PAP leaders. The continuous drive to educate the population increased the number and intellectual quality of the educated persons with each successive generation of citizens. The effect of education was socially accumulative. Over time, educated Singaporeans became increasingly reluctant to readily concede supremacy in knowledge and wisdom to new PAP leaders. The well-educated were increasingly able to imagine and articulate their versions of desired futures for themselves, if not for the nation. Even if they did not choose to contest the PAP vision directly, they were able to pursue their own versions of this vision. Realizing that the electorate would no longer accept the government's uncompromising top-down imposition of what the PAP ministers had decided were sound policies, Prime Minister Goh began his term by emphasizing his difference from Lee Kuan Yew. As we have seen in Chapter 3, he sought an ideologically new social compact with the citizens through "Shared Values;" redefined governance as trusteeship with a more consultative, participatory and a more human side of government; and promoted the cultural development of Singapore towards a more gracious society and a kinder and gentler nation, instead of one with highly competitive and self-serving citizens.

To heed increasing clamor from the electorate for more alternative voices, Goh introduced two new categories of MPs:

- the Non-Constituency MP (NCMP)—non-PAP contestants who have garnered the highest number of votes among contestants who have lost in a general election; and
- the Nominated MP (NMP), consisting initially of independent minded individuals but progressively made up of nominees from different interest groups, such as the NTUC, employer's associations and women's organizations.

The addition of these new MP categories was an attempt to head off the potential election of opposition party members to parliament. Against Lee Kuan Yew's vehement anti-welfarism, Goh introduced: an SGD 5 billion Edusave fund to provide extra-curricular activities for all students; Medifund and Medisave to provide subsidies to the lower income group; and distribution of cash through "Singapore Shares" of the annual budget surplus of the government.

To expand consultation and participation, he introduced the Feedback Unit, which regularly convened discussion sessions on emergent issues, to draw opinions from cross-sections of Singaporeans. He also convened two government commissions—the Singapore 21 Committee and the Remaking Singapore Committee—which solicited public opinions on the "future" of Singapore (Latif 2009). Civil Society organizations, partly emboldened by the slide of PAP's popular support and partly encouraged by Goh's style of government, became more assertive and were, in fact, given more room. For example, the Nature Society won the battle over the conservation of the coastal area of Chek Jawa in Pulau Ubin (Koh 2009). Finally, the government adopted a suggestion from the short-lived political discussion group, Roundtable, to establish the Hong Lim Park Free Speech Area in 2000. This area has since become the place for public demonstrations for both ad hoc and organized groups to voice their grievances or conduct celebrations.

To develop a "gracious" society, several cultural institutions were successively established, namely:

- the Ministry of Culture and the Arts in 1990;
- the National Arts Council, which established a Singapore Film Commission that supports a fledgling local film industry;
- the National Heritage Board;
- a new Singapore Art Museum;
- the Asian Civilization Museum;
- major renovation to the Singapore National Museum;
- new campuses for the Nanyang Academy of Fine Arts and the LaSALLE College of the Arts;
- the secondary School of the Arts;
- a new National Library; and
- a multi-billion-dollar performing arts center, The Esplanade – Theatres on the Bay.

Beyond the infrastructure hardware, direct or in-kind financial assistance to artistic groups and individual artists also increased, enabling some of the art workers to earn a living wage. Two major international arts events were launched: the annual Singapore Arts Festival, showcasing international, including Asian, performances in music, theater and dance; and the first Singapore Biennale of international contemporary visual arts (in 2006 after Goh's prime ministership). At both high- and low-ends of the cultural spectrum, variety was increased and censorship relaxed: nudity on stage, bar-top dancing and a movie rating system that includes an "R" rating for adult entertainment. Censorship was not lifted completely and continues till today as a site of contention between the government and the arts community. While professional associations were either enjoying the benefits of economic growth, such as business organizations, or legally restrained by the government from being critical, such as the Law Society (Rajah 2012: 161–218), theater groups have always borne the disproportional responsibility of playing the role of social critic (Chua 2004). This palpable "cultural liberaliza-tion" was much appreciated by the educated middle class, and it also attracted international notice. A cover story of the Asian edition of *Time* magazine (19 July 1999) declared "Singapore Swings" and that the "city state is getting competitive, creative and even funky;" this for a place that was long governed by the ascetic, strait-laced, no nonsense and morally righteous PAP and best known as a "cultural desert." To this change Goh declared, "But having fun is important. If Singapore is a dull, boring place, not only will talent not want to come here, but even Singaporeans will begin to feel restless" (quoted in Kwok and Low 2002: 149).

Notably, alongside liberalizing culture, Goh continued to reinforce PAP's hold on power (Rodan 2009). In the 1997 general election, he reiterated the threat that public housing estates in constituencies that elected non-PAP MPs would be deprived of government-subsidized estate upgrading. He also expanded both the size and number of Group Representative Constituencies (GRCs), which compounded opposition parties' difficulties in contesting elections as they had neither the financial resources nor the number of "quality" candidates to contest in the enlarged GRCs. Goh remained steadfast to the PAP's belief that Singapore is best governed by a single party, namely itself. All the processes and gestures of consultation, public participation and accommodation of different voices in parliament were undertaken as indices of the government's responsiveness and accountability to the electorate, in the hope of convincing them that there was no need to vote for opposition parties in general elections. They were therefore primarily undertaken to avoid political party competition, with the message "Have your desire for opposition fulfilled, but never to the extent of changing the government" (Goh quoted in Chin 2009: 79). Nevertheless, together with Goh's own genuinely friendly personality, these gestures enabled him to recover the PAP's lost ground and stem the slide in popular electoral support. In the 1997 general election, the PAP garnered 65 percent of the popular vote, an increase of 4 percent from the 1991 election. By the 2001 election, it jumped to 75.3 percent (Chin 2009). The recovery was significant as it reflected, firstly, that the PAP government could endure the departure of Lee Kuan Yew from the helm (Devan 2009) and, secondly, that Singaporeans appeared to be willing to continue supporting the PAP in government as long as it was prepared to listen and take them into account. However, the regained strength of popular support was not to last; it slipped back to 66 percent in the 2006 general election.

The Third Generation

In 2004, leadership in the PAP government was smoothly transferred to a third generation of younger ministers, with Lee Hsien Loong as

Prime Minister. This third generation faced its first general election in 2006. During the election, Goh Chok Tong, then Senior Minister, was tasked to mentor the two new PAP candidates who were contesting the two single-seat constituencies held by Low Thia Khiang of the Workers' Party (WP) and Chiam See Tong of the Singapore Democratic Party, respectively. In both, the two opposition parties retained their respective seats.

More interesting contests were happening elsewhere. The Workers' Party, under the leadership of Low Thia Khiang, had been quietly rejuvenating itself. In this election, it fielded two teams of young and untested candidates in two heavy weight GRCs. One team contested in the Ang Mo Kio GRC against Prime Minister Lee's team and the other contested in the Aljunied GRC, against the team led by the Minister for Foreign Affairs, George Yeo, possibly the most popular of the PAP ministers. The PAP teams won both GRCs readily; the Prime Minister's team received 66 percent and George Yeo's team received 56 percent in the respective GRCs. However, that the two WP teams of complete neophytes could snatch a substantial percentage of votes from the two heavy weight and popular cabinet ministers was clearly disappointing to both men. The results were clearly indicative of sympathetic electoral support for the young challengers to the PAP establishment. This was to be an early intimation of things to come.

Meanwhile, cultural liberalization continued apace. One of the first acts of Lee Hsien Loong as Prime Minister was to exempt all indoor activities, except those involving religion and race, from the need to obtain licenses from the Public Entertainment Licensing Unit in the Police Department. Public consultation processes were further expanded through REACH (Reaching Everyone In Active Citizenry @ Home), which replaced the Feedback Unit. However, the most notable liberalization was in the area of LGBT politics.

The discovery of the first few victims of HIV/AIDS in 1985 was enough to raise the government's concern. It provided funding to voluntary groups, such as Action for AIDS, which assist the patients and educate the public about the disease. The voluntary groups provided contact points for gays and the seed for the gay movement (L.J. Chua 2014: 49). Meanwhile, English language theater groups using "aesthetics as critique" actively produced gay-themed plays, the most explicit of which was *Completely With/Out Character* by The Necessary Stage in 1998. It chronicled the life of Paddy Chew, the first AIDS gay patient to go public. The public airing of gay issues gathered momentum quickly. In 2003, then Prime Minister Goh Chok Tong publicly stated that the government had relaxed its negative stance against gay individuals and was quietly hiring them into the civil service. Such positive developments in the government attitude towards gays opened up a political discursive space for the gay community to push their agenda publicly. To cut a long story short (L.J. Chua 2014), gay politics cumulated in two significant events.

The first happened in October 2007. Invoking a little used parliamentary procedure, the LGBT community, with the help of a liberal NMP, lawyer Siew Kum Hong, managed to introduce a petition in parliament for the repeal of Section 377A of the penal code, which criminalizes oral and anal sexual activities between men. As parliament was sitting to debate other changes in the penal code, including the removal of Section 377A, the petition was given immediate deliberation for two days. The outcome, perhaps the best that could be hoped for, was a parliamentary consensus that homosexuality should no longer be criminalized and a declaration from Prime Minister Lee Hsien Loong that, in view of the conservative character of the society, Section 377A would remain but the law would not be enforced against consenting adults in private. This "policy of non-enforcement" (L.J. Chua 2014: 114) was a major symbolic and substantive victory for the gay community.

The second event involved Hong Lim Park. The availability of this free speech space spawned the idea for a "pride parade" to be held there. It evolved to become the annual Pink Dot Day, a festival of "love" in which members of the public who are supportive of the LGBT community would turn up in pink. The first Pink Dot Day was held on Valentine's Day, 14 February 2009 (L.J. Chua 2014: 119–22). The PAP government's acceptance of the festival and the LGBT community's expansion of gay politics signify, practically and symbolically, the liberalization of culture and the expansion of space for civil society.

The changing attitude of the government was further evidenced by what has come to be known as the AWARE (Association of Women for Action and Research) Saga (Chong 2011). On 28 March 2009, a group of conservative Christian women successfully staged a coordinated takeover of AWARE, the 25-year-old women's organization that champions issues of gender equality. They were motivated by their objection to AWARE's school sex education program which contained lessons on homosexuality. The group had prepared its ground by having a significant number of its supporters taking out membership in AWARE. On the evening of the general assembly, when the executive committee members were being elected, the group was easily elected by the presence of large numbers of the new members, capturing 9 out of the 12 seats on the executive committee. The Christian connection was exposed by the local media; 6 of the 9 were members of the same Anglican Church and had the same mentor who is well-known for her homophobia. Issues of religion and sexuality were conjoined; the most conservative segment of the population was engaged in battle with the most liberal members of the feminist and LGBT movements, a very potent mix (L.J. Chua 2014: 122–5). The conservative Christian connection spurred some founding members of AWARE, now known as the "old guard," to start a petition to call an emergency general assembly (EGM), as permitted by AWARE's constitution. The EGM was scheduled on 2 May 2009. Meanwhile, AWARE membership swelled from 300 to 3,000; on the day of the EGM, individuals were still signing up for membership at the door. At the EGM, the Christian group confronted

> the groundswell of liberal Singaporeans, male and female, turning out to protect their own rights to belief, self-expression, self-formation and self-identity, regardless of whether they are sexually conservative or adventurous, hetero-normal or otherwise "queer".…The result was a thorough routing of the conservatives. The liberals won the day. The government shut out AWARE from schools and conservative education on sexuality was reinstated. (Chua 2011b: 23–4)

Throughout the entire event, the nation was enthralled and very likely waiting for the government to intervene. Several cabinet ministers expressed concern for the polarizing tendency of the contest and specifically warned against religion becoming embroiled in politics. This warning was critical because the pastor of the Anglican Christian group had from his pulpit exhorted fellow church members to attend the EGM to support their "Christian sisters." The response from the Anglican Archbishop, who was also the head of the National Council of Churches, was immediate and to the point: "We do not condone churches getting involved in this matter; neither do we condone pulpits being used for this purpose" (quoted in Chong 2011: 5). The rebuke drew a public expression of "regret" from the Anglican pastor and possibly reduced the attendance of Christians at the EGM, thus averting turning it into a religion issue. The disavowal of the National Council of Churches isolated the group that took over AWARE, making state intervention and potential criminalization for disrupting religious harmony unnecessary. As for the rumor that the government was orchestrating events in the background, Prime Minister Lee Hsien Loong clarified during the 2009 National Rally Speech that he only spoke to the religious leaders after the event.

The progressive liberalization of the cultural sphere across successive generations of PAP government leaders is there for all who care to see. By the time of Lee Hsien Loong's prime ministership there was no more talk of a "social compact," as obvious differences in an increasingly economically, culturally and socially differentiated population have made explicit common ideological ground untenable. However, cultural liberalization that is indicative of a proliferation of cultural values and practices does not mean that the PAP government accepts the development of political liberal pluralism; the same politically repressive laws such as the Internal Security Act and the libel legislation remain in place. Significantly, there also appears to be little interest among the majority of Singaporeans in political liberal pluralism. National politics has never abandoned its materialist issues as the results of the 2015 general election showed.

Continuation of Materialist Politics

In the 2008 global recession created by a financial crisis in the US, Singapore attracted significant foreign direct investment inflow because of its stable political and economic conditions. From 2006 to 2008, the total foreign direct investment (FDI) in Singapore grew from SGD 370 billion to SGD 496 billion.[1] The employment opportunities created by these investments could only be filled by the rapid importation of foreign labor. The population rose from below 4 million in 2005 to approximately 5.18 million in 2011, with the heaviest inflow during the last three of the seven years. One in four of the 5.18 million residents was a foreigner, which included CEOs of multinational companies as well as unskilled workers and domestic helpers.[2] The government

---

[1] From Singapore Statistics "Foreign Direct Investments in Singapore by Country/ Region, 20052009" http://www.singstat.gov.sg/stats/themes/economy/biz/foreign investment.pdf [accessed 3 Nov. 2011].

[2] *Monthly Digest of Statistics*, Singapore, October 2011: 16. http://www.singstat. gov.sg/pubn/reference/mdsoct11.pdf [accessed 31 Oct. 2011].

defended its aggressive immigration policy giving the reason that "for every one foreign worker employed…1.5 local jobs were created" (*Straits Times* 22 Apr. 2011). Faced with an aging population and a sustained declining birth rate, Singaporeans generally accept that new immigrants are necessary to maintain and grow the economy. However, the speed with which the inflow happened and the large number of incoming migrants became a public issue as Singaporeans found themselves having to compete more intensely for all public services, from school enrollment to public transport to healthcare facilities, housing and employment.

An example was public housing. By the end of 2011, there were close to a million public housing units with an average household size of 3.5. Using this number as the base, it was estimated that there were 1.6 million additional people to be housed. To accommodate these people, rules for renting out public housing flats and rooms were relaxed. This was reflected in the increase of household size to 4.4 by mid-2013 (*Straits Times* 11 May 2013). Among the new arrivals were new citizens and permanent residents who were entitled to purchase resale flats, thus increasing competition and pushing up prices steadily between 2006 and the second quarter of 2011 (Chua 2014: 525). Demand for public housing among citizens became acute by the end of the 2000s. Among those who were looking to buy their first home, the mismatch of housing price increases relative to income increases caused widespread anxiety about affordability of public housing.

In the midst of the housing crisis, among other grievances, the government released a White Paper with its population projection of 6.5 million for the future, which could only be realized by accepting more immigrants. Public dissatisfaction was instant. This was translated into disaffection against not only the government but also the immigrants, generating xenophobic excesses especially on the Internet. The government responded by bringing down the immigrant numbers, reducing it from a high of 19 percent in 2008 to 4.1 percent in 2010. However, it could not act as decisively to bring down public housing prices without causing unhappiness among the existing homeowners, which comprised the majority of the population. Instead, to maintain affordability, it increased cash housing grants to first time homeowners to offset the rising cost and also extended the mortgage period from between 20 to 25 years to 30 years. As new homeowners generally buy their flats when they are in their mid-thirties, they will be paying mortgage until they retire at the current statutory retirement age of 62.

The minor changes did not pacify the electorate. Immigration, housing affordability and public transport, along with high ministerial wages, became issues in the April 2011 general election. Unlike previous general elections when opposition parties tended to leave many constituencies uncontested, this time all constituencies, except the GRC helmed by Lee Kuan Yew, were contested. The PAP proclaimed that it was out to win a "clean sweep" of all the seats. The Workers' Party (WP) returned to contest in the GRCs of both Prime Minister Lee Hsien Loong and Foreign Minister George Yeo. Its leader, the popular Low Thia Khiang, abandoned his safe seat in the Hougang constituency to run against George Yeo, in the Aljunied GRC. The nightly political rallies of the WP drew crowds of literally tens of thousands, across gender, race, religion, age and class divisions. The PAP dismissed this as "business as usual" because similar phenomena had been seen in previous general elections, yet on voting day the crowds did not translate into votes for the opposition parties. Meanwhile, attendance at PAP rallies was so paltry that the pro-government mainstream print and television media refrained from printing/screening photographs of the rallies. However, images of the WP rallies were ubiquitous on the Internet and social media, where emotionally charged opinions and alternative viewpoints on current affairs were being circulated.[3]

The PAP's dismissal of the crowd in WP rallies proved misplaced. Halfway through the campaign period, Minister George Yeo, who is

---

[3] The emergence of social media has radically transformed the relations between media and politics. Declining dependence of Singaporeans, especially the young, on mainstream media for political opinions and information has reduced the efficacy of the PAP government's control over media. The mainstream media, especially the newspapers, now finds itself constantly perusing social media sites and blogs to discover what is being debated, and it is compelled to report the issues when the debate reaches a certain level of intensity, in order to stay relevant to its audience and reading public. Consequently, control of the press is becoming increasingly more symbolic than real, even as control extends into policing specific websites, with what the government considers a "light touch," which includes gazetting public affair sites as "political sites," with specific legal constraints. One website, The Real Singapore, operated out of Australia by a Singaporean husband and Japanese wife team, was shut down by the Media Development Authority. The husband and wife team was charged and jailed for sedition for intentionally inciting "ill feelings and hostilities" among Singaporeans against foreigners, specifically Filipino migrant workers, in its postings (*Straits Times* 11 May 2015).

genuinely well liked and highly respected by Singaporeans in general, publicly commented that he was experiencing a sense of deep "frustration, anger and resentment" against the PAP among the electorate that was never there before (*Straits Times* 6 May 2011). He suggested that the opposition parties were acting as the "loudspeaker" for these negative sentiments, which appeared to be the case, given the massive turnouts at the WP rallies. Sensing the public anger, Prime Minister Lee apologized for not taking earlier action on housing demands and public transport problems; the public apology was a first for a PAP minister, let alone the Prime Minister (*Straits Times* 4 May 2011). The WP leader, Low Thia Khiang, who led his team against Minister Yeo, summed up the deep frustration among Singaporeans as the result of the PAP's "arrogance and overconfidence when they think they have successfully stripped all the power away from Singaporeans" (*Straits Times* 6 May 2011). The sense of powerlessness among Singaporeans in determining the trajectories of their lives had arguably been building up over the years. The pent-up frustrations, anger and resentment had all been waiting for tangible targets to focus on and the right moment to burst forth. That moment came on 7 May 2011.

The electorate delivered its message and it was a shock to all Singaporeans. The PAP received 60 percent of the popular votes cast, the lowest it had ever received since 1959. It lost seven contested seats, the greatest number lost since 1959. It also lost one GRC, the Aljunied GRC, the first time since GRCs had been introduced in 1989. The defeated PAP team was led by George Yeo. It included the only woman cabinet minister Lim Hwee Hua, one Malay senior minister of state, an incumbent MP and a first-time candidate who was touted to be destined for ministerial office. They were defeated by the WP team headed by Low Thia Khiang, the only veteran MP, and five untested individuals. The defeat of the popular George Yeo was particularly poignant as many who voted against him did so reluctantly, given the circumstances. If the WP had lost both the Hougang and Aljunied GRCs, the PAP would have had a clean sweep. The Aljunied GRC voters in particular thus had an additional national "responsibility" to keep opposition voices alive in parliament. An immediate consequence of the result was the announced resignation of Lee Kuan Yew from his cabinet position.

The election result was immediately hailed as a "watershed" by commentators proclaiming a "new normal" for Singapore's immediate future. The newly elected parliament immediately responded to the grievances raised during electioneering with a series of substantive policy changes. For instance, the pre-election reduction of migrant workers had resulted in a serious labor shortage, which badly affected labor-intensive industries, particularly the retail service sector. Nevertheless, against pressure from the business sector the government continued to hold down the number of new arrivals as it restructured the economy to increase technological and capital input, and intensify job training and retraining for local workers. In response to criticism that it habitually seeks economic growth at all costs, the government began to accept a "slow growth" future of 3 to 4 percent.

In public housing, the incumbent minister was replaced and the new minister immediately sped up supply, commissioning 100,000 units to be built by 2015. Additionally, new stringent rules on homeowner-ship were imposed on permanent residents, including the demand to dispose of any properties they might hold outside the country, if they were to buy a public housing flat. To reduce speculation, the down payment for second and third property purchases was increased from 10 percent to 30 percent. Furthermore, the total debt of an individual, including mortgage and credit card payments, should not exceed more than 60 percent of his/her monthly income. After all these "market cooling" regulations, the price increase in public housing finally slowed down in mid-2013. It began to fall in 2014 for successive financial quarters and to stabilize by the second half of 2016. Meanwhile, restrictions on foreign labor inflow also dampened rents in the private housing sector, discouraging speculative investments.

Social redistribution was also stepped up. Finance Minister Shanmugaratnam declared categorically, "we must redistribute" (2012: 3). Consequently, the following changes took place.

- Workfare that was introduced in 2008 as a temporary measure to supplement income for workers who earned below set income levels was made a permanent program.
- Additional cash grants for new home purchasers were extended to include the middle class.
- More welfare expenditure was directed towards the poor and the aged.
- A one-off SGD 8 billion dollars Pioneer Generation Fund was established to assist the aging generation who had earned low incomes in their youth during the 1950s and 1960s and now in their old age had little savings.

- A national healthcare system, Medicare Life, was put in place for the first time in 2014.
- To address class inequalities in educational achievement, a pre-school program in public school system was initiated.

Given these changes, the Finance Minister noted that the new parliament was tilting towards the "left of center."

In response to the criticism that it lacked consultation, the government embarked on a year-long, nationwide public consultation program called the "Our Singapore Conversation." A 26-member committee, which included newly elected PAP MPs, was set up to gather feedback from 50,000 Singaporeans regarding their opinions and aspirations for the future. Further, to continue "humanizing" the government, in his public speeches Prime Minister Lee began to showcase actual individuals who were self-resilient in spite of difficulties and handicaps and who benefited from government policies as illustrative "exemplary" Singaporeans, instead of displaying cold hard statistics as his predecessors were wont to do. Finally, in response to the increasing significance of the Internet and social media, every cabinet minister developed his/her own website and blogged on various platforms to engage the public. In these websites, they uploaded bits of personal routine life including photographs, just like other Internet users, but they also used these sites to announce public policies being considered by the government and draw public attention and discussion. All these efforts that the PAP government put in to address popular grievances did not go unnoticed. However, it was widely recognized that it was hard for the PAP government to regain the electorate's trust.

In 2015, Singapore commemorated the fiftieth anniversary of its independence with a year-long string of "SG50" celebration events at all levels of government—from special birth certificates for children born in 2015 to the return of the national day parade to the Padang, as in the year of independence. The nation lamented that Lee Kuan Yew did not live to see the parade as he died on 23 March. The outpouring of grief by Singaporeans was overwhelming: a non-stop queue filed past his body that lay in state for four days at Parliament House; every community center set up a memorial space for citizens who did not make it to Parliament House to pay their last respects and sign the book of condolence, and the route of his cortege on the day of his funeral was lined with Singaporeans, braving the rain, saying their final goodbye. Amidst the SG50 celebrations and the outpouring of affection for the founding Prime Minister, the PAP called for a general election on September 11, one year before it was necessary to do so. The result was another shock to Singaporeans.

This time all the seats, including the Tanjong Pagar GRC which had been headed by Lee Kuan Yew, were contested. The same massive crowds turned up at WP nightly rallies. The PAP introduced a string of new candidates who, the electorate was told, were destined for ministerial rank. It campaigned hard, focusing on face-to-face contacts with the electorate rather than media events. The WP argued that the responsiveness of the PAP government was due to its enlarged presence in parliament and, therefore, Singaporeans should vote to "entrench" the presence of the opposition party in there as well. Chee Soon Juan, the secretary general of the Singapore Democratic Party (SDP), who had been kept out of election for more than a decade due to bankruptcy caused by libel suits from PAP leaders, emerged as the leader of the SDP team that contested in the Holland-Bukit Timah GRC, which included a very articulate doctor/academic of public health, Paul Tambyah. The quality of candidates in the opposition parties had improved greatly, although among the smaller opposition parties, there were candidates whom most Singaporeans would not consider "qualified" for political office. There was a high public expectation that the opposition, especially the WP, would improve in their performance and even win additional GRCs.

The result: the PAP returned to power with a sharp increase in the popular vote, from 60 percent in 2011 to 69.8 percent in 2015. The WP clung to its six seats, narrowly escaping defeat in the Aljunied GRC by a very thin margin, which would return the country to the days of a purely PAP parliament. Pundits tried to come up with various "analyses" of the election outcome, such as the result being a sympathy vote for Lee Kuan Yew and a feel-good factor due to the SG50 celebrations. However, ultimately, it was likely because the PAP government had in the preceding four years successfully addressed the material grievances of Singaporeans by doing the following:

- improving public transport;
- bringing down prices of public housing;
- reducing immigration numbers;
- introducing Singaporean-first policies in various areas, including jobs;
- increasing social welfare spending and social transfer to the poor, needy and aged;

- introducing a universal medical care system; and,
- experimenting and planning for government-run early childhood education centres.

In other words, the PAP had succeeded in taking care of the so-called "bread and butter" issues or the material concerns of the citizens' everyday life, which it had always promised to deliver. The 2011 election turned out to be not only a "watershed" but possibly a brief aberration.

Conclusion

Decades of economic development and higher education attainment among the population, much to the credit of the PAP government, have spawned a middle-class society which increasingly demands a greater say in the ways it is governed. The cumulative number of middle-class educated individuals, constantly augmented by successive generations, no longer readily concedes leadership and accepts the decisions of their contemporaries in the PAP government, unlike the largely uneducated population during the time of the first-generation PAP leaders. As the gap in achievement between successive generations of politicians and the electorate has narrowed, all politicians have had to work harder to convince and persuade the electorate, rather than to decide "what was best" for them as Lee Kuan Yew's generation was able to do and, in fact, did. The need to consult, persuade, invite participation, and be inclusive and accountable in governance has progressively intensified since the early 1990s, when the Prime Minister's post was handed over to Goh Chok Tong and then to Lee Hsien Loong, who is now facing with increased urgency the task of selecting the next fourth generation of PAP leaders. It is estimated that by the time Lee steps down, his successor would have been in political office for slightly over a decade, a very short time relative to his own 20 years of "training" in different ministerial posts under Goh Chok Tong. After the 2015 general election, the widespread view among educated Singaporeans is that there is no identifiable Prime Minister-in-training among the fourth generation who are already cabinet ministers.

Meanwhile, as argued elsewhere, Singapore society has become too complex to be contained by authoritarianism—social class differences have become more visible; consumerism has affected everyone, generating a plethora of lifestyle choices; and personal beliefs have varied and "self-identity" has become a work in progress, subject to constant revisions because of exposure to different cultural beliefs and practices, not the least liberal Western ideas. This liberalization of culture and liberal self-formation is a dynamic process that does not look back but only looks forward; personal preferences and desires keep expanding and changing, transgressing limit after limit (Chua 2011b: 18). However, as the 2015 general election demonstrated, the political future of the nation will not be determined by the liberalizing cultural sphere but by the same "bread and butter" or materialist issues, such as affordable housing, employment and economic stability, issues which the PAP government has proven very adept at managing, judging from the institutions it has put in place since its early social democratic days. As a very frustrated cosmopolitan liberal law professor, playwright and public intellectual, Eleanor Wong (2015), ventilated after the 2015 general election, "This is a vote confirming the type of system that Singaporeans want to live under."

CONCLUSION
An Enduring System

It is an open world. But let's not think that we are all moving teleo-
logically towards that destination that you now see in the US or UK.
We all have to evolve and we all need some humility as to how we
progress democracy. (Tharman Shanmugaratnam, Second Deputy
Prime Minister and Minister for Finance, quoted in the *Straits Times*
20 May 2015)

IN 2015, SINGAPORE CELEBRATED ITS 50 Years Anniversary of Independence. On 23 March of the same year, Lee Kuan Yew, the man who
made building Singapore his life's work, passed away. There was a massive outpouring of grief among the citizens. It was an event of solidarity,
a materialization of the imagined nation. Inevitably, the question that
had been asked throughout his years as Prime Minister, Senior Minister
and finally, Minister Mentor from 1959 until 2011, was raised again
at home and abroad, "What will happen to Singapore after Lee Kuan
Yew?" The PAP government may be said to have already provided the
answer. Since Lee had stepped aside as the Prime Minister little had
changed. Over its more than 50 years in government, the PAP has put
in place an administrative and institutional system to ensure stable political and economic growth. This system will endure for the foreseeable
future, adjusting to changing contingencies but without upheaval.

Among the many reasons for the PAP government's self-confidence,
in addition to incorruptibility and technical executive competency, are:

- a highly selective process of inducting individuals into politics;
- an electoral parliamentary system that advantages itself as the incumbent government;

- an elected presidency that safeguards the national reserve;
- the national public housing program; and
- the state-capitalist wealth that makes a significant financial contribution to the annual national budget.

Each of these institutions has its own contingent problems and systemic contradictions. The induction system shows an increased narrowing of its recruitment base, with ministerial candidates drawn from the higher ranks of the civil service and military, and rank-and-file MP candidates chosen from individuals who have links with PAP leaders—for example, as former private secretaries, loyal grassroots organizers or, recently, as the children of past politicians. Although the PAP insists it selects only the best people for leadership positions, this practice has the potential for creating leaders who are out of touch with citizens and insensitive to their needs, and who view themselves as a privileged elite. Yet, even the harshest critics of elitism have to concede that Singapore should be governed by the best (Tan 2014). The process for electing the president is open to criticism as the rules for candidature are so restrictive and undemocratic that each election has a dearth of candidates for the position; indeed, there have been calls from the PAP ranks to scrap the elected presidency and return to an appointed president who is the ceremonial head of state. The public housing program has over the years developed systemic contradictions that require the government to make constant and vigilant policy adjustments to

- avoid situations that lead to either an over-supply or an under-supply of housing;
- maintain housing prices that ensure adequate retirement funds for an aging population; and
- keep housing prices affordable for new entrants into the housing market.

Finally, the state-capitalist sector is vulnerable to the vicissitudes of the trough and peaks of global capitalism. All these contingent and systemic problems require a high degree of alert maintenance. However, they are not reasons enough for the PAP government to abandon any of the institutions as the cost to the incumbent government's legitimacy would be too high.

The most important institution sustaining the legitimacy of the PAP government is the electoral parliamentary system. The government has never tried to capitalize on its hegemonic hold on power by abolishing the electoral system, in spite of Lee Kuan Yew's deep frustration with the fact of having to be elected and Prime Minister Goh Chok Tong's likening electoral politics to a spectator sport in which the spectators choose the team. While the PAP government has undoubtedly manipulated the rules of election to its advantage, there remains room for different political parties to field candidates. Moreover, the electioneering period allows the parties to voice public grievances on behalf of the electorate as the big turn-outs at opposition party rallies during every election attest to. The expression of these grievances in turn serves as feedback for the PAP government to demonstrate its responsiveness and sense of accountability in ameliorating the conditions of the aggrieved and to recover lost electoral ground. Skepticism regarding the PAP's willingness to subvert the electoral system was significantly reduced when the WP defeated George Yeo, a popular and capable minister. That Senior Minister Goh Chok Tong deemed Yeo too important for the Cabinet to lose (*Straits Times* 6 May 2011), his defeat lent credence to the PAP's claim that Singapore is a democracy and it governs by popular mandate.

The importance of the electoral parliamentary system in sustaining the legitimacy of the PAP government is often underestimated, even dismissed as a sham, because of what critics regard as the authoritarian excesses of Lee Kuan Yew. However skewed, the political significance of Singapore's electoral parliamentary system is brought into relief when one compares it with the other authoritarian states in East Asia. The military-backed, first-generation presidents of Taiwan and Korea set the stage for each nation's subsequent political development. In spite of their respective impressive economic development, without an electoral system to provide the mandate to govern, the two authoritarian regimes could not avoid popular demands for democratization, which eventually led to the introduction of elections as the basis of government legitimacy. Even if China transforms itself into a market economy, cleans up corruption and adheres more closely to the rule of law, the Communist Party will continue to suffer from a "democratic deficit" at home and abroad because it has yet to institute a process of popular elections. This point was emphasized by the commentator on China affairs, Pei Minxin (2015), who used the occasion of Lee Kuan Yew's passing to pen a message, presumably to the Chinese government that has been looking to Singapore for practical lessons:

By holding regular competitive elections, Mr. Lee effectively established a mechanism of political self-enforcement and accountability—he gave Singaporean voters the power to decide whether the PAP should stay in power. This mechanism has maintained discipline within the ruling elite and makes its promises credible.... Regrettably, most of the rest of the world has never given Mr Lee proper credit for crafting a hybrid system of authoritarianism and democracy that vastly improved the well-being of his country's citizens without subjecting them to the brutality and oppression [to] which many of Singapore's neighbours have resorted...Mr. Lee may have been sceptical about the benefits of democracy, but he was not viscerally hostile to it; he understood its usefulness.

This is an open secret that every analyst of Singapore's political development knows but will not always admit so nakedly.

In the cultural sphere, freedom of expression has been a major arena of contention. Limits on freedom of expression and the freedom to hold public gatherings have always been partly a response to the multiracial composition of the citizenry. The specter of racial violence as an imaginable perennial phenomenon in Singapore has turned the need to maintain racial and religious harmony into an instrument for controlling freedom of expression. Public discussions of race and religion are severely circumscribed. Any act that is perceived as potentially disruptive of racial and/or religious harmony, intended or otherwise, can be criminalized as sedition. In the new century, there are signs of intensified religiosity across all religions practised in Singapore. Consequently, the boundaries of contact zones between religions, and by extension race, continue to be vigilantly policed by the state because the large number of new immigrants and new citizens has unsettled the taken-for-granted multiracial tolerance among Singaporeans. This is reflected in the increasing use of the Sedition Act to deal with foreign individuals, who are deemed to have threatened racial and religious peace in speeches and especially in Internet postings. With the demise of communism, the only detainees held without trial have been alleged members of Islamic fundamentalist organizations. Significantly, in contrast to protests against the use of libel suits and detention to quash political dissenters, the increase in sedition charges and the detention of Islamic fundamentalists have received little public outcry.

Beyond race and religion, freedom of expression has continued to expand as cultural liberalization has increased in Singapore, which has led to more freedom of expression through life-style choices. The government's ability to constrain life-style choices is highly limited. For example, the government despairs at its limited ability to change the low marriage rate and low birthrate, especially among the tertiary-educated Singaporeans. It can only coax individuals to take responsibility for producing more children to maintain a stable population. Related to freedom of expression is freedom to sexuality and the increasingly open expression of LGBT relations. The right to polymorphous sexual preferences has alarmed the religious right wings of both the Christian and Muslim religions. As the LGBTs and religious conservatives are entirely within their rights to express their respective beliefs about sexuality (Chong 2011), the clash between these two groups leaves the government on the sidelines. For example in 2014, the government could not and did not intervene when Christian and Muslim individuals were exhorted to wear white on Pink Dot Day, which is a celebration of LGBT lifestyles in Hong Lim Park.

On the other hand, withholding of funds to theater groups that stage homosexual themes or the withdrawal of grants for graphic novels that satirize Singapore politics is a crude instrument that exposes the heavy hand of the state in censorship, discrediting the government's claim to promote arts for a "gracious" Singapore. There is one area where the PAP government appears to be intransigent in using heavy-handed suppression—the reinterpretation of Singapore's political history. Historical reinterpretations which raise doubts about the veracity of the Barisan leaders as communists have been actively countered by the government, which insists on the objectivity of the official history. The careers of some young revisionist historians in Singapore have ended before they began as they have been unable to secure academic positions in local universities.

Beyond the politically correct call for social cohesion and inclusivity, the current generation of PAP ministers is no longer concerned with establishing a common ideological framework for the nation, as it is increasingly obvious that the government's attempts to shape Singaporeans' social cultural values are no more than ineffective symbolic gestures. The government can state its stands but is unable to get citizens to abide by them. Culture will always remain a terrain of contestation with the government as one party in the contest, as it should be. While cultural liberalization will go a long way to satisfy the less politically minded and dissipate their frustration with the PAP government, continuing censorship will have exactly the opposite effect.

Freedom of choice and freedom of expression are highly individualistic in all areas of high and popular culture. However, there are no institutional structures that can act to shape the liberal side of cultural pluralism into a force for creating political pluralism.

In the balance between authoritarianism, electoral democracy and cultural liberalism, Singapore has been shifting closer to the electoral democratic and culturally liberal end. As international tolerance is replaced by condemnation for all modes of excessive repression and as Singapore's footprint in global affairs becomes more pronounced, each successive generation of PAP political leaders has been moving away from the style and substance of overt authoritarian/paternalistic governance. Although it is unlikely that the PAP will lose control of parliament in the next decade or beyond, there is nevertheless room to politicize different issues, singularly or in constellation. Each successive general election has seen the electorate using their votes to either put pressure on the government to change its policies and practices or to endorse them.

The instruments and institutions for democracy are already in place, albeit frequently manipulated to the advantages of the incumbent PAP government. However, a question remains: will there be greater political competition resulting in political pluralism in parliament? The answer will depend heavily on whether or not the other political parties are able to make inroads into the PAP's hegemony by winning more seats in general elections. Since 1984, evidence from past elections has shown that the electorate stands ready to register, with their votes, dissatisfaction with government policies which were unreasonably imposed on them. However, it remains an uphill task not because of authoritarianism but because of the PAP's proven capacity to recruit talent, execute long-term policies and plans, and improve the material lives of ordinary Singaporeans. The reversal of popular support for the PAP, from the low of the 2011 general election to 69.8 percent of the vote cast in the 2015 general election, attests to this. Paraphrasing the words of one of the WP candidates, there was not the same anger as there was in the 2011 election among the electorate. The electorate was heard, its unhappiness was addressed, and its everyday life problems were ameliorated. This led citizens to once again endorse the government for its efficiency and effectivity. The desire for political and parliamentary pluralism was put aside. All this suggests that the PAP has created an enduring political system—an electoral democracy that:

- disavows liberalism and promotes national and collective interests over individual freedoms, especially in the governing of race where mutual tolerance is paramount as a minimal necessary condition for social stability;
- restricts the rights to property by nationalizing land and regularly intervenes in the housing market to maintain affordability of housing for all;
- asserts the right of the state as an active entrepreneur in domestic and global economy, in order to generate income for social redistribution; and
- has shifted democracy away from politics of representation to politics of trusteeship couched in a vocabulary of accountability based on a morality of trust between the governing and the governed.

The voting behavior of Singaporeans suggests that they understand the electoral process and cast their votes rationally, which raises the question of whether or not the other political parties can offer or surpass the PAP's ability to govern. There appears to be no alternative political bases to be organized to challenge the political hegemony of the PAP in the foreseeable future for three reasons:

- Singapore does not have a capitalist class that is willing and able to fund alternative political parties;
- organized labor unions are firmly under the government's control; and
- the middle class is highly conservative for various reasons, including being directly or indirectly dependent on the extensive civil service and state enterprise network for employment, and the desire to protect their investments in property.

After more than 50 years of evolution, these three above features are likely to remain as the basic foundational institutions of Singapore's polity, economy and society.

Another hypothetical but heuristic question is: should another political party manage to unseat the PAP in parliamentary power, is it likely to dismantle the public housing program, privatize the state-enterprises, dissolve the sovereign wealth funds, remove the race-identity of Singaporeans and ideologically encourage the flourishing of liberal individualism and political pluralism? The answer would be "no" for four reasons.

- Public housing, is now effectively institutionalized and regarded by Singaporeans as a citizenship entitlement, and it will continue to be fundamental to the legitimacy of any future incumbent government. Furthermore, it will be useful in enabling the incumbent government to leverage it for other social policies.

- Dismantling the state-capitalist sector and sovereign wealth funds would deprive a future incumbent government of a very significant source of revenue which enables the politically popular low income tax regime and system of social redistribution. This is particularly important as globally successful companies are capitalizing on the highly varied tax regimes of different nations to avoid paying a significant level of tax on their profits to any government.

- The call by liberal Singaporeans for the government to remove the race marker on individual Singaporeans has ironically become a conservative gesture in a world in which multiple identities are being celebrated, where having an additional identity marker is a strategic cultural resource for the individual.

- The geopolitical and geospatial reality of Singapore's smallness and its multiple vulnerabilities weigh heavily in the beliefs of every Singaporean and militate against excessive individualism that could pull the country in different directions, unravelling the materially prosperous and socially secure life that Singaporeans know. Since the beginning of the twenty-first century, liberal democratic capitalism has lost much of its attractiveness globally. The problem is partly political and economic in nature as illustrated by gridlock politics in the US, lack of regulation and the socially unconscionable greed of individuals in the financial sector that led to the 2008 global financial crisis, from which debt-laden developed nations have found it difficult to recover, especially those in the European Union. The sustained financial stagnation has led to the rise of right-wing xenophobic political parties in liberal Europe as a response to massive migration from the collapsing Islamic states in the Middle East and financially failed states of Africa.

All these factors would suggest that the success of the political economic system put in place by the PAP government is likely to survive for the foreseeable future, even if the PAP loses control of parliament.

Singapore as a Model?

Russian and European socialism has failed and the individualizing tendencies of global capitalism and the ideological hegemony of liberalism have conceptually de-territorialized all locations into a trajectory of sameness of liberal democratic capitalism. Singapore's apparent success in building an electoral parliamentary system without liberalism might suggest another path to political development, which shows why social and collective responsibility is preferable to the atomizing tendency of liberal capitalism. However, the Singapore story is frequently dismissed as "interesting" but "unique" on account of the country's small size and is thus assumed to bear no lessons for larger-sized countries. To the extent that a nation's development is an aggregate effect of the historical contingencies that it faces, no nation's development can be wholly replicated elsewhere; Singapore cannot be cloned. Nevertheless, more and more city mayors, business leaders, civil society activists, journalists and others from developing nations see Singapore as a model (Chua 2011). For example, after the Crimea's violent breakaway from Ukraine, the head of the Crimea Affairs Ministry was reported to have said, "I blew the dust off the book *Singapore: From Third World to First* by Lee Kuan Yew to have another read when I became minister.... We will pursue Singapore's model in Crimea, we will ensure a comfortable business environment here" (*Straits Times* 24 May 2014). Such statements are used for different purposes by different categories of social actors: civil society activists use it to indict their governments' failures in governance; mayors use it to project an imagined future to entice investment; and capitalists use it to push different levels of government into supporting the development of infrastructure. Such moves are not necessarily followed by concrete action.

However, interest in "the Singapore model" is not all rhetoric. For example in 1992, the late Deng Xiaoping, the man responsible for the marketization of the Chinese economy, instructed Chinese state bureaucrats to study Singapore: "Singapore's social order is rather good. Its leaders exercise strict management. We should learn from their experiences, and we should do a better job than they do."[1] Since then, joint government urban projects between China and Singapore have been initiated. Among these projects are the Suzhou Industrial Park (Pereira 2003) and an urban management training program for potential Chinese mayors, which has been running for more than two decades at the Nanyang Technological University. (A similar program can also be found in the Lee Kuan Yew School of Public Policy at the National

---

[1] http://www.nytimes.com/1992/08/09/weekinreview/the-world-china-sees-Singapore-as-a-model-for-progress.html [accessed 20 Apr. 2015].

University of Singapore.) More generally, according to George Yeo, a former Singapore Minister for Foreign Affairs, China's

> …interest in the Singapore experiment is episodic. From time to time when it confronts issues and it scours the world for solutions, it looks at what Singapore does. Sometime it likes what it sees, sometimes it does not like what it sees. And then it draws and abstracts the relevant lessons. This of course puts Singapore in a rather interesting position vis-à-vis China.[2]

That the largest nation in Asia is studying the smallest for useful lessons is not entirely surprising. As the governing party of a single-party state, the Chinese Communist Party would like to replicate the PAP's success in using capitalist principles and practices for economic development to maintain a relatively even economic distribution while providing widespread upward social mobility for most citizens and creating a very large middle class without having to share political power.

However, "Singapore as a model" does not refer to the mode of governance that is so central to Singapore's success story. Overburdened by a legacy of authoritarianism, no one will publicly proclaim the desire to replicate Singapore's one-party dominant parliamentary system, although one may silently envy and wish for a single-party government's efficacy and efficiency in executing government plans. If "Singapore as a model" were to be put into practice, it would translate into a question of how some policies and practices of the PAP government might be productively transferred and reconfigured elsewhere according to local conditions. Of the three foundational institutional practices discussed above, state multiracialism is perhaps the most locally context bound and least mobile; the planning and programming of housing estate developments and the organization of state-capitalism through SOEs and SWFs can be, and have been, emulated in other countries, especially those with developing economies.

State Multiracialism

Singapore's state multiracialism is not easily transferable because few new post-colonial nations have populations with an overwhelming

---

[2] http://beyondsg.typepad.com/beyondsg/2010/07/speech-by-minister-george-yeo-chinas-reemergence-on-the-global-stage-at-the-futurechina-global-forum.html [accessed 20 Apr. 2015].

majority of non-indigenous people who are not descendants of the colonizing race. It is this demographic characteristic that made the state multiracialism policy a political necessity in the founding of independent Singapore. The merit of the policy is that the explicit recognition of racial and ethnic differences provides the rationale for emphasizing racial harmony as a public good, which is socially and morally desirable. Equality among all racial groups requires the majority race-group to accept that it is just one among many race groups and, in principle, it has the same status and entitlements as the smallest race group. It also requires the government to stay above all race-groups, even if its leadership is drawn largely from the majority group, to not only adjudicate potential conflicts of interests among the groups fairly but also to vigilantly police, and intervene if necessary, when race-related concerns and issues between the races arise with the view of sustaining harmony for the long term. These necessary conditions for state multiracialism are difficult to fulfill in practice. Consider the following examples in Singapore:

- Although the presence of minority MPs in parliament is guaranteed, the numerical superiority of Singapore's Huaren MPs makes this guarantee a rescindable concession.
- The Huaren have to contend with the progressive atrophy of Chinese languages and cultural competence with the passing of each successive generation because of the increasing dominance of English as the economically advantageous language.
- The Malay minority has had to suffer doubts about their loyalty to the nation, one manifestation of which is that most Malay young men are not conscripted into the armed forces.

These and other grievances are tolerated by the Huaren and Malays as prices to be paid for the desired, and sometimes enforced, racial harmony.

If the maintenance of state multiracialism is already fraught with contradictions in Singapore, it is difficult to imagine how and why it would be adopted and adapted elsewhere. The situation in most newly independent nations is typically the following. The majority of the population is the indigenous people who have proprietary claim to the new nation. Because the former colonial government displaced or suppressed all indigenous cultural symbols, including language, the indigenous majority immediately legislates its culture and language as the nation's main culture and language while actively suppressing cultures and languages of the minority groups or simply neglecting them. The leaders of the indigenous majority population often feel duty bound to advantage their constituency over minority groups, especially if the latter are of migrant stock, regardless of how localized they may be. A moderate manifestation of these two factors is the case of Singapore's neighbor, Malaysia, where the demand for Malay supremacy in politics and culture has become increasingly aggressive in recent years. A more extreme manifestation is the case of Sri Lanka. The Sri Lankan government precipitated a protracted civil war with the Tamil Tigers from 1983 to 2009 when it sought to reverse the privileges granted to the Tamil minority by the British colonial regime by instituting measures that would give advantages to the indigenous Sinhalese majority.

However, it is now widely recognized that the supposed race-blindness of liberal democracy is itself a denial of racism and thus an ideological obstacle for ethnic or racial minorities to raise their grievances against racism. The behavior of Western Europeans in recent years has also lifted the veil of liberal multiculturalism as a gloss, if not a pretense, for cultural assimilation of minority groups into the majority population. Political leaders of the mainstream political parties have called for education to inculcate national values in minority groups who are unwilling and unable to negotiate and modify the basic values which are fundamental to their identities, as exemplified by Islamic migrant communities. Far right-wing nationalist parties, once confined to the fringes of European political life, are gaining popular electoral support through increasingly vociferous and violent means of fanning of xenophobia and racism. These developments suggest that the European experiment with liberal multiculturalism has all but collapsed.

Such developments behoove us to explicitly recognize the dangers of both the mainstream liberal and far right responses to the presence of minority ethnic and racial groups. The issue is how to design a race management system in which such explicit recognition does not lead to discriminatory racial profiling and official racism that create racial conflict. At its minimal practical level, Singapore's multiracialism policy explicitly recognizes the differences between the races but leaves the substance of the differences to groups and individual themselves to work out, beyond official gestures of equal distribution of national resources, for example, providing public holidays for all race groups. Its primary concern is with the maintenance of racial harmony, and doing so has given rise to systemic contradictions that it has to manage continuously, including occasionally curtailing a group's or an individual's rights. This has possibly made state multiracialism in Singapore an object of criticism rather than emulation.

Exporting Urban Planning Practices

To any visitor, Singapore's overall economic success is immediately visible in the total physical and spatial image of the island as a modern metropolis. Singapore is frequently mentioned as a model for emulation by city mayors, urban planners and big private developers in Asia. According to urban historian Janaki Nair, since the 1980s, "Singapore has dominated the vision of Bangalore's future" because

> Singapore is an achievable ideal, a realizable utopia as the city-state shares the common legacy of colonial rule with Bangalore, is an Asian society with some common social features, and above all, has transformed its spatial and economic identity in less than 40 years. (Nair 2005: 124)

At a more critical level, the recognition of Singapore as an illustration of a successful global city by state actors and private developers represents "a certain ideal characterized by a strong state, a global orientation, a master-planned urban environment and a technocratic and market-oriented mode of planning" (Shatkin 2011: 80).

> In practice, Singapore planners, in and outside the state-planning office have ... transformed home-grown contingent efforts at nation-building into abstract, technical lessons of urban economic development that can be imparted internationally, that can be exported as urban planning expertise and management know-how, either as good-will in the form of international aid [on the part of the government] or as profit-driven commercial consultancies. (Chua 2011: 36)

The totality of the urban planning experience and practices of Singapore has been disaggregated and abstracted as a set of formulae of best practices that can be dispersed, singularly or in constellation, across space and time to be reassembled in new configurations in completely new contexts. The technocratic, master-planning practices in the highly integrated infrastructure system and so apparent in the ubiquitous public housing estates are being exported to many developing economies in Asia and the Middle East. As of 2008, Jurong International, a subsidiary of the Jurong Town Corporation with experience of industrial park developments domestically, had a "project presence spanning 139 cities across 37 countries, amassing more than 1,000 projects worldwide."[3] Surbana, initially the planning arm of the HDB, was transferred as an independent enterprise to Temasek Holdings and currently has projects in China, India, Qatar, the United Arab Emirates, South Africa and all the ten members in the Association of Southeast Asian Nations. The consultancy services provided by these companies include: master planning; concept planning; infrastructure planning; architectural design; and mechanical, civil, structural and electrical engineering. The scale of the projects ranges from building single industrial commercial buildings and residential estates to reconceptualizing city districts to designing whole towns that have yet to be built (Shatkin 2014: 134). To date, the most comprehensive urban development project is the Suchou Industrial Park (SIP), located outside Shanghai, a joint-venture between China and Singapore (Pereira 2003). Its apparent success was such that, according to Prime Minister Lee Hsien Loong, in every city he visited during his week-long tour of inland China in September 2010, "the local Chinese government leaders want an SIP-like park of their own" (*Straits Times* 12 Sept. 2010). In 2015, four of the biggest state-owned planning and development enterprises were merged into a single entity, with an aggregate value of approximately SGD 5 billion: Surbana-Jurong International will provide building and engineering services while Ascendas and Singbridge will invest and hold assets.[4] In the same year, the Singapore government was appointed by Chandrababu Naidu, the chief minister of the Indian state Andhra Pradesh, to develop the master plan for a new capital city, ten times the size of the island of Singapore, because its existing capital, Hyderabad, was transferred to the new split-away state of Telangana. The master planning was completed by Surbana-Jurong International in 2016. However, projected capital investments for Singbridge's residential property development and Ascendas' industrial property development have yet to proceed at this time of writing.[5]

---

[3] This quotation was taken from the Jurong International website which the company closed after it was incorporated into Surbana-Jurong.
[4] http://areit.listedcompany.com/newsroom/PRESS_RELEASE_JTC_AND_TEMASEK_TO_CREATE_INTEGRATED_URBAN_SOLUTIONS_PLATFORM_16_FEB_2015.pdf [accessed 27 Apr. 2015].
[5] http://news.asiaone.com/news/singapore/singapore-consortium-develop-andhra-pradeshs-new-capital [accessed 25 Apr. 2015].

The prevailing social and political conditions of each of the Singapore-aspiring locations differ significantly. Consequently, each new assemblage generates unintended consequences that deviate greatly from developments in Singapore. For example, when transferred to Vietnam and China, the guidelines and practices for comprehensively planned self-sufficient public housing estates were applied to develop gated communities for the privileged. The politically motivated social redistribution and the integration of class and race in Singapore's public housing estates was replaced by the accentuation of class distinction, segregation and exclusion. In another instance, an effort to develop a Housing Provident Fund modeled after Singapore's CPF system for homeownership in China failed completely to directly assist personal home purchases. Instead, the fund was used largely as loans to developers to finance construction of affordable housing (Chen and Deng 2014: 940–1). Without the social democratic motivation that undergirds Singapore's public housing system, the knowledge transfer from Singapore to China has produced diametrically opposite social and political consequences. Closer to the spirit of Singapore's public housing program is a slum upgrading project in São Paulo, Brazil. Labeled "Cingapura," the project "is the image of the future, the formal, brightly painted, ordered housing that is the counter-world to the Brazilian *favela* and its constellations of informality" (Roy 2011: 332). The project recalls the similar "emergency flats" that were the humble beginnings of the Singapore public housing system, and hopefully also embraces the ambition to house the whole nation.

State Capitalism

All varieties of capitalism are heavily dependent on the specificities of national history and institutional culture (Peck and Theodore 2007). Nevertheless, the PAP government's processes for growing state-owned enterprises (SOEs) can be adopted by others. As analyzed in Chapter 6, there were three paths to establishing SOEs in Singapore. Of these, the first pathway—joint-ventures with foreign partners—is the most conventional and ubiquitous path. The second pathway is direct investment by the state and requires no further elaboration. The third pathway is the transformation of suppliers of public and government services into profitable SOEs. This is more controversial politically. It might be argued that it is morally reprehensible for a government to profit from its citizens in providing necessary services, such as electricity, water and telecommunication services. However, it is evident that society-wide undifferentiated public subsidies for essential services produce a very un-equal distribution of benefits, favoring those who are better off relative to those who are poor. Additionally, sustained long-term subsidies can drain away financial resources that are desperately needed for social development.

For example, in Indonesia and Malaysia, annual state subsidies for fuel have amounted to tens of billions in each government's local currency. Attempts by both governments to reduce subsidies have been consistently met with public protests, forcing the governments to rescind any price increase in the interest of being re-elected. However, the Indonesian government, under the current incumbent President Joko Widodo, who is not part of the endemically corrupt political economic establishment, successfully reduced fuel subsidies by 30 percent as of January 2015, six months after his election. He promised to use the savings for health and education spending. In contrast, profits derived from Singapore's SOE suppliers remain in the public coffers, a signifi-cant portion of which is used to annually defray the costs of governance and enhance social redistribution to the socially disadvantaged, particu-larly the elderly in a rapidly aging population.

The success of Singapore's SOEs has a potential unintended socio-political effect. Once a successful SOE has consolidated its position in the domestic market, it is able to discourage and keep out competitors from local and foreign entrepreneurs in the same business. The aggre-gated effect of successful SOEs thus dampens the emergence of a domestic industrial capitalist class, which is capable of exercising power over the government/state in self-interest. This is in sharp contrast to the case of South Korea, where the government intervened with indus-trial policies that assisted selective privately owned export industries with a definite potential to succeed (Johnson 1982; Wade 1990; Amsden 1989; Stubbs 2009). As a consequence, the Korean state has over time helped to engender a powerful local capitalist class that owns globalized enterprises. Members of this class use its financial power to influence public policies, align themselves with different political parties or fac-tions and ultimately, place themselves beyond the control of the state (Chang 2010: 101–28). This difference in capitalist class formation accounts for the absence of one of the organized contestants for power that the PAP has had to face in Singapore (Pereira 2008).

Successful Singapore SOEs hold important lessons, particularly for centrally-planned socialist economies in transition to a market economy.

In such transitions, the critical question is how to reform the generally inefficient SOEs. The Russian experience of wholesale privatization resulted in the emergence of oligarchs who took control of the economy away from the state. This was a negative lesson quickly learned by China and Vietnam. China opted for the gradual shrinking of the presence of SOEs in the market (Guthrie and Wang 2007: 102–3), allowing smaller and non-strategic SOEs to be merged or acquired by the private companies, thus enabling the new private sector to grow in the economy (Wen and Xu 1997). Similar processes were undertaken in Vietnam (Fforde and deVylder 1996). The Chinese state has retained SOEs in strategic sectors, such as banking, telecommunication and energy industries (Cornish 2012), and injects capital to grow them into successful multinational enterprises. Big SOEs within a specific industry are also merged in order to compete for projects globally. For example, two state-owned train-makers, the China CNR Corp. and CSR Corp., are to be "combined into a single huge conglomerate to compete with foreign players and prevent infighting between them" (*Straits Times* 28 Apr. 2015).

Just like successful Singapore SOEs transforming themselves into publicly listed corporations, the Chinese government has progressively transformed retained SOEs into "shareholding companies" (Guthrie and Wang 2007: 105), with investments from the private sector. The four wholly state-owned banks—Construction Bank, Commercial and Industrial Bank, Agricultural Bank and Bank of China—have been corporatized and publicly listed, with the China Investment Corporation, a sovereign wealth fund, retaining the majority share (Li 2009: 1510). With corporatization, the banks are now accountable not only to their major shareholder, the Chinese state, but more importantly to their international investors, like Singapore's Temasek Holdings which has significant stakes in all four banks. Corporatization thus ensures international standard accounting practices, transparent transactions and the payment of regular dividends to the shareholders. In this way, corporatization has inadvertently become an additional instrument to weed out corruption among the Chinese SOEs.

There appears to be a significant operational difference between China's and Singapore's SOEs. Singaporean SOEs act like capitalist enterprises, fully focused on profit-making. Half of the aggregated profits generated by all the SOEs are channeled subsequently to the annual national budget for social redistribution by the government. The practice is to first generate profits and then redistribute. In contrast,

Chinese SOEs are directly held responsible for their employees' social welfare and the political concerns of the state. For example, laying off redundant employees creates economic hardship for laid-off employees while increased unemployment also creates a political problem for the state. Chinese SOEs are expected to avoid both causing economic hardship for their workers and contributing to the failure the state's economic policies. Forced into having to manage two different sets of often conflicting functions reduces the SOEs ability to maximize profits. From a strictly capitalist enterprise point of view, this failure to maximize profit is seen as a flaw, largely caused by state intervention in the management of companies by the Communist Party-appointed directors, whose duty it is to ensure that the social and political concerns of the state are taken care of. However, this balancing of social responsibility and profit-making may be read as part of an experiment to build a market socialism with Chinese characteristics.

In recent years, the Chinese government has been keenly studying different aspects of Singapore (Ortmann and Thompson 2014). Part of the rapid and massive accumulation of foreign reserves derived from the export-oriented industrialization was reorganized as SWFs, after studying Singapore's GIC and Temasek Holdings (Cognato 2008). Xiao Yaqing, the head of China's State-Owned Assets Supervision and Administration Commission (SASAC), stated, "Temasek has always been a role model" (*Sunday Times* 13 Mar. 2016). A state-capitalist sector is being forged out of the retained SOEs and new SWFs, just as in Singapore. If China is able to successfully transform and institutionalize its state capitalism, despite its lack of democracy, liberal free market capitalism may be said to have met its match. We will see the emergence of China as a hegemonic single-party state with a strong state capitalist sector in a developed market economy which is an integral part of global capitalism where the material life of the majority of its population is progressively improving—in short, a Singapore writ large.

Conclusion

After close to six decades of continuously governing Singapore, the PAP government is now in its transition to a fourth generation of political leadership, and it has developed a very stable political system. This system features a decidedly anti-liberal social management system that places social interests above individual rights and freedoms and an economy that is a mix of state-owned and private capital. Singapore's cultural sphere has been expanded and liberalized, but the political sphere has not made any concession to ideological pluralism. It is a system that will endure for the foreseeable future because it has the general popular support of Singaporeans, who have come to believe in the efficacy and efficiency of a single-party dominant government, as long as it is responsive to their largely material demands, which the PAP government is. Although Singaporeans have become adept in using their electoral support to negotiate with the PAP, as reflected in the fluctuating levels of support during general elections, they have not shown any desire to push the PAP out of its ruling position.

Internationally there appear to be separate evaluations of the Singapore political and economic systems. Politically, there is recognition that there is in place a competitive election system, which is inching towards a more level playing field. However, in a world where democracy and liberalism are conceptually inseparable, the PAP government is considered non-democratic, especially in light of the PAP's explicit disavowal of liberalism. At best, it is seen as a case of contested authoritarianism. This, however, appears to be of no consequence to the PAP leadership, which, if anything, is more confident of its ideological beliefs and above all its own nationalist policies and practices. This confidence is reinforced by the warm reception that the PAP government has received internationally from all types of governments and global institutions, especially financial ones. It is also reinforced by the frequent references to Singapore as a model of development for emerging and developing economies. In this last context, the Chinese government's close observation of Singapore's state capitalist system and replication of some of its best practices is most consequential. Should China succeed in developing a robust state capitalist sector which contributes significantly and steadily to its annual revenue, it could demonstrate that state capitalism is a more stable system than a liberal democracy which is dependent entirely on the willingness of enterprise in the free market to live up to its social responsibilities through taxes. Should that happen, the Singapore political economic system under the PAP is likely to be even more resistant to change, without a significant global political and/or economic upheaval.

BIBLIOGRAPHY

Alagappa, Muthiah, ed. *Taiwan's Presidential Politics: Democratization and Cross-straits Relations in the Twentieth-first Century*. Armonk, NY: M.E. Sharpe, 2001.

Aljunied, Syed Muhd Khairudin. *Colonialism, Violence and Muslims in Southeast Asia: The Maria Hertogh Controversy and its Aftermath*. London: Routledge, 2009.

Amsden, A.H. *Asia's Next Giant: South Korea and Late Industrialization*. New York: Oxford University Press, 1989.

Asher, G. Mukul. *Social Adequacy and Equity of the Social Security Arrangements in Singapore*. Singapore: Times Academic Press, 1991.

Asher, M. and Nandy, A. "Singapore's Policy Responses to Aging, Inequality and Poverty: An Assessment." *International Social Security Review* 81 (2008): 43–60.

Back, Les and Shamser Sinha. "New Hierarchies of Belonging." *European Journal of Cultural Studies* 15, no. 2 (2012): 139–54.

Bain, William. *Between Anarchy and Society: Trusteeship and the Obligation of Power*. Oxford: Oxford University Press, 2003.

Baker, Jim. *Crossroads: A Popular History of Malaysia & Singapore*. Singapore: Times Books International, 1999.

Balin, Bryan J. *Sovereign Wealth Funds: A Critical Analysis*. 2009. https://jscholarship.library.jhu.edu/bitstream/handle/1774.2/32826/Sovereign%20Wealth%20Funds%20A%20Critical%20Analysis%20032008.pdf [accessed 11 June 2009].

Barr, Michael. *The Ruling Elite of Singapore: Networks of Power and Influence*. London: I.B. Tauris, 2014.

Bell, Daniel. *The End of Ideology*. Glencoe, Illinois: Free Press, 1960.

Bell, Daniel A. "Communitarian Philosophy and East Asian Politics." In *Communitarian Politics in Asia*, ed. Chua Beng Huat, 25–45. London: Routledge, 2004.

————. *China's New Confucianism: Politics and Everyday Life in a Changing Society*. Princeton: Princeton University Press, 2008.

Bell, Daniel A., et al. *Towards Illiberal Democracy in Pacific Asia*. London: Macmillan Press, 1995.

Bell, Daniel A. and Hahm Chaibong, eds. *Confucianism for the Modern World*. Cambridge, UK: Cambridge University Press, 2003.

Blackburn, Kevin and Karl Hack. *War Memory and the Making of Modern Malaysia and Singapore*. Singapore: NUS Press, 2012.

Bloodworth, Dennis. *The Tiger and the Trojan Horse*. Singapore: Times Books International, 1986.

Bowen, John. "On the Political Construction of Tradition: *Gotong Royong* in Indonesia." *Journal of Asian Studies* 45, no. 3 (1986): 545–61.

Brown, David. *The State and Ethnic Politics in South-East Asia*. London: Routledge, 1996.

Case, William. *Politics in Southeast Asia: Democracy or Less*. Richmond: Curzon Press, 2002.

Chalmers, Ian. "Loosening State Control in Singapore: The Emergence of Local Capital as a Political Force." *Southeast Asian Journal of Social Science* 20 (1992): 57–84.

Chan Heng Chee. *Singapore: The Politics of Survival*. Singapore: Oxford University Press, 1971.

————. *A Sensation of Independence: A Political Biography of David Marshall*. Singapore: Oxford University Press, 1984.

————. "The PAP and the Structuring of the Political System." In *Management of Success: The Moulding of Modern Singapore*, ed. K.S. Sandhu and P. Wheatley, 70–89. Singapore: Institute of Southeast Asian Studies, 1989.

Chan, Joseph. *Confucian Perfectionism*. Princeton: Princeton University Press, 2014.

Chang Chin Chiang and Yi Yan. *History of Clan Associations in Singapore*. Singapore: Federation of Chinese Clan Associations, 2005.

Chang Kyung Sup. "Chaebol: The Logic of Familial Capitalism." In *South Korea under Compressed Modernity: Family Political Economy in Transition*, ed. Chang Kyung Sup, 101–28. London: Routledge, 2010.

————. "The Anti-communitarian Family? Everyday Conditions of Authoritarian Politics in South Korea." In *Communitarian Politics in Asia*, ed. Chua Beng Huat, 57–77. London: Routledge, 2009.

Chatterjee, Partha. *The Nation and its Fragments*. Princeton: Princeton University Press, 1993.

————. *Lineages of Political Society: Studies in Postcolonial Democracy*. New York: Columbia University Press, 2011.

Chen, Jie and Lan Deng. "Financing Affordable Housing through Compulsory Saving: The Two-decade Experience of Housing Provident Fund in China." *Housing Studies* 29, no. 7 (2014): 937–58.

Cheng, Siok Wah. "Economic Change and Industrialization." In *A History of Singapore*, ed. Ernest C.T. Chew and Edwin Lee, 182–215. Singapore: Oxford University Press, 1991.

Cheong Yip Seng. *OB Markers: My Straits Times Story*. Singapore: Straits Times Press, 2012.

Chia, N.C. "Retirement Financing Options for Singaporeans: Issues and Challenges." Paper presented at the Launch of the Singapore Research Nexus, National University of Singapore, 1 Mar. 2011.

Chin, James. "Electoral Battles and Innovations: Recovering Lost Ground." In *Impressions of the Goh Chok Tong Years in Singapore*, ed. Bridget Welsh, James Chin, Arun Mahizhnan and Tan Tarn How, 71–82. Singapore: NUS Press, 2009.

Chin, Peng. *My Side of History*. Singapore: Media Masters, 2003.

Chong, Terence, ed. *The AWARE Saga: Civil Society and Public Morality in Singapore*. Singapore: NUS Press, 2011.

Chua Beng Huat. "Looking for Democratization in Post-Soeharto Indonesia." *Contemporary Southeast Asia* 15, no. 2 (1993): 131–60.

————. *Communitarian Ideology and Democracy in Singapore*. London: Routledge, 1995.

————. *Political Legitimacy and Housing: Stakeholding in Singapore*. London: Routledge, 1997.

————. "'Asian Values' Discourse and the Resurrection of the Social." *Positions: East Asian Culture Critiques* 7, no. 2 (1999): 573–92.

————, ed. *Consumption in Asia: Lifestyles and Identities*. London: Routledge, 2000a.

————. "Public Housing Residents as Clients of the State." *Housing Studies* 15, no. 1 (2000b): 45–60.

————. "Multiculturalism in Singapore: An Instrument of Social Control." *Race and Class* 44, no. 3 (2003a): 58–77.

————. "Maintaining Housing Values under the Condition of Universal Home Ownership." *Housing Studies* 18, no. 5 (2003b): 765–80.

————. "Communitarianism without Competitive Politics in Singapore." In *Communitarian Politics in Asia*, ed. Chua Beng Huat, 78–101. London: Routledge, 2004.

————. "The Cost of Membership in Ascribed Community." In *Multiculturalism in Asia*, ed. Will Kymlicka and Baogang He, 170–95. Oxford: Oxford University Press, 2005.

————. "Singapore as model." In *Worlding Cities: Asian Experiments and the Art of Being Global*, ed. Ananya Roy and Aihwa Ong, 29–54. Chichester: Wiley-Blackwell, 2011a.

————. "Making Singapore's Liberal Base Visible." In *The AWARE Saga: Civil Society and Public Morality in Singapore*, ed. Terence Chong, 14–24. Singapore: NUS Press, 2011b.

———. "Navigating between Limits: Future of Public Housing in Singapore." *Housing Studies* 29, no. 4 (2014): 520–33.

Chua, Lynette J. *Mobilizing Gay Singapore: Rights and Resistance in an Authoritarian State*. Singapore: NUS Press, 2014.

Clark, G.L. and A. Monk. "Government of Singapore Investment Corporation (GIC): Insurer of Last Resort and Bulwark of Nation-state Legitimacy." *The Pacific Review* 23, no. 4 (2010): 429–51.

Clutterbuck, Richard. *Conflict and Violence in Singapore and Malaysia 1945–1983*. Singapore: Graham Brash (Pte) Ltd., 1984.

Cognato, Michael H. "China Investment Corporation: Threat or Opportunity." *NBR Analysis* 19, no. 1 (2008): 9–36. Seattle, WA: National Bureau of Asian Research.

Cohen, Benjamin J. "Sovereign Wealth Funds and National Security: The Great Tradeoff." *International Affairs* 85, no. 4 (2009): 713–31.

Cornish, M. "Behaviour of Chinese SOEs: Implications for Investments and Cooperation in Canada." Ottawa, Ontario: Canadian International Council and Canadian Council of Chief Executives, 2012.

Dallmayr, Fred. "Democracy and Multiculturalism." In *Democracy and Difference: Contesting the Boundaries of the Political*, ed. Seyla Benhabib, 278–94. Princeton: Princeton University Press, 1996.

Davis, Deborah. "Urban Consumer Culture." In *Culture in Contemporary China*, ed. M. Hockx and J. Strauss, 170–87. Cambridge: Cambridge University Press, 2005.

Devan, Janadas. "Succeeding Charisma." In *Impressions of the Goh Chok Tong Years in Singapore*, ed. Bridget Welsh, James Chin, Arun Mahizhnan and Tan Tarn How, 27–33. Singapore: NUS Press, 2009.

Duruz, Jean and Gaik Cheng Khoo. "Making Rojak…or Eating 'Together-in-difference'?" Introduction to *Eating Together: Food, Space and Identity in Malaysia and Singapore*. Lanham: Rowman and Littlefield, 2015.

Edelstein R.H. and Lum Sau Kim "Housing Prices, Wealth Effects and the Singapore Macro-economy." *Journal of Housing Economics* 13, no. 4 (2004): 342–67.

Esping-Andersen, Cøsta. *The Three Worlds of Welfare Capitalism*. Cambridge: Polity Press, 1990.

Etzioni, Amitai, ed. *The Essential Communitarian Reader*. Boulder: Rowan and Littlefield Publishers, 1998.

Favell, Adrian. "Applied Philosophy at the Rubicon: Will Kymlicka's 'Multicultural Citizenship'." *Ethical Theory and Moral Practice* 1, no. 2 (1998): 255–78.

Fforde, Adam and S. de Vylder. *From Plan to Market: The Economic Transition in Vietnam*. Boulder, CO: Westview Press, 1996.

Fish, Stanley. "Boutique multiculturalism, or why liberals are incapable of thinking hate speech." *Critical Inquiry* 23, no. 2 (1997): 378–95.

Fong, Sip Chee. *The PAP Story: The Pioneering Years.* Singapore: Times Periodicals, 1980.

Fukuyama, Francis. *The End of History and the Last Man.* London: Penguin, 1992.

George, Cherian. "Consolidating Authoritarian Rule: Calibrated Coercion in Singapore." *Pacific Review* 20, no. 2 (2007): 127–45.

————. *Freedom from the Press: Journalism and State Power in Singapore.* Singapore: NUS Press, 2012.

Glazer, Nathan. *We Are All Multiculturalists Now.* Cambridge, MA: Harvard University Press, 1997.

Goh Chok Tong. "Speech at the Congratulatory Dinner given by Marine Parade GRC Grassroots Leaders." National Archives of Singapore, gct\1991\gct0208.doc, 1991.

————. "Singapore: Global City of Buzz, Home for Us." http://www.nas.gov.sg/archivesonline/speeches/view-html?filename=20101105002.htm [accessed 11 Nov. 2014].

Goh Keng Swee. "A Socialist Economy that Works." In *Socialism that Works,* ed. C.V. Devan Nair, 77–85. Singapore: Federal Press, 1976.

————. "Socialism in Singapore." In *The Economics of Modernization,* ed. Goh Keng Swee, 209–15. Singapore: Asia Pacific Press, 1972.

Gow, David. "German Government Seeks Power to Veto Takeovers by Sovereign Wealth Funds." *The Guardian,* 21 Aug. 2008. http://www.guardian.co.uk/world/2008/aug/21/germany.mergersandacquisitions [accessed 19 Oct. 2009].

Gray, John. *Enlightenment's Wake: Politics and Culture at the Close of the Modern Age.* London: Routledge, 1995.

Guthrie, Doug and Junmin Wang. "Business Organizations in China." In *Handbook of Research in Asian Business,* ed. Henry W.C. Yeung, 99–121. Cheltenham: Edward Elgar Publishing, 2007.

Gunew, Sneja. *Haunted Nations: The Colonial Dimensions of Multiculturalisms.* London: Routledge, 1960.

Gwee Yee Hean, "Education and the Multi-racial Society." In *Modern Singapore,* ed. Ooi Jin Bee and Chiang Hai Ding, 208–15. Singapore: Singapore University Press, 1969.

Habermas, Jürgen. *Legitimation Crisis.* Boston: Beacon Press, 1973.

Han, Fook Kwong, et al. *Lee Kuan Yew: Hard Truths to Keep Singapore Going.* Singapore: Straits Time Press, 2011.

Hartz, Louis. *The Liberal Tradition in America.* New York: Harcourt Brace and Company, 1955.

Harvey, David. *A Short History of Neoliberalism.* Oxford: Oxford University Press, 2005.

Hassan, Riaz. *Families in Flats.* Singapore: Singapore University Press, 1997.

Hutchcroft, Paul D. and Joel Rocamora. "Strong demands and weak institutions: the origins and evolution of the democratic deficit in the Philippines." *Journal of East Asian Studies* 3, no. 3 (2003): 259–92.

He Jin. *The Mighty Wave*. Translated by Tan Jin Quee, Loh Miaw Gong and Hong Lysa. Kuala Lumpur: Strategic Information and Research Development Centre, 2011.

Heryanto, Ariel. "Pop Culture and Competing Identities." In *Popular Culture in Indonesia: Fluid Identities in Post-authoritarian Politics*, ed. Ariel Heryanto, 1–36. London: Routledge, 2008.

Hong, Lysa and Huang Jianli. *The Scripting of a National History: Singapore and its Past*. Hong Kong: Hong Kong University Press, 2008.

Hopkins, Katherine. "Sovereign Funds are Cash Kings." *The Guardian*, 29 Apr. 2008. http://www.guardian.co.uk/business/2008/apr/29/sovereignwealth funds.useconomy [accessed 19 Oct. 2009].

Huang Jianli. "Positioning the Student Political Activism of Singapore: Articulating Contestation and Omission." *Inter-Asia Cultural Studies* 7, no. 3 (2006): 403–30.

Huntington, Samuel. "A Clash of Civilizations?" *Foreign Affairs* 72, no. 3 (2004): 22–49.

Human Rights Watch. *"Unkept Promise:" Failure to End Military Business Activities in Indonesia*. New York: Human Rights Watch, 2010.

Hussain, Zakir. "Raffles, MM Lee and the Rule of Law." *Straits Times*, 28 Oct. 2008.

Hussin, Dayang Istiaisyah. "School Effectiveness and Nation-Building in Singapore: Why Madrasahs Stand out from National Schools." MA thesis, Department of Sociology, National University of Singapore, 2003.

Hutchcroft, Paul D. and J. Rocomora. "Strong Demands and Weak Institutions: The Origins and Evolution of the Democratic Deficit in the Philippines." *Journal of East Asian Studies* 3, no. 2 (2003): 252–92.

Imran bin Tajudeen. "From Riau to Singapore 1700–1870s: Trade Ports and Urban Histories." In *Singapore Dreaming: Mapping Utopia*, ed. H. Koon Wee and J. Chia, 102–26. Singapore: Asian Urban Lab, 2016.

Ismail, Nizam. "Civil Society in Singapore: Revisiting the Banyan Tree." In *Singapore Perspectives 2013: Governance*, ed. Gillian Koh, 53–8. Singapore: Institute of Policy Studies, 2014.

Jayasuriya, Kanishka. "The Rule of Law and Capitalism in Asia." *The Pacific Review* 9, no. 3 (2007): 367–88.

Jayasuriya, K. and Garry Rodan. "New Trajectories for Political Regimes in Southeast Asia." *Democratization* 14, no. 5 (2007): 767–72.

Johnson, Chalmers. *MITI and the Japanese Miracle: The Growth of Industrial Policy, 1925–1975*. Stanford, CA: Stanford University Press, 1982.

Joppke, C. and S. Lukes, eds. *Multicultural Questions*. New York: Oxford University Press, 1999.

Kadir, Suzaina. "Islam, State and Society in Singapore." *Inter-Asia Cultural Studies* 5, no. 3 (2004): 357–71.

Kahn, Joel. *Other Malays: Nationalism and Cosmopolitanism in the Modern Malay World*. Singapore: Singapore University Press, 2006.

Kaye, Barrington. *Upper Nanking Street*. Singapore: University of Malaya Press, 1960.

Keane, John. "Introduction." In Claus Offe, *Contradictions of the Welfare State*. Cambridge, MA: MIT Press, 1984.

Kennedy, J. *A History of Malaya*. London: MacMillan, 1970.

Kim Dae Jung. "Is Culture Destiny? The Myth of Asia's Anti-democratic Values." *Foreign Affairs* 73, no. 6 (1994): 189–94.

Koh, Gillian. "Pruning the Banyan Tree? Civil Society in Goh's Singapore." In *Impressions of the Goh Chok Tong Years in Singapore*, ed. Bridget Welsh, James Chin, Arun Mahizhnan and Tan Tarn How, 93–106. Singapore: NUS Press, 2009.

Koh, Tommy. "A Small but Extraordinary Fish in the Ocean." *The Straits Times*, 6 Jan. 2013.

Koh, T.T.B. "The Law of Compulsory Land Acquisition in Singapore." *The Malayan Law Journal* 35 (1967): 9–22.

Kuo, Eddie C.Y. "The Promotion of Confucian Ethics in Singapore: A Sociological Analysis." *Commentary* 7 (1989): 24–5.

————. "Confucianism as Political Discourse in Singapore: The Case of an Incomplete Revitalization Movement." Working Paper No. 113, Department of Sociology, National University of Singapore, 1992.

Kuo, Eddie C.Y., Jon Quah and Tong Chee Kiong. *Religion and Religious Revivalism in Singapore*. Singapore: Ministry of Community Development, 1988.

Kundnani, Arun. "Multiculturalism and its Discontent: Left, Right and Liberal." *European Journal of Cultural Studies* 15, no. 2 (2012): 155–66.

Kwa Chong Guan, Derek Heng and Tan Tai Yong. *Singapore: A 700 years history: From Emporium to World City*. Singapore: National Archives of Singapore, 2009.

Kwok Kian Woon and Low Kee-Hong. "Cultural Policy and the City State: Singapore and the New Asian Renaissance." In *Global Cultures: Media, Arts, Policy and Globalization*, ed. Diane Crane, Nobuku Kawashima and Kenichi Kawasaki, 149–68. London: Routledge, 2002.

Kymlicka, Will. *The Rights of Minority Cultures*. Oxford: Oxford University Press, 1995.

————. *Multicultural Odysseys: Navigating the New International Politics of Diversity*. Oxford: Oxford University Press, 2007.

Lai Ah Eng. *Meanings of Multiethnicity: A Case Study of Ethnicity and Ethnic Relations in Singapore*. Kuala Lumpur: Oxford University Press, 1995.

Lal, Brij V., Peter Reeves and Rajesh Rai, eds. *Encyclopedia of Indian Diaspora*. Singapore: Didier Millet, 2006.

Latif, Asad Iqbal. "Re-imagining the Nation: Goh Chok Tong's Singapore." In *Impressions of the Goh Chok Tong Years in Singapore*, ed. Bridget Welsh, James Chin, Arun Mahizhnan and Tan Tarn How, 40–9. Singapore: NUS Press, 2009.

Lau, Albert. "The Historical Context: High-stakes Talk." *Straits Times*, 11 Oct. 2014.

Lee Boon Hiok. "The Bureaucracy." In *Management of Success: The Moulding of Modern Singapore*, ed. K.S. Sandhu and Paul Wheatley, 90–101. Singapore: Institute of Southeast Asian Studies, 1989.

Lee, Edwin. "The Colonial Legacy." In *Management of Success: The Moulding of Modern Singapore*, ed. K.S. Sandhu and Paul Wheatley, 3–50. Singapore: Institute of Southeast Asian Studies, 1989.

———. *The British as Rulers: Governing Multiracial Singapore 1819–1914.* Singapore: Singapore University Press, 1991.

———. *Singapore: The Unexpected Nation.* Singapore: The Institute of Southeast Asian Studies, 2008.

Lee Kuan Yew. *Battle for Merger.* Singapore: Ministry of Culture, 1962.

———. "A Tale of Two Cities—Twenty Years On." Li Ka Shing Lecture, University of Hong Kong, 14 Dec. 1997.

———. "Why Singapore Is What It Is." Keynote address to the International Bar Association. *Straits Times*, 15 Oct. 2007.

———. "A Chance of a Lifetime." Interview with Liu Thai Ker in *A Chance of a Lifetime: Lee Kuan Yew and the Physical Transformation of Singapore*, 16–9. Singapore: Centre for Liveable Cities and the Lee Kuan Yew Centre for Innovative Cities, 2016.

Lentin, A. and Gavan Titley. "The Crisis of Multiculturalism in Europe: Mediated Minarets, Intolerable Subjects." *European Journal of Cultural Studies* 15, no. 2 (2012): 123–38.

Leong, David. "Clan Associations of Singapore and their Roles in the Small Business Sector." In *Handbook of Research on Ethnic Minority Entrepreneurship*, ed. Leo-Paul Dana, 669–977. London: Edward Elgar, 2007.

Levitsky, S. and Way, L.A. "The Rise of Competitive Authoritarianism." *Journal of Democracy* 13, no. 2 (2002): 51–65.

Levitsky, Steven and Lucan A. Way. *Competitive Authoritarianism: Hybrid Regimes After the Cold War.* New York: Cambridge University Press, 2010.

Lew, Seok-Choon, Woo-Young Choi and Hye Suk Wang. "Confucian Ethics and the Spirit of Capitalism in Korea: The Significance of Filial Piety." *Journal of East Asian Studies* 11, no. 1 (2011): 171–96.

Li, Hong. "China Investment Corporation: A Perspective on Accountability." *The International Lawyer* 43, no. 4 (2009): 1495–513.

Li, Tania. *Malays in Singapore: Culture, Economy and Ideology.* Singapore: Oxford University Press, 1989.

Lim, Ivan. "The Singapore Press and the Fourth Estate." In *Press Laws and Systems in ASEAN States*, ed. Abdul Razak, 102–18. Jakarta: The Garuda Metropolitan Press, 1985.

Liow, Joseph Chinyong. "Ketuanan Melayu: What's in a Name?" *Straits Times*, 5 Jan. 2015.

Locke, John. "Second Treatise of Government." In *Two Treatises of Government*, ed. Peter Laslett, sec. 149, 3rd ed. Cambridge: Cambridge University Press, 1988.

Lodge, George and Ezra Vogel. *Ideology and National Competitiveness: A Study of Nine Countries*. Boston: Harvard Business School Press, 1987.

Loh Kah Seng. *Squatters into Citizens: The 1961 Bukit Ho Swee Fire and the Making of Modern Singapore*. Singapore: NUS Press, 2013.

Loh Kah Seng, et al. *The University Socialist Club and the Contest for Malaya: Tangled Web of Modernity*. Amsterdam: University of Amsterdam Press, 2012.

Low, Hwee Cheng Adeline. "The Past in the Present: Memories of the 1964 'Racial Riots' in Singapore." *Asian Journal of Social Science* 29, no. 3 (2001): 431–55.

Low, Linda. "Sustaining the Competitiveness of Singapore Inc. in the Knowledge Based Global Economy." In *Sustaining Competitiveness in the New Global Economy*, ed. Ramkishen S. Rajan, 135–50. Cheltenham, UK: Institute of Policy Studies, 2003.

Loh, Linda and T.C. Aw. *Housing a Healthy, Educated and Wealthy Nation through the CPF*. Singapore: Times Academic Press, 1997.

Lowe, Lisa. *Mapping Multiculturalism*. Minneapolis, MN: University of Minnesota Press, 1996.

Lukes, Steven. *Individualism*. New York: Harper and Row Publishers, 1973.

Lydgate, Chris. *Lee's Law: How Singapore Crushes Dissent*. North Carlton, Victoria, Australia: Scribe Publications, 2003.

Mauzy, Diane K. and R.S. Milne. *Singapore Politics under the People's Action Party*. London and New York: Routledge, 2002.

MacFarquar, Roderick. "The Post-Confucian Challenge." *Economist*, 9 Feb. 1980.

Mudhall, Stephen and Adam Swift. *Liberals and Communitarians*. Oxford: Oxford University Press, 1992.

Nair, Janaki. *The Promise of Metropolis: Bangalore's Twentieth Century*. New Delhi: Oxford University Press, 2005.

Nasir, Kamaludeen Mohamed and Syed Muhd Khairudin Aljunied. *Muslims as Minorities: History and Social Realities of Muslims in Singapore*. Bangi: Universiti Kebangsaan Malaysia Press, 2009.

National Convention of Singapore Malay/Muslim Professionals. *Forging a Vision: Prospects, Challenges and Directions: Malays/Muslims in 21st Century Singapore*. Singapore: Association of Muslim Professionals, 1990.

Ngiam Kee Jin. "Coping with the Asian Financial Crisis: The Singapore Experience." Singapore: Institute of Southeast Asia, Visiting Researchers Series No. 8, 2000.

Niskanen, William A. "Reaganomics." *Library of Economics and Liberty*, 1988. http://www.econlib.org/library/Enc1/Reaganomics.html [accessed 9 April 2009].

Obama, Barack. *The Audacity of Hope*. New York: Canongate, 2006.

O'Connor, James. *The Fiscal Crisis of the State*. New Brunswick: Transaction Publications, 2002.

Offe, Claus. *Contradictions of the Welfare State*. Cambridge, MA: MIT Press, 1984.

Ong, Aihwa. *Neoliberalism as Exception: Mutations in Citizenship and Sovereignty*. Durham, NC: Duke University Press, 2006.

Ortmann, Stephen and M.R. Thompson. "China's Obsession with Singapore: Learning Authoritarian Modernity." *The Pacific Review* 27, no. 3 (2014): 433–55.

Ow Chin Hock. "Singapore." In *The Role of Public Enterprise in National Development in Southeast Asia: Problems and Prospects*, ed. Nguyen-Truong, 153–254. Singapore: Regional Institute of Higher Education Development, 1976.

Pang Cheng Lian. *Singapore's People's Action Party: Its History, Organization and Leadership*. Singapore: Oxford University Press, 1971.

Phang, Sock Yong. "Public Housing—Appreciating Assets?" In *Singapore Perspectives 2012*, ed. Kang Soon Hock and Leong Chan-Hoong, 81–8. Singapore: Institute of Policy Studies, 2013.

Pech, Laurent. "Rule of Law in France." In *Asian Discourses of Rule of Law: Theories and Implementation of Rule of Law in Twelve Asian Countries, France and the US*, ed. Randall Peerenboom, 79–112. London: Routledge, 2004.

Peck, Jamie and Nik Theodore. "Variegated Capitalism." *Progress in Human Geography* 31, no. 6 (2007): 731–72.

Pei, Minxin. "The Real Singapore Model." *Straits Times*, 31 Mar. 2015.

Pereira, Alexius A. "Whither the Developmental State: Explaining Singapore's Continued Developmentalism." *Third World Quarterly* 29, no. 6 (2008): 1189–203.

————. *State Collaboration and Development Strategies in China: The Case of China-Singapore Suchou Industrial Park: 1992–2002*. London: Routledge, 2003.

Peterson, William. *Theater and the Politics of Culture and Contemporary Singapore*. Middletown, CT: Wesleyan University Press, 2001.

Phongpaichit, Pashuk and Chris Baker. *Thaksin*. Chiangmai: Silkworm Press, 2009.

Poh Soo Kai. "Living in a Time of Deception." In *The 1963 Operation Coldstore in Singapore: Commemorating 50 Years*, ed. Poh Soo Kai, Tan Kok Fang and Hong Lysa, 161–202. Kuala Lumpur: Strategic Information and Development Centre, 2013.

Poh Soo Kai, Tan Kok Fang and Hong Lysa, eds. *The 1963 Operation Coldstore in Singapore: Commemorating 50 Years*. Kuala Lumpur: Strategic Information and Development Centre, 2013.

Poon, Angela. "Pick and Mix for a Global City: Race and Cosmopolitanism in Singapore." In *Race and Multiculturalism in Malaysia and Singapore*, ed. Daniel P.S. Goh, M. Gabrielpillai, P. Holden and Gaik Cheng Khoo, 70–85. London: Routledge, 2009.

Prasad, M. "Fun with Democracy: Election Coverage and the Illusive Subject of Indian Politics." In *Elections as Popular Culture in Asia*, ed. Chua Beng Huat, 139–54. London: Routledge, 2007.

Preston, Alex. 2010. "Sovereign Wealth Funds are the new Kings of Markets" in *New Statesman*, 30 Aug. 2010. http://www.newstatesman.com/economy/2010/08/swfs-banks-financial-funds [accessed 30 Aug. 2010].

Purushotam, Nirmala. *Negotiating Language, Constructing Race: Disciplining Difference in Singapore*. Berlin, New York: Mouton de Gruyter, 1997.

———. "Disciplining Difference: 'Race' in Singapore." In *Southeast Asian Identities: Culture and Politics of Representation in Indonesia, Malaysia, Singapore and Thailand*, ed. Joel S. Kahn, 51–94. Singapore: Institute of Southeast Asian Studies, 1998.

Puthucheary, Dominic. "James Puthucheary, his Friends and his Times." In James Puthucheary, *No Cowardly Past: Writings, Poems Commentaries*, ed. D. Puthucheary and Jomo K.S., 3–38. Kuala Lumpur: Insan Press, 1998.

Quah Sy Ren. *Kuo Pao Kun 1939–2002: Plays in English*. Singapore: The Theatre Practice, Global Publishing, 2012.

Rahim, Lily Zubaidah. *The Singapore Dilemma: The Political and Educational Marginality of the Malay Community*. Singapore: Oxford University Press, 1998.

Rajah, Jothie. *Authoritarian Rule of Law: Legislation, Discourse and Legitimacy in Singapore*. Cambridge: Cambridge University Press, 2012.

Rajaratnam, S. *Singapore: Global City*. Singapore: Ministry of Culture, 1972.

Ramage, Douglas. *Politics in Indonesia: Democracy, Islam and the Ideology of Tolerance*. London: Routledge, 1995.

Ramakrishna, Kumar. *Original Sin? Revising the Revisionist Critique of the 1963 Operation Coldstore in Singapore*. Singapore: Institute of Southeast Asian Studies, 2015.

Robison, Richard. "The Politics of Asian Values." *The Pacific Review* 9, no. 3 (1996): 309–27.

Rodan, Garry. *The Political Economy of Singapore's Industrialization: National State and International Capital*. Basingstoke: Macmillan, 1989.

————. "The Internationalization of Ideological Conflict: Asia's New Significance." *The Pacific Review* 9, no. 3 (1996): 328–51.

————. *Transparency and Authoritarian Rule in Southeast Asia.* London: Routledge, 2004.

————. "Goh's Consensus Politics of Authoritarian Rule." In *Impressions of the Goh Chok Tong Years in Singapore,* ed. Bridget Welsh, James Chin, Arun Mahizhnan and Tan Tarn How, 61–70. Singapore: NUS Press, 2009.

————. "Competing Ideologies of Political Representation in Southeast Asia." *Third World Quarterly* 33, no. 2 (2012): 311–32.

Rodan, Garry and Caroline Hughes. *The Politics of Accountability in Southeast Asia: The Dominance of Moral Ideologies.* Oxford: Oxford University Press, 2014.

Rodan, Garry and K. Jayasuriya. "New Trajectories for Political Regimes in Southeast Asia." *Democratization* 14, no. 2 (2007): 767–73.

Rodan, G. and K. Jayasuriya. *Beyond Hybrid Regimes.* Special Issue in *Democracy* 14, no. 5 (2007).

Ronald, R. and J. Doling. "Shifting East Asian Approaches to Homeownership and the Housing Welfare." *Journal of Housing Policy* 10, no. 3 (2010): 233–54.

Roy, Ananya and Aihwa Ong, eds. *Worlding Cities: Asian Experiments and the Art of Being Global.* Chichester: Wiley-Blackwell, 2011.

Sandhu, K.S. and Paul Wheatley, eds. *Management of Success: The Moulding of Modern Singapore.* Singapore: Institute of Southeast Asian Studies, 1989.

Sassen, Saskia. *The Global City: New York, London, Tokyo.* Princeton, NJ: Princeton University Press, 1991.

Saunders, Peter. *A Nation of Home Owners.* London: Unwin and Hyman, 1990.

Schein, Edgar H. *Strategic Pragmatism: The Culture of the EDB.* Cambridge, MA: MIT Press, 1996.

Seah, Chee Meow. *Community Centres in Singapore: Their Political Involvement.* Singapore: Singapore University Press, 1973.

Seow, Francis. *To Catch a Tartar: A Dissident in Lee Kuan Yew's Prison.* New Haven, CT: Yale Southeast Asia Studies, 1994.

————. *The Media Enthralled: Singapore Revisited.* Boulder: Lynne Rienner Publishers, 1998.

————. "The Judiciary." In *The Singapore Puzzle,* ed. Michael Haus, 107–24. Westport, CT: Praeger, 1999.

Shanmugaratnam, Tharman. "Building an Inclusive Society." In *Singapore Perspectives 2012,* ed. Kang Soon Hock and Leong Chan-Hoong, 1–4. Singapore: World Scientific Press, 2012.

Shatkin, Gavin. "Planning Privatopolis: Representation and Contestation in the Development of Urban Integrated Mega-projects." In *Worlding Cities: Asian Experiments and the Art of Being Global,* ed. Roy Ananya and Aihwa Ong, 77–97. Chichester: Wiley-Blackwell, 2011.

Shatkin, Gavin. "Reinterpreting the Meaning of the 'Singapore Model': State Capitalism and Urban Planning." *International Journal of Urban and Regional Research* 38, no. 1 (2014): 116–37.

Shih, V. "Tools of Survival: Sovereign Wealth Funds in Singapore and China." *Geopolitics* 14, no. 2 (2009): 328–44.

Sin, Chih Hoong. "Segregation and Marginalization with Public Housing: The Disadvantaged in Bedok New Town, Singapore." *Housing Studies* 17 (2002a): 267–88.

Sin, Chih Hoong. "The Quest for a Balanced Ethnic Mix: Singapore's Ethnic Quota Policy Examined." *Urban Studies* 39, no. 8 (2002b): 1347–74.

Singapore Economic Review. "Special Issue Report of the Central Provident Fund Study Group." Vol. 31, no. 1 (1986).

Singh, Bilveer. "Southeast Asia in 1987: Hope amidst Problems." *Southeast Asian Affairs* (1988): 3–21.

Solebo, Dami. "Sleeping Giants Awake? Sovereign Wealth Funds." *Hedge Fund Spotlight v4 (4).* http://www.preqin.com/docs/newsletters/HF/Hedge_Fund_Spotlight_April_2012.pdf [accessed 16 Apr. 2012].

Stubbs, Richard. "What Ever Happened to the East Asian Developmental State? The Unfolding Debate." *The Pacific Review* 22, no. 1 (2009): 1–22.

Szelenyi, I. *Urban Inequalities under State Socialism.* New York: Oxford University Press, 1983.

Tan, Kelvin and Cherian George. "Civil Society and the Societies Act." *Straits Times*, 27 Mar. 2001.

Tan, Kenneth Paul. "Meritocracy and Political Liberalization in Singapore." In *The East Asian Challenge for Democracy: Political Meritocracy in Comparative Perspective*, ed. Daniel A. Bell and Chenyang Li, 314–39. Cambridge: Cambridge University Press, 2013.

Tan, Tai Yong. "Singapore: Civil-military Fusion." In *Coercion and Government: The Declining Political Role of the Military in Asia*, ed. M. Alagappa, 276–93. Stanford, CA: Stanford University Press, 2001.

———. *Creating "Greater Malaysia:" Decolonization and the Politics of Merger.* Singapore: Institute of Southeast Asian Studies, 2008.

Tan Yew Soon and Soh Yew Peng. *The Development of Singapore's Modern Media Industry.* Singapore: Times Academic Press, 1994.

Taylor, Charles. "Cross-purposes: The Liberal-communitarian Debate." In *Philosophical Arguments*, 181–203. Cambridge, MA: Harvard University Press, 1995.

The Economist. "The Invasion of the Sovereign Wealth Funds." 17 Jan. 2008.

Teo, Soh Lung. *Beyond the Blue Gate: Recollection of a Political Prisoner.* Singapore: Function 8, 2011.

Teo Youyenn. *Neoliberal Morality in Singapore: How Family Policies Make State and Society.* London: Routledge, 2011.

Thio, Li-Ann. "Rule of Law within a Non-liberal 'Communitarian' Democracy." In *Asian Discourses of Rule of Law: Theories and Implementation of Rule of Law in Twelve Asian Countries, France and the US*, ed. Randall Peerenboom, 183–224. London: Routledge, 2004.

Tremewan, Christopher. *The Political Economy of Social Control in Singapore.* London: St Martin's Press, 1994.

Truman, Edward M. *Sovereign Wealth Funds: Threat or Salvation?* Washington, DC: Peterson Institute for International Economics, 2010.

Tu Weiming, ed. *The Triadic Chord: Confucian Ethics, Industrial East Asia and Max Weber.* Singapore: Institute of East Asian Philosophy, 1991.

Urban Redevelopment Authority (URA). *Concept Plan 2001.* Singapore: Urban Redevelopment Authority, 2001.

Vasu, Norman. "Governance through Difference in Singapore." *Asian Survey* 52, no. 4 (2012): 734–53.

Visscher, Sikko. "Actors and Arenas, Elections and Competition: The 1958 Election of the Singapore Chinese Chamber of Commerce." *Journal of Southeast Asian Studies* 33, no. 2 (2002): 315–32.

———. *The Business of Politics and Ethnicity: A History of the Singapore Chinese Chamber of Commerce and Industry.* Singapore: NUS Press, 2007.

Vogel, Ezra. *Japan as Number One: Lessons for America.* Cambridge, MA: Harvard University Press, 1979.

Wade, Robert. *Governing the Market: Economic Theory and the Role of Government in East Asian Industrialization.* Princeton, NJ: Princeton University Press, 1990.

Wang Gungwu. "The Chinese as Immigrants and Settlers." In *Singapore: The Management of Success*, ed. K.S. Sandhu and Paul Wheatley, 552–62. Singapore: Institute of Southeast Asian Studies, 1989.

Watt, Nicholas. "David Cameron Unveils Plans to Sell Off Roads." *The Guardian*, 19 Mar. 2012. http://www.guardian.co.uk/politics/2012/mar/19/david-cameron-sell-off-roads [accessed 18 Apr. 2012].

Wen, G.J. and D. Xu, eds. *The Reformability of China's State Sector.* Singapore: World Scientific Press, 1997.

Williams, Leonard. *American Liberalism and Ideological Change.* DeKalb, IL: Northern Illinois University Press, 1997.

Wolfe, Alan. *The Limits of Legitimacy: Political Contradictions of Contemporary Capitalism.* New York: The Free Press, 1977.

Wong, Aline K. and Stephen H.K. Yeh, eds. *Housing a Nation: 25 Years of Public Housing in Singapore.* Singapore: Housing and Development Board, 1985.

Wong, Benjamin. "Political Meritocracy in Singapore: Lessons from the PAP Government." In *The East Asian Challenge for Democracy*, ed. Daniel A. Bell and Chenyang Li, 288–313. Cambridge: Cambridge University Press, 2013.

Wong, Eleanor. "Liberal Reflections on Loss and Acceptance in GE 2015." *Straits Times*, 16 Sept. 2015.

Wong, Evelyn S. "Industrial Relations in Singapore: Challenges for the 1980s." In *Southeast Asian Affairs*, ed. Pushpa Thambipillai, 258–69. Singapore: Institute of Southeast Asian Studies, 1983.

World Bank. *The East Asian Miracle: Economic Growth and Public Policy*. World Bank Policy Research Report 4, no. 4. Washington, DC: World Bank, 1993.

Yao, Souchou. *Singapore: The State and the Culture of Excess*. London: Routledge, 2007.

Yeung, Henry Wai-chung. "Strategic Governance and Economic Diplomacy in China: The Political Economy of Government-linked Companies from Singapore." *East Asia* 21, no. 1 (2004): 40–64.

———. From National Development to Economic Diplomacy? Governing Singapore's Sovereign Wealth Funds." *The Pacific Review* 24, no. 5 (2011): 625–52.

Zakaria, Fareed. *The Future of Freedom: Illiberal Democracy at Home and Abroad*. New York: W.W. Norton, 2003.

———. "Culture Is Destiny: A Conversation with Lee Kuan Yew." *Foreign Affairs* 73, no. 2 (1994): 109–26

Zhao, B. "Consumerism, Confucianism, Communism: Making Sense of China Today." *New Left Review* 222 (1997): 43–59.

INDEX

PSIA information can be obtained
www.ICGtesting.com
inted in the USA
VOW12s2009101017
51005LV00001B/105/P